OK!

THE STORY OF *OKLAHOMA!*

OK!

THE STORY OF *OKLAHOMA!*

MAX WILK

Grove Press ❦ New York

Published by Grove Press
A division of Grove Press, Inc.
841 Broadway
New York, NY 10003-4793

Published in Canada by
General Publishing Company, Ltd.

Due to limitations of space,
permissions appear on page 272,
which constitutes an extension of
this copyright page.

Library of Congress Cataloging-in-Publication Data

Wilk, Max.

    OK! : the story of Oklahoma! / Max Wilk.— 1st ed.

       p.   cm.

    ISBN 0-8021-1432-6 (acid-free paper)

    1. Rodgers, Richard, 1902–   Oklahoma!   I. Title.

ML410.R6315W5   1992

782.1′4—dc20   92-11454

                                          CIP

                                         MN

Manufactured in the United States of America

Printed on acid-free paper

Designed by Richard Hendel

First Edition 1993

10 9 8 7 6 5 4 3 2 1

TO

RICHARD RODGERS

AND

OSCAR HAMMERSTEIN,

who created a masterpiece and

made this book possible

CONTENTS

ACKNOWLEDGMENTS

No work of history such as this can be solely the product of the author. He needs the willing assistance of many others, and I would like to bring out a large cast to take proper bows for their kind help.

In no particular order of billing, then, may I express my deep gratitude to Agnes de Mille, who graciously shared her recollections with me. Alfred Drake, Celeste Holm, Kate Friedlich, Bambi Linn, Paul and Vivian Shiers, George Church, Marc Platt, and Hayes Gordon from far-off Australia were all lavish with their oral histories, with valuable keepsakes, private diaries, precious photos, and clippings.

Jay Blackton's insights about the musical score of *Oklahoma!* are vivid and should be an endowment for future generations. Further thanks to George Irving, John Fearnley, and Joan Roberts for their anecdotes.

Elaine Steinbeck has almost total recall about backstage events during the show's production, for which she receives fervent thanks.

Miles White's generosity with his memories and his expertise as to the costuming and decor of the show provided this history with necessary facts. His personal files were a treasure trove, and his generosity in permitting precious memorabilia to be reproduced is rare. Again, thanks.

Helene Hanff was lavish with her wry memories of working in the Theatre Guild press department, circa 1943. Mary Hunter Wolf helped me with incisive recollections about playwright Lynn Riggs, as did Miranda Levy. Edmund Hartmann had marvelous insight into Oscar Hammerstein's character.

Abe Samuel, of Allentown, Pennsylvania, is a miraculous source of valuable sheet music. Al Remsen has continually unearthed other show business ephemera. Thanks to both of them.

Hal Prince has much to say about musical comedy and was willing to interrupt a busy schedule to share some of his observations with me. Likewise, Stephen Sondheim took time out from his work to offer some cogent thoughts. And William Hammerstein has often offered encouragement and helped point me towards others who could supply more necessary history.

Patricia Willis and her staff at the Beinecke Library at Yale, where the Theatre Guild archives are stored for posterity, have been constantly helpful with their knowledge and time. Katherine Metz at the Museum of the City of New York was also generous, as was Robert Taylor at the Performing Arts Library of Lincoln Center.

The Westport Historical Society unearthed the original program of the revival of *Green Grow the Lilacs* and permitted me to reproduce it, and the Westport Playhouse allowed me to reproduce the rare poster for that summer production.

For transcribing what must have seemed endless hours of oral history for me with loving care and patience, a bow to Lois Porro of Westport.

My editor, Walter Bode, has been remarkably patient and caring throughout this project, even during such times when he certainly must have wondered what sort of theatrical tiger he had by the tail.

My wife, Barbara, has listened to anecdotes, complaints, et al. and retained her equanimity throughout, for which she earns, as always, a special citation.

Last, but far from least, my thanks to the reliable and endlessly helpful Ruth Nathan, far more than a literary agent, who has willingly shared this ride from the onset, through potholes, detours, and an occasional skid, ever since the beautiful morning when that surrey with the fringe on top hove into view with this author somewhat nervously holding on to the reins.

February 1992

SHUBERT THEATRE

New Haven's Center of Entertainment

INTRODUCTION

Just another Thursday-night opening.

That's what the Elm City audience assumed. Those paying customers filed into the New Haven Shubert Theatre that blustery winter night in 1943, the second year of World War II.

The usual cross section of New Haven burghers, solid citizens, Yale faculty members, plus a sprinkling of affluent haberdashers and salesmen from the local Chapel Street tailoring emporia. A few Yale undergraduates who hadn't yet been drafted by the army, or who were finishing up accelerated courses before shipping off with the navy. And, of course, that regular delegation piling in from New York. The "wrecking crew." Those theatrical agents, ticket brokers, movie company executives and scouts, all the "wise money"—the denizens of the Brill Building, or Little Lindy's,

"21," and the Cub Room at the Stork, here to check out the Theatre Guild's latest offering, a musical called *Away We Go!*

What did anyone know about this new show? Only that it had been written by Richard Rodgers and Oscar Hammerstein, that it was directed by Rouben Mamoulian, from Hollywood, and that it starred absolutely nobody's name above the title.

So far, what did that tell you?

Not much, but it didn't matter—Shubert regulars were dedicated gamblers from way back. They had to be. For years, they had been betting their cash ticket money on a constant game of theatrical roulette to get the first look. A weekly temptation offered to them by those equally optimistic producers who proffered their latest attractions fresh from the Manhattan rehearsal halls. Interspersed with touring companies who had exhumed such hardy chestnuts as *Maytime*, *The Student Prince*, or *Blossom Time* from the Shubert warehouse in New York, magicians known as Sim-Sala-Bim, or pirated Gilbert and Sullivan operettas, this stream of new plays and musicals would stop off in New Haven to use the theatre as a launch pad. The company had three days to hang and set up the scenery, rehearse the music, and to run through technical and full dress rehearsal. Thursday night, ready or not, curtain up . . . a harrowing schedule, one which only the toughest could survive. Then, thriving or dying, muscles flexed, the fledgling show staggered on its hopeful trek to Boston, Philly, and (possibly) Broadway.

Shubert openings customarily provided as much drama on one side of the proscenium as the other. Pushing through the crowded lobby around eight, one might easily spot the nervous playwright, already well fortified by several double whiskies from Kaysey's Restaurant across Church Street, smiling wanly at his fond wife and relatives. That chap over there certainly was the director; gaunt, eyes reddened by lack of sleep, followed by his faithful assistants, each holding at the ready clipboards, pocket flashes, and a supply of aspirin and Tums. Here came a group of well-dressed civilians, obviously backers, greeting each other heartily and preparing to cheer on their investment, no matter what.

Behind the last row of orchestra seats, in that space customarily reserved for the standees who paid a dollar to peer through velvet drapes, one found oneself surrounded by a convention of nervous pacers, a cadre of show staff, headed by the producer, sometimes sober, often not. As the evening wore on, one could hear from the rear of the house muttered curses at missed cues up there onstage, or anguished groans over the malfunctioning scenery being mishandled by the local stagehands. It was all a familiar game to the New Haven theatregoers, and in a perverse sort of way they relished the opening night madness. To be here tonight as witnesses made them midwives at the birth of what might be a major hit show, did it not? For years to come one could say, "Hey, I was there."

This particular Thursday was a new musical, and if there was anything that tickled Shubert audiences it was a good old rip-roaring razzmatazz song-and-dance show. Over the last few decades they had been treated to some of the very best. What a pleasure to have sat through the first performance of Cole Porter's *Leave It to Me!* with Sophie Tucker belting out "Most gentlemen don't like love, they just want to kick it around!" and then a piquant Mary Martin doing her cheerful striptease to "My Heart Belongs to Daddy." The Shubert audiences could call back the fond memories of such witty Rodgers and Hart musicals as *Too Many Girls*, or *The Boys from Syracuse*, and what about that riotous night when Billy Gaxton and Victor Moore wowed them in Irving Berlin's happy *Louisiana Purchase*? Bert Lahr and Ethel Merman in *DuBarry Was a Lady*, also by Yale's own Cole—oh what a night that had been. Beloved Merm in *Panama Hattie*, Merm and the great Jimmy Durante in Schwartz and Dietz's *Stars In Your Eyes*—oh yes, that was a night when the Shubert rocked with laughter as Jimmy tossed pieces of his grand piano into the orchestra pit, yelling "Don't raise da bridge, boys, lower da river!"

True, there were other nights when the curtain rose, the music struck up a jolly beat, and what ensued was pure disaster. A turkey. A lead balloon. A stinkeroo from the first notes of the overture. Openings in which the Shubert stage ran red with the blood of failed jokes, unreprised duets, creaky and witless libretti, and a gang of flop-sweated performers up there, fighting gamely, desperately, to make it through to the final curtain.

On such nights the Shubert audience would sit it out respectfully, optimists to the end (when it blessedly came). Then they'd stagger their way out into the New Haven night, past the numb and silent producer and his coterie, the backers shaking their heads in stunned anguish and the weary production crew bracing itself for an all-night council of war up in some suite at the Taft. And as the Shubert faithful left, ever optimists, they might be muttering softly to each other . . . who knew? Perhaps they might be able to fix this one. Stranger things had happened, right here in New Haven, right? And they had been there, witnesses to miracles. *"Hey, I was there . . ."*

On this particular March night in New Haven, the Shubert optimists were out in full force. If there were no marquee names up there, well, here was the newly formed partnership of Richard Rodgers and Oscar Hammerstein. Rodgers? Everybody could hum something by Dick Rodgers, all those bright happy hits he and Lorenz Hart had crafted, like *Babes in Arms*, which featured the lovely ballads "My Funny Valentine" and "Where or When," or *I Married an Angel*, with that gorgeous Zorina, who'd been such a knockout. With Dick and Larry at work you always knew something terrific would emerge, even in *Pal Joey*, though it had been a little gamey— some very rough stuff in those Hart lyrics; but the show had introduced a wonderful leading man, name of Gene Kelly, he made up for everything. Songs, laughs, dances, ballads, oh, yes, Rodgers and Hart certainly could please an audience.

But tonight it was Rodgers without Hart. How come? Nobody knew. Oscar Hammerstein? How long had it been since he'd had something memorable on a stage? *Show Boat*, with Jerome Kern, sure, but nothing really successful lately. Maybe four or five years since his *Very Warm for May*, another show he'd done with Kern. A nice show, lovely music and lyrics, but it certainly hadn't stayed around. Produced by Max Gordon; yes, the same Max Gordon who was standing out there in the lobby, a short man, staring gloomily through his spectacles at the customers as they entered. Hammerstein had done some other shows since. In fact, he'd come through the Shubert here in 1941 with some operetta he'd done with Sigmund Romberg, a piece called *Sunny River*, good, but not really good enough. It had gone on to New York and folded very quickly.

But tonight's show was the product of the Theatre Guild, and New Haven audiences had always respected that group; for years the name had been synonomous with quality. Since the twenties, the Guild had brought plays by O'Neill and Ferenc Molnár and Shaw, stars such as the Lunts, Helen Hayes—always class acts. On the other hand, when was the last time anyone could remember Lawrence Langner, tiny Theresa Helburn, and Armina Marshall, all three of whom were welcoming their friends and associates in the Shubert lobby, ever showing up before with a musical? It simply wasn't their style, was it? Matter of fact, if one wished to be captious, it had been a very long time between hits for the Guild. The rumor had it they were in deep trouble. The rumor was, for once, correct.

Now what about the director? This man Mamoulian, supposed to be a big Hollywood talent?

Sure, he'd directed *Porgy and Bess*, that wonderful Gershwin opera, back in the thirties, but did that mean he could still cut it on the stage? Plenty of those big-time Hollywood types had tried it, and hadn't they regularly landed flat on their cans?

So once again, another opening, another evening of Shubert roulette. The cash customers had placed their bets, and the ushers were herding everyone inside to the gaming table.

In the Broadway theatre of the 1920s, the Theatre Guild had become truly a class operation. What other management could advertise such an imposing history as this one?

Playwright Sidney Howard had brought them his moving The Silver Cord and the successful melodrama Ned McCobb's Daughter. The great Italian playwright Luigi Pirandello had given them his puzzling work Right You Are If You Think You Are. The English writer A. A. Milne was not only the author of every child's favorite, Winnie the Pooh, but also a deft playwright capable of such successes as Mr. Pim Passes By.

S. N. Behrman had vaulted to the front rank of American playwrights with his sparkling comedy The Second Man. He would join such important talents as George Bernard Shaw as a Guild standby. ("When in doubt, revive Shaw" was a Guild motto.)

Was it any wonder that Guild subscribers signed up, Pavlovian-like, for their tickets year after year? (Remembering, of course, that this advertisement omits the Guild's other crown jewel, Mr. Eugene O'Neill.)

THE SILVER CORD

RIGHT YOU ARE IF YOU THINK YOU ARE

THE SECOND MAN

NED McCOBB'S DAUGHTER

PYGMALION

MR. PIM PASSES BY

8:31. Magic time. From the orchestra pit came the sound of clarinets practicing trills, the echoes of fiddled arpeggios, the rumtumtum of the drummer with his snares and cymbals. And now, that electric moment when the conductor raised his arms, tapped softly on the podium with his baton, and called his musicians to attention.

The houselights were down, the footlights went up, it was time for Mr. Rodgers's overture.

The audience waited, expectant for a bright, well-orchestrated piece, a new ballad, then perhaps one of Rodgers's lovely waltzes, building to a finale.

Not this night. What they heard was a brief run-through of several songs, almost perfunctory, one which ended almost as quickly as it had begun. (In truth this "overture" had been patched together by the arranger, Robert Russell Bennett, a scant few hours ago.)

And then the curtain rose.

To total silence.

Astonishing, completely unexpected, deafening.

There, on the Shubert stage, was a drop revealing a view. A Southwestern mesa? Or was it the prairie? Beyond, a mountain range, with a vista of rolling hills. Bright, yellow, wondrous sunlight flooded the set and warmed the proscenium.

Still, silence.

Strange. Not a single dancing girl in sight.

Okay, then, if we were supposed to be out West, where were the dancing cowboys twirling their customary ropes, doing a fast tap routine with their usual tricks while singing about the good life out here on the range?

Nope. Not a single boy dancer.

The only sign of life on that Shubert stage seemed to be some old lady sitting there, wearing her poke bonnet; in her hand was a stick; she was pumping away . . . at a butter churn?

Silently.

She wasn't even singing.

What sort of a way was this to open a musical?

———————

From the orchestra, more silence. No rich choirs of fiddles from the pit, no brass figures, no chords of any kind. Just golden silence and that old lady with her churn, pumping away.

The Shubert regulars were, to say the least, perplexed.

Was this a musical?

Where the hell was the music?

Then, offstage, there could be heard the sound of a pleasant male voice. He seemed to be singing some sort of a ballad.

A ballad?

No, no! You didn't open a musical with a ballad, you started with a song that was upbeat, jazzy, that told the people this was a wonderful old world, especially when you had a nifty girl on your arm, and if you didn't have a penny in your pocket what did it matter so long as she was by your side— that's how you opened a musical!

The voice sang:

> There's a bright golden haze on the meadow,
> There's a bright golden haze on the meadow.
> The corn is as high as a elephant's eye,
> And it looks like it's climbin' clear up to the sky.

". . . As high as a elephant's eye?" Would Larry Hart have ever written anything like that?

Then the young man came strolling onstage; nice-looking chap, dressed in simple cowboy clothes, nothing fancy, but he sang like a leading man so he had to be one. In the program it said he was Curly, and as Curly, Alfred Drake was now singing:

Oh, what a beautiful mornin',
Oh, what a beautiful day.
I got a beautiful feelin'
Everything's goin' my way.

And the lady pumping the churn, a character named Aunt Eller, played by Betty Garde, looked up and smiled at Curly and went on churning her butter while he kept right on singing.

Some peculiar kind of an opening number . . .

It's a safe bet that nobody in the audience of Shubert veterans that night in March 1943 had ever seen anything like it, nor what would follow that lovely opening song.

Max Gordon sure as hell hadn't.

He sat there in his down-front aisle seat staring, with far more than ordinary interest, at what was transpiring up there on the stage.

Everyone in the small world of the Broadway theatre knew that Max, a veteran of many years in and out of the red, was a born worrier. How about the story of the night he'd brought Robert Sherwood's *Abe Lincoln in Illinois* to Washington and there had been a special performance for President and Mrs. Roosevelt, followed by an after-theatre White House reception? When FDR had congratulated Max on the remarkable production and lavished praise on Raymond Massey's performance of Sherwood's play, Max's glum response had been, "Yeah, Mr. President, but will it make a quarter?"

Max had far more than casual concern about the future of *Away We Go!* Max had invested hard cash in this show. His own dollars, and also those of Hollywood dynast Harry Cohn, the boss of Columbia Pictures. Cohn, whose favorite comment about his business practices was "I don't get ulcers, I *give* them!" Cohn, who'd become impressed with Max Gordon's track record—it included, along with *Abe Lincoln in Illinois*, such smash hits as *Junior Miss*, *My Sister Eileen*, and Clare Boothe's *The Women*—had made an arrangement with Gordon to represent Columbia on Broadway. Max represented Class; Cohn thirsted for some so he could compete with L. B. Mayer, or Darryl Zanuck. Max's advice would assist Cohn in investing in forthcoming shows and getting the jump on the competition from Metro or Warners when the bidding started on some promising Broadway hit.

Months earlier Max had suggested *Away We Go!*, a Theatre Guild musical, written by Richard Rodgers and Oscar Hammerstein, as something that might interest Columbia. It sounded classy enough to Cohn, a noisy rough-and-tumble type who'd begun his career many years earlier as a song-plugger in New York saloons and who never lost his taste for popular music.

"You think this turkey has a chance?" he'd asked Max.

Gordon, never given to hyperbole, had said that he thought so. "But I'm not making any guarantees, Harry," he'd added, glumly. Cohn had presented the project to his New York board, which turned him down.

"Okay," said Cohn, ever the gambler. "Then I put my own money in— not the stockholders. That way nobody can bitch if it's a flop, and if it's a hit, I'm a hero. Now—are you going in with me, Max?"

Gordon, as much of a gambler as his new boss—hadn't he already lost one fortune in the 1929 stock market crash?—understood the name of the game. "Sure, why not?" he'd told Cohn.

Now, tonight at the Shubert, in his official capacity as Harry Cohn's eyes and ears—as well as his own—Max sat staring and listening.

So did the rest of the Shubert gamblers. As the first act of *Away We Go!* continued, Curly and Laurey, his intended, went for a ride in "The Surrey with the Fringe on Top." The backers patiently sat and waited, anticipating some excitement on that stage. They finally got some, forty-odd minutes into the show, when there came a rousing number called "Kansas City," sung and danced by a kid named Lee Dixon.

Later on a pleasant girl named Celeste Holm, playing Ado Annie, launched into a crowd-pleaser called "I Cain't Say No." There were some

laughs at her wide-eyed delivery of Hammerstein's deft and witty lyrics, but so far the Shubert hadn't exactly exploded with excitement.

Then came a song for Laurey and the other girls called "Many a New Day." A lilting ballad for her and her intended, "People Will Say We're in Love." Certainly this score was first-class Rodgers and well-crafted Hammerstein, but where was the smash hit? It certainly didn't come at the end of Act One, when something quite remarkable happened. The young Laurey, now danced by a ballerina, embarked on a dream ballet by Agnes

de Mille in which she tried to make up her mind whether or not she was in love with Curly. Remarkable. New and totally different from anything the Shubert audience had ever seen.

And then the first act curtain fell.

There was some applause, but nothing earthshaking. You can't blame those Shubert gamblers for being somewhat confused; they'd never seen a show remotely like this one. Forty minutes had passed before there'd been an ensemble of girls, and even then not one of them had revealed as much as her shapely calf! And as far as those ballerinas were concerned, well, maybe they could toe-dance, but who ever figured a musical show about homesteaders in Oklahoma was the proper setting for some high-class ballet?

Max Gordon made his way up the aisle and out through the lobby doors. His face was impassive, revealing none of what he truly felt, which was sheer, unadulterated panic.

This first act, this remarkable concoction, with its simple storyline of two young lovers in turn-of-the-century Oklahoma, homesteaders working out their problems against the stark plains, farmers and cowhands, surreys, old ladies churning butter—and ballet!—all of it was foreign. Not in all the time he'd been producing—not in the decades when he and Al Lewis had produced vaudeville sketches, nor in the years since, when Max had worked with them all, Kaufman, Moss Hart, Dietz and Schwartz, the greats and near-greats, with their flops and their smashes—had he ever sat through a first act such as this.

And to cap off matters, he had money in this. His own.

So did his employer, Harry Cohn.

People lighting cigarettes were passing Max, heading for the outer lobby. Some of the "wrecking crew" were carrying their overcoats, an ominous sign; it meant they were headed for the early train back to New York. One of them was producer Mike Todd, on his way out, silently turning thumbs down.

"So, whaddaya think?" asked one acquaintance.

Max shrugged. "Too early to tell," he said. "How do you like it?" "Interesting," said another one of the Broadway boys. "Needs work," said a third. "What doesn't?" asked Max.

Nobody was prepared to commit. Except for one, who said, "I think it's amazing—never saw anything like it!"

"You really think so?" asked Max.

"I loved it!"

"You loved it enough to buy a piece of it?" pressed Max.

"Yeah. Yeah, I could!" came the response.

Max beckoned him closer and lowered his voice. "Would you be willing to buy, say, twenty-five hundred dollars worth?" he suggested.

"From whom?" asked the lobby acquaintance.

Max pulled out a pocket pad and a pencil. "Show me a check and you've bought yourself a piece," he said. Then he held out his hand. A second's hesitation and then a handshake closed the deal.

Another passerby had been listening. He was a diminutive chap named Al Greenstone, another Broadway type, whose special niche in show business consisted of the printing of glossy theatrical souvenir books, which he sold in the theatre lobby before and after the performance.

"Hey, Max, can I get in on this?" he asked.

"As long as your check cashes," said Max. "You like the show, how much do you want?"

"I'll take another twenty-five hundred dollars," said Greenstone.

Gordon scribbled out another slip.

By the time the lobby lights were flashing on and off, signaling the beginning of Act Two, Max Gordon had divested himself of a good-sized piece of the investment he had made in the show.

And as he walked towards his seat, ready to sit through the rest of this peculiar—well, could you truly call it a musical?—this hybrid stew by Dick Rodgers and Oscar Hammerstein, he nodded sympathetically toward the two of them. He knew exactly what the authors were going through, oh, how well he knew. Hadn't he been in the same exact spot, here in the Shubert lobby, with his own productions?

Walter Winchell's faithful secretary, Rose, who'd been sent by her boss to New Haven to scout this new Theatre Guild musical, did not return for the second act. Instead she dropped by the Taft Hotel, where she sent a wire to the office before taking the 10:00 P.M. train back to New York.

Her wire, which Winchell ran in his column the following day, read NO LEGS NO JOKES NO CHANCE.

The second act of *Away We Go!* gave the audience a rouser, "The Farmer and the Cowman," and then came a lovely Rodgers ballad, "Boys and Girls Like You and Me." Ado Annie and her boyfriend Will Parker did a joyful duet, "All er Nothin," and then came a spirited number in praise of the new state of Oklahoma, sung by a quartet and danced, in a solo spot, by George Church. Curly and Jud got into a fight over Laurey; it ended with Jud falling on his knife and Curly accused of murder! Strange . . . but it all ended happily, when Curly was exonerated and he and Laurey embraced. Music up, and curtain. More polite applause.

The New Haven gamblers were already reaching for hats and coats and mufflers and heading for the outer lobby doors.

Max Gordon came up the aisle, listening to the comments around him. Some of the crowd had enjoyed their evening. Not spectacularly, mind you. The general consensus was that this *Away We Go!* could use work, plenty of work. Some brave souls were saying they loved it; others merely shrugged. Then there was that favorite New Haven reaction: "Nice . . . but who knows?"

As Max Gordon hurried through the frigid winter night looking for a cab to take him down to the station, he must have felt better. He'd managed at least to lighten up his investment in this strange mishmash of a show, this exhibit that would shortly go on up to the Colonial in Boston, then come down to the St. James on West Forty-fourth Street, probably have a couple of weeks' run, and then quietly expire.

Too bad about Dick and Oscar, two very talented guys. They'd worked hard, done their usual capable job, but somewhere along the line the whole thing hadn't come together, it had collapsed like a failed soufflé. Those girls in their long dresses, those arty ballets—no high-kicking, nothing but that little love story. It was all too . . . different. If the Theatre Guild, which everyone knew was having a bad case of the shorts, was counting on this piece to bail them out, well, too bad.

Who knew how shows like this went wrong? Who knew, indeed. That was show business. You try for a hit with the best people around rowing the boat, the way Max had done with *Very Warm for May*, you and the crew give it your best shot and you end up striking out with the paying customers. So who can fault Max Gordon for having impulsively sold off those pieces of *Away We Go!* that night in New Haven, at intermission, to such fortunate people as Al Greenstone, who would for years to come cash fat weekly checks because he'd taken a wild $2,500 flyer to buy a piece of a show that would become *Oklahoma!*

Luckily, Max Gordon hadn't managed to sell off all his investment, and Harry Cohn's, that night in New Haven.

Within a few short weeks the show would have a new title, a revamped second act, and a rousing next-to-closing second act number and become a landmark American musical comedy.

And make a liar out of Winchell's Rose.

THE BEGINNING

urtain time, 8:27 P.M., on a pleasant summer's evening in 1940, in Westport, Connecticut. Outside the rambling, remodeled faded red barn that was now the Westport Country Playhouse, an apprentice began to ring the bell. Slowly, reluctantly, continuing to chat and gossip, the gathering of relaxed summertime theatregoers down below in the garden started to climb the creaking wooden stairs that led to the lobby doors.

Outside, there were posters heralding tonight's play: a revival of *Green Grow the Lilacs*, by Lynn Riggs, starring Betty Field and Winston O'Keefe, with Mildred Natwick. DIRECTED BY JOHN FORD proclaimed the bold type, but in fact that eminent film craftsman had not appeared for the rehearsals, nor would he even make it to Westport. But the show had gone on, in tradi-

This is the original window card heralding the revival of Green Grow the Lilacs at the Westport Playhouse. A half century later this same window card remains on the wall in the Green Room at Westport, backstage. (And for a half century visitors have had the mistaken impression that director John Ford was responsible for the revival of Lynn Riggs's play.)

The window card has been removed from its place on the wall only once: when the Westport management was good enough to entrust it to this author for the specific purpose of having it photographed. It is now back safely in place, where it will hopefully remain for the next half century.

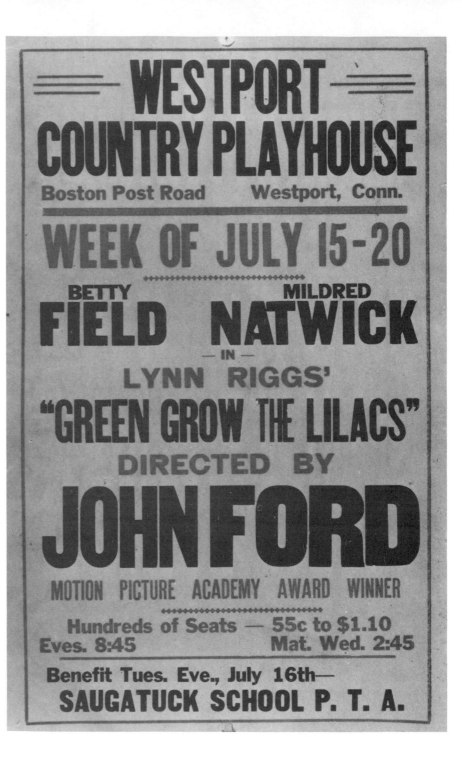

tional summer stock fashion (whatever happens, we get the curtain up by Monday night!), with producer John Haggott filling in for the absent Ford.

Up the steps, in the crowd, came Theresa Helburn of the Theatre Guild, a diminutive middle-aged lady with startling, cerulean-blue hair. Known to everybody in the New York theatre as "Terry," the soft-spoken and gracious lady was respected for her artistic acumen and her ability to squeeze the last dollop of fat out of a production budget.

Helburn and her husband lived here in Westport during the summer months, a scant few miles away from the Wilton home of her partners in the Guild, Lawrence Langner, a balding, portly gent who'd combined a career as a man of the theatre with his thriving practice as a patent lawyer, and Langner's wife, Armina Marshall, tall and striking, who hailed from far-off Oklahoma and who could proudly trace some of her Cherokee Strip forebears back to the Native Americans of that area.

They composed the troika that controlled the Theatre Guild, a powerful and prestigious American theatrical management team that, for the past two decades or so, had thrived in New York and on the road across America. Langner and his wife also owned the Westport Playhouse, where annual summer stock seasons brought upscale revivals to Fairfield County and where the Guild could also, at reduced production cost, try out new and promising plays.

The Theatre Guild specialized in distinguished work studded with stars; it was synonymous with Shaw, O'Neill, the Lunts, Gershwin, Helen Hayes —in short, the best. That was the general view of the Theatre Guild, and it had been so for years. But behind Theatre Guild office doors, Terry Helburn, Lawrence, Armina, and their accounting department knew how bad things actually were. There had been an oversupply of flops lately, well-mounted shows that hadn't gone well either artistically or, more important, financially. Business was bad; subscribers were unhappy. How much longer could they sustain themselves? But it's an old show business tradition that no matter how much red ink is flowing through your balance

sheets, you smile and exude optimism to the civilians you meet in the lobby. To paraphrase Wilkins Micawber, *the next hit is bound to turn up.*

It might even be tomorrow. Who knows?

So, on this summer night, smiling and waving to friends, Terry Helburn climbed the stairs, stopped off in the lobby to offer best wishes to the two young Harvard men, John Haggott and John Cornell, who'd leased the theatre for this summer, greeted old friends and acquaintances, and then made her way down the aisle on her husband's arm to take her seat on those venerable, hard Westport Playhouse benches.

The house lights went down, the footlights came up, and the curtain parted. There, on the Westport stage, sat an old farm woman in a poke bonnet: Aunt Eller, bathed in the bright Oklahoma sunlight, methodically working on her butter churn.

Terry Helburn knew this play well. Nine years back, in 1931, thirty-two-year-old Lynn Riggs had brought it to the Guild. She'd liked it then; she and Langner had hoped it would succeed. They'd taken a chance with this young Oklahoma playwright who seemed to have a true poetic gift, but back in the depths of the Depression audiences hadn't been too receptive to the charming love story of the young cowboy and the feisty ranch girl. After 64 performances the show had closed; now it was getting its second chance.

Terry Helburn sat and watched as up on the stage Curly began to romance young Laurey, the high-spirited, independent Oklahoma lass. The Westport audience was having a good time, but then, summer audiences were notoriously easy to please. The young assistant stage manager, twenty-six-year-old Elaine Anderson Scott, a Texan who later married John Steinbeck, would remember that summer evening's events vividly even a half century later:

> Johnny Haggott had found Gene Kelly, who was working around the neighborhood doing a summer musical called *Two Weeks with Pay* down at the Ridgeway Theatre in White Plains, to come up and stage some square dances for us. You see, in Riggs's play there's that big party scene, and it's full of country music and dancing. So Gene put it on for us; this was just before he went to New York to become such a big hit in Rodgers and Hart's *Pal Joey*. Since John Ford hadn't showed up, Haggott directed, and it was a smashing evening. I was backstage, but naturally, being a Texan, I had to dance in the square dances! And since I knew Lynn Riggs, it was even nicer for me. He'd come down to the University of Texas when my then husband, Zachary Scott, and I had been at the Drama School, and we'd met him down there. Anyway, the revival was delightful, and with that good cast, why not?

Terry Helburn was enjoying tonight's revival, and her producer's antennae, always tuned in to the ticket buyers around her, told her that Riggs's play was deeply satisfying her neighbors. Who knows when the idea began

Lynn Riggs, the Oklahoma-born playwright whose 1931 play would become, twelve years later, the basis of one of our greatest and most enduring American musicals. Could young Riggs ever have imagined, on that night when his play closed, in 1931, that it would someday rise again, phoenixlike, to such triumph? Hardly . . .

to flicker in her subconscious? Just the vaguest sort of notion, perhaps, but one that wouldn't go away. As the actors onstage went through the complications of their love story, which Lynn Riggs had so artfully set to turn-of-the-century American folk music, Terry Helburn's mind must have begun to fill with possibilities.

"After the show, Terry came backstage to see everybody," remembers Elaine. "No matter what anybody tells you today, I was there when it happened, and I remember, it was strictly *her* idea. She said to us all, 'This would make a good musical!' " Everyone agreed. It was seductive to think of the show being transformed into a musical. Most ideas in the theatre are seductive. In the helter-skelter world of show business, such fantasies are common. They're everyone's stock-in-trade, the coin of the realm, the dream world from which all creative minds draw daily sustenance. Take away the "what if," the euphoria and the seductive possibilities, and what have you got left? Your unemployment insurance.

Sometimes the best antidote to such ideas is to lie down until they go away. Or to let them drop back into the subconscious. But on this night in 1940, Terry Helburn had come up with a "what if" that was solid. It would be two years before the project would actually start. Even after that it would be a truly Sisyphean journey before Terry's idea bore any fruit. No one, not even such hardened theatrical veterans as the three partners in the Guild, could ever have imagined how long and pot-holed the road ahead would be.

Before she was done, all the wise boys around town would refer to her project as Helburn's Folly. And she herself somewhat ruefully wrote "I don't remember when I became convinced that *Green Grow the Lilacs* was what I had been looking for. What I do remember is trying to make other people share my conviction. When you're trying to raise a lot of money, people reminded me, you ought to offer them a sure-fire success, not a play that hasn't done so well in the past. Musicals, they said in disgust, don't have murders in the second act."

Not that Helburn was unaccustomed to the travails of sustaining a theatrical venture as healthy as the Theatre Guild had been over the years. She and her partners had been through struggles and difficulties aplenty. Survival in theatre is an art that commingles creativity with karate. "The difference between the Theatre Guild and the Shuberts," Agnes de Mille once noted sharply, "is that the Theatre Guild gives you tea."

All through the post–World War I years of the New York theatre, no single production group had had as much effect on public taste nor had done so much to raise the level of American theatre as the Guild. Into a show business famous for cheap melodramas, star vehicles, maudlin, tear-jerking love stories, crook plays, and star-and-garter burlesques, the Guild introduced a theatre based on literacy, talent, and intellect. It had been founded in 1918 by Langner, Helburn, actress Helen Westley, director Philip Moeller, designer Lee Simonson, and banker Maurice Wertheim. The young group went through an intense period of birth-pangs. "For the record," remembered Helburn, "we were all people with strong convictions, creative impulses, and considerable personal ambition, and we were noisily articulate about these things.

"What Lawrence and I and a handful of others had in mind was an art theatre, in its best sense. But we wanted to take the curse off the word 'artistic' and provide something real and beautiful, not merely the trappings of culture and the pseudo-cleverness and the exotic unreality that are attached to the word 'artistic.'"

The Guild's first play was produced in the Garrick Theatre on Thirty-fifth Street. It was *The Bonds of Interest* by Jacinto Benavente. It cost $1,100 to open. "Five hundred dollars from Lawrence," said Helburn, "and the rest of the group chipping in one hundred dollars apiece." They were fortunate to have as their landlord financier Otto H. Kahn, a true patron of the arts. "When you make the rent," he told them, "you pay the rent. When you don't make it, you need not pay it."

With the first production the Guild did not make the rent. But they had signed up a few faithful subscribers. Their second venture was *John Ferguson* by the young British playwright St. John Ervine, a dramatist whose well-made plays would be staples for theatregoers on both sides of the Atlantic during the next three decades. "By that time," said Helburn, "there was the lump sum of nineteen dollars in the treasury. But it got done. The play put the Guild on its feet and started it on its career. The only other capital we had was enthusiasm for our idea and faith in the public."

The Ervine play, a stark tragedy, was an immediate hit. Subscribers began to sign up, the box office was busy, and from 1920 on the Guild was well and truly launched. For seasons to come, Guild productions in New York and on tour would stimulate American theatregoers and develop their tastes for avant-garde drama. The Guild produced Shakespeare, Strindberg, Tolstoy, and Leonid Andreyev. From the beginning the emphasis was on content, not stars. Helen Westley made the group's position clear. "The popular play presents the actor," she said. "The actor of the art theatre presents the play." The Guild envisioned a permanent acting company, capable of performing anything, and it proceeded to develop such a group.

Beginning with his massive *Heartbreak House*, the Guild became George Bernard Shaw's American producers. In England the fiery Shaw was in disgrace because of his antiwar stand. In America, on the Broadway stage, he was soon restored to a position as a major satiric playwright. Soon Langner, Helburn, et al. ventured to do Shaw's interminable *Back to Methuselah*, losing $20,000 instead of the $30,000 they'd expected to. Which prompted Shaw to suggest to them that they'd actually made $10,000! And for this act of faith Shaw gave his Guild supporters the rights to do *Saint Joan* and all of his ensuing works. Over the years so many of Shaw's plays were a part of the Guild's repertory that "When in doubt, revive Shaw" became the Guild credo.

Ferenc Molnár, a great Hungarian playwright, gave them his sparkling and witty comedy *The Guardsman*. Alfred Lunt and Lynn Fontanne played the leads; the play had flopped once before, but now, in 1924, it launched the young couple's career with a brilliant success. During the twenties the Guild produced the plays of Sidney Howard, who won a Pulitzer Prize for *They Knew What They Wanted*, (later to become the basis for Frank Loesser's *The Most Happy Fella*), Elmer Rice, whose *The Adding Machine* became a major force in symbolic theatre, S. N. Behrman, whose gift for high comedy raised social satire to an art form, and, finally, the works of Eugene O'Neill. The list of Theatre Guild subscribers grew longer with each successful season. Certainly those faithful audiences were assured again and again of the most venturesome plays, performed by the best actors and actresses available. These were the golden years.

By 1925 the Guild was financially secure enough to build its own theatre, on West Fifty-second Street just off Broadway (now called the Virginia). Before the new theatre opened, a special production, created by talented Broadway newcomers, was scheduled downtown at the Garrick. *The Garrick Gaieties* offered singing and dancing, sketches and special material performed by a cast that included young Lee Strasberg, Harold Clurman, Edith Meiser, Sterling Holloway and Philip Loeb. The purpose was to raise funds for tapestries that would decorate the new Guild Theatre uptown. The ever-waspish critic Alexander Woollcott sagely quipped "The Gobelins will get you if you don't watch out," and in years to come the paucity of productions that turned a profit in the new Guild Theatre seemed to prove him correct.

Theresa Helburn later said "Sitting on the empty stage of the Garrick, Dick Rodgers played the songs and Larry Hart, a slight, frail youth not over five feet tall in spite of his elevator shoes, sang them for us. When they came to the song 'Manhattan,' I sat up in delight. These lads had ability, wit, and a flair for a light, sophisticated kind of song. The first night's response was so terrific that we put *The Garrick Gaieties* into a regular run for our subscribers, and so one promising group of young people was launched on its professional way."

Years later, seated in the Guild Theatre, Hart nudged his partner Rodgers. "See those tapestries?" he muttered. "We're responsible for them."

"Hell, they're responsible for *us*," corrected Rodgers.

Between April 1926 and October 1928 the Guild presented no fewer than fourteen plays. By now Theresa Helburn had become the executive director, a post she shared with Langner, who was often absent dealing with his considerable legal practice. In a *New Yorker* profile Helburn was described as "the power behind the throne. She is the terror of actors, the bane of playwrights, and the thorn of agents, managers, and kindred mortals."

In 1929 the golden years of New York legitimate theatre began to fade. The first blow was the invention of the talking picture, which ran three and four times a day in vast movie palaces; there, for far less than 52nd Street box-office prices, thousands applauded such famous former stage actors as John Barrymore, Edward G. Robinson, and Paul Muni. Much more damaging to the legitimate theatre would be the loss of many contemporary playwrights, who would travel out West by the trainload to become highly paid "dialoguers" for the various studios. Then came that black October day when the stock market crashed, and overnight the affluent Harding-Coolidge-Hoover years ended.

Still waving the banner of theatrical excellence, the Guild managed to remain solvent through the ensuing Depression years, but it would become more and more of a struggle. Gone were the Lunts; they'd become managers themselves and toured across America as their own bosses. A new producing venture, the Playwrights Company, siphoned away Guild stalwarts. It was formed by playwrights Maxwell Anderson, Sidney Howard, S. N. Behrman, Elmer Rice, and Robert E. Sherwood, all of whom had previously brought their plays to Helburn and Langner; but these powerful dramatists now desired autonomy and a larger share of the profits. True, the Guild retained O'Neill, and thus produced his *Strange Interlude*, and *Mourning Becomes Electra, Desire Under the Elms*, and his remarkable attempt at nostalgic comedy, *Ah, Wilderness!* There was the remarkable Heyward-Gershwin opera, *Porgy and Bess.* Critical kudos poured in, but financially the Guild was beginning to float unsteadily through seas of red ink. By 1939 it was sixty thousand preinflationary dollars in debt.

Then Katharine Hepburn, who had been dubbed "box-office poison" by movie exhibitors, came back to Manhattan with a new Philip Barry script in her hand. It was the charming and sophisticated *Philadelphia Story.* With Langner and Helburn as her partners ("the Guild, disrupted in management and tottering on its feet," Helburn later described it), Hepburn's gamble became a smash hit. The Guild was saved, albeit temporarily, by the Hollywood belle.

In 1940 the Guild produced Robert Sherwood's *There Shall Be No Night.* It starred their old standbys, Alfred Lunt and Lynn Fontanne, and while it was a major success it was only one hit amid a batch of other ventures that quietly expired.

So on that summer night at the Playhouse in Westport, Terry Helburn was well aware that she and her partners were on a dizzying financial tightrope, trying hard not to fall off. Where would the next successful idea come from to rescue them?

———————

"I don't remember who exactly thought of this, but somebody said 'Let's get Dick Rodgers over here,'" recalls Elaine Steinbeck today. "After all, Dorothy and Dick were right nearby, up the road in Fairfield. He was called, and he came down, sat through *Green Grow The Lilacs*, and I was also there afterwards, at the discussion with Terry and Lawrence. Dick said 'Yes, it's a good idea.'"

In her memoirs, Helburn summed up her intuitive response to *Green Grow the Lilacs* that warm summer night in Westport. "For years," she said, "I had been groping my way toward a new type of play with music, not musical comedy, not operetta in the old sense, but a form in which the dramatic action, music, and possibly ballet could be welded together into

A scene from Lynn Riggs's play Green Grow the Lilacs, as produced by the Theatre Guild. Curly is played by young Franchot Tone, Aunt Eller by Helen Westley, and young Laurey by June Walker. Unfortunately, no picture is available of Ali Hakim, the peddler, played in the original production, in 1931, by none other than the legendary Lee Strasberg, who would go on to found the Actors Studio. (Courtesy of Beinecke Library)

a compounded whole, each helping to tell the story in its own way. This was an idea which was finally crystallized years later, in *Oklahoma!*"

Now Terry Helburn had found herself a project. One that was still 90 percent fantasy and 10 percent fact. But she had the definite interest of Dick Rodgers, a major musical talent, and it was hardly a problem to secure an option on the rights to Riggs's play. Two firm assets. Or perhaps it would be more realistic to gauge them at one and a half. Dick Rodgers may have been bankable to potential Broadway investors, but Riggs's Oklahoma love story was far from the hottest property around town.

Even after Helburn called Riggs's agent at Samuel French with the notion of adapting *Green Grow the Lilacs* into a Broadway musical, Riggs's career in the theatre remained evidence of Robert Anderson's dry summary: "You can make a killing in the theatre, but you can't make a living." Helburn's option money was welcome indeed. Riggs, as usual, was working on another play, and whatever dollars came from the Guild would go to keeping him at his typewriter.

Years later, when *Oklahoma!* was established as a mammoth success, Ev Simms, one of Riggs's neighbors on Shelter Island, where the playwright had settled in the fifties, remembers him one day at his mailbox ripping open an envelope to remove a check. The money represented Riggs's share of the sale of the motion picture rights to *Oklahoma!* "My God!" cried Riggs. "I'm rich! This is seventy-five thousand dollars! It's more money than I've ever had in one piece all my life!"

We have few regional playwrights in today's theatre. Over the years we have become homogenized, and original dramatic voices with a local accent are few and very far between. But even back in the thirties Lynn Riggs was a rarity. Born in 1899 in Indian territory that would become a part of the state of Oklahoma in 1907, he grew up on the same open prairie that was the background, the essence, the wellspring of his writings.

His father had been a cowboy who turned to farming. (Appropriate enough in view of the Hammerstein lyric which would open the second act

```
                  GREEN GROW THE LILACS
                  ̲̲̲̲̲̲̲̲̲̲̲̲̲̲̲̲̲̲̲̲̲̲̲̲̲̲̲

MUSIC
MUSIC                                            BOOK

Rodgers & Hart                          Russell Crouse

Kern                                    Ira Gershwin

Bowles                                  Ben Hecht

Irving Berlin                           Morris Ryskind

Cole Porter                             Fields

Kurt Weill            LaTouche          Rose Franken

                                        Philip Barry

                                        S.N.Behrman

                                        Cecil Holm

Martin Flavin                           Jerome Chodorov

Paul Green

Moss Hart                               Valentine Davies

Mark Reed                               Paul Osborn

Belle Spewack                           Cornelia Otis Skinner

Michael Blankfort                       Pat Collinge
```

Early on in the planning stages of Away We Go! *Terry Helburn drew up a list, for discussion with her partners, of potential composers, lyricists, and librettists who could be considered for the future musicalization of Lynn Riggs's* Green Grow the Lilacs.

Theatre buffs should have a field day identifying some of the less famous potential talents who were being suggested by Helburn, Langner, et al. circa 1942. But what today seems most remarkable about this creative shopping list is not the talent that is on it but the one who is not, namely Oscar Hammerstein II!

of *Oklahoma!*—"The farmer and the cowman should be friends.") Young Lynn worked on the family farm but soon developed an attraction to the theatre that would continue all his life. When he left Oklahoma for the first time it was on a train carrying cattle to the Chicago stockyards. There he made an abrupt career reversal; he found a job singing in a local movie theatre. He moved on to New York, where his career was mainly a succession of dead-end jobs that supported him but led nowhere in particular. He returned to his native Oklahoma and began to write, first poetry, then drama. Soon he was trying to merge both into one form.

His plays met with predictable rejections. His first production, a love tragedy called *Big Lake*, had no success but did draw some attention to his talent. In 1930 he achieved his first professional production, under the aegis of the distinguished New York producer-director Arthur Hopkins. The play, *Roadside*, flopped, but it would earn Riggs a Guggenheim Fellowship. He used that welcome endowment to underwrite a trip to Paris, and there he wrote his next play, *Green Grow the Lilacs*.

With the sturdy homesteaders of turn-of-the-century Oklahoma, Riggs was writing about his own kind, celebrating his homeland and the people he knew intimately.

When his script reached the Theatre Guild, Terry Helburn became one of its staunchest supporters. This was precisely the sort of play the Guild needed—it had a fresh setting, it was peopled by robust characters, there were folk songs and dancing, a touching love story, and a dramatic climax in the second act when Jud (originally "Jeeter," in *Green Grow the Lilacs*) Fry was stabbed. It was far more than entertainment; it was truth. Helburn prevailed, and the Guild bought Riggs's play.

Cheryl Crawford, the Guild's casting director—she would later become a major Broadway producer with the Group Theatre—found the right actors for the 1931 production; the two leads were played by Franchot Tone and June Walker. The venerable Aunt Eller, shrewd and salty-tongued, was played by Helen Westley, one of the original founders of the Guild. For the supporting cast Crawford hired several genuine cowboys who happened to be in New York for the Madison Square Garden Rodeo; their presence added to this folk play an authenticity rarely found on Broadway.

Audiences enjoyed Riggs's love story and responded warmly to the folk ballads and Western cowboy laments interspersed through the production, but *Green Grow the Lilacs* did not exactly set New York on fire. Perhaps the 1931 audiences were more involved in their own day-to-day survival amidst the financial wreckage of the 1929 crash than they were with the problems of Curly's pursuit of Laurey in another, simpler time. Or perhaps a Western story was more suited to the screen, where cowboys roamed the range in search of justice. Whatever the reason, after its allotted sixty-four performances for the Guild's subscription audiences the play closed and went on tour. It finally ended up between the covers of Burns Mantle's *Ten Best Plays of 1931*, and in the Samuel French catalog of plays available for stock and amateur groups, and there it would remain until Terry Helburn called to discuss her plans for a musical version.

When the play was first printed Riggs supplied some very perceptive notes for future producers and directors. "My play might well have been retitled *An Old Song*," he wrote.

> My intent was to recapture in a kind of nostalgic glow . . . the great range of mood which characterized the old folk songs and ballads I used to hear in my Oklahoma childhood, their quaintness, their sadness, their robustness, their simplicity, their hearty or bawdy humors, their sentimentalities, their melodrama, their touching sweetness. . . . For this reason, I considered it wise to throw away the conventions of ordinary theatricality—a complex plot, swift action, etc., and to try to exhibit luminosity in the simplest of stories, a wide area of mood and feeling. After the people are known, I let them go ahead, acting out their simple tale, which might have been the substance of an ancient song.

Later these notes would be vital to the eventual conception, so simple and effective, that is the keynote of Oscar Hammerstein's libretto and the style of the Rodgers and Hammerstein score. Not only did his adaptors start from Riggs's original concept, they strengthened it.

After *Green Grow the Lilacs* closed, Riggs migrated west to Santa Fe, where the standard of living was so modest that he could afford to write more plays.

"Lynn loved it out there," says Mary Hunter Wolf, a director who was his friend and neighbor at the time.

He found it a very congenial atmosphere. Remember, there was a thriving artistic colony in the town and up north in Taos; painters, writers, poets, all working and enjoying the simple life, which in those days certainly didn't cost much. It was much more conducive to work than, say, his Oklahoma family background. Lynn's father resented Lynn's "artistic" background; it wasn't somehow fitting to have a son who wrote. In those days people weren't anywhere as openminded about such things as they might be today.

Out in Santa Fe nobody challenged one's life-style, or one's appetites, whatever they might be. So Lynn could go on living in a very modest style, supporting himself by tending the chickens of his neighbors, a very wealthy Santa Fe family! The family traveled a lot, and I suspect the job they'd given Lynn was a sort of endowment. But no matter, it kept him writing, and at the same time he took to studying those chickens every day. He loved to describe to me their social structure; which rooster ruled the flock and which hen stood where in the community pecking order. He took to treating them like characters in one of his scripts—that was the sort of wonderfully imaginative mind Lynn had!

Riggs's next play, *Cherokee Night*, a group of seven connecting scenes dealing with the life of the American Indian, would be produced in 1935 by the WPA Federal Theatre Project. The following season, his comedy *Russet Mantle,* which starred John Beal, had another respectable but barely profitable Broadway run.

Like so many other playwrights of that depressed period (and, alas, of our own times) Riggs could barely rely on the theatre for any livelihood. His theatre royalties were sporadic, if they came at all, and his periods of teaching, both at the University of Oklahoma and in North Carolina for his friend Paul Green, did not bring in very much money.

During those dark thirties and forties there was, however, one well at which writers could draw sweet sustenance. If Broadway was a depressed area, Hollywood had desks equipped with typewriters waiting for play-wrights. Studio executives were quite prepared to pay out weekly checks for infusions of literate dialogue. So in 1936 Riggs journeyed West to labor as cowriter on a very peculiar film epic for producer David O. Selznick that starred Charles Boyer and Marlene Dietrich. It was called *The Garden of Allah*, and it was a lushly romantic "saga" set in the Sahara (read Mojave) desert. What Riggs was doing attempting to make sense out of that totally garbled storyline has only one answer: the size of his paycheck.

The following year Riggs went to work for another Hollywood legend, the monumental Cecil B. DeMille (uncle to Agnes, who would later cho-reograph the ballets for *Oklahoma!*). DeMille decided that the young Oklahoma playwright was precisely the right talent to provide the proper feeling for his new epic, to be called *The Plainsman*. Once again it was a matter of economics, not art. Riggs did the job, took his salary, and left Hollywood for Santa Fe to continue his playwriting.

By the time Terry Helburn had begun her campaign to turn Riggs's play into a Broadway musical, he'd finished another play, *The Cream in the Well*. Directed by Mary Hunter Wolf, it opened in New York in 1941 and received respectable notices, but once again it added no black ink to Riggs's assets.

Even though Riggs could take a certain measure of confidence in the knowledge that Terry was a determined lady with sufficient drive and energy to bring her fantasy to eventual commercial life, he was also a realist. If the show ever happened, it might earn him a decent weekly royalty; after all, his new contract with the Guild called for 1 percent of whatever weekly gross the musical version of *Green Grow the Lilacs* took in. But being a man who'd had considerable experience on Broadway, and more important, with those chickens out in Santa Fe, Riggs was wisely not counting on anything—not until it happened.

Back he went to Los Angeles, where he would spend the first year of World War II in a writer's office at Universal. There, in one intense period of work, he completed four screenplays, highly forgettable films such as *Madame Spy*, *Destination Unknown*, and two scripts that were particularly divorced from the prairie, *Sherlock Holmes in Washington* and *Sherlock Holmes and the Voice of Terror*.

———————

But before there was Rodgers and Hammerstein there was Rodgers and Hart, and there Terry Helburn encountered her first roadblock. She'd discussed *Green Grow the Lilacs* as a project for Dick Rodgers and Larry Hart, and Rodgers had been enthusiastic. With such talents as these two the future for her project seemed very rosy indeed. It would be a reunion of the Guild with the pair whose career had begun with their success at *The Garrick Gaieties*. A natural, right?

Wrong. While Dick was willing, he could not commit Larry's participation.

Worse than that, it didn't seem as if the team of Rodgers and Hart could last much longer.

And so Terry Helburn's dream of a smash-hit musical, born that 1940 summer night in Westport, had to be put on hold until Dick Rodgers settled his future with Larry Hart.

RODGERS & HART & HAMMERSTEIN

ole Porter once penned a lyric ("A Picture of Me Without You") in which he slyly cited famous symbiotic pairings: Henry Ford and his car, Philadelphia and its Biddles, Fritz Kreisler and his fiddle, et al. He might well have added Rodgers and Hart.

LARRY

Rodgers without Hart was as improbable and difficult to imagine as, say, Mr. Sears without Mr. Roebuck. Or Mr. Rolls without Mr. Royce.

For the past two decades, ever since *The Garrick Gaieties*, they'd been a team. They were *the* team. They'd turned out a stream of love lyrics, brilliant comedy songs, gorgeous waltzes, and charming ballads for adoring audiences.

Irving Berlin himself had encapsulated their qualities years before.

> Tuneful and tasteful,
> Schmaltzy and smart.
> Music by Rodgers,
> Lyrics by Hart.

Praise from Caesar indeed.

Young and prolific, they were capable of turning out not only sharp and witty songs such as "Mountain Greenery," "Manhattan," and "Thou Swell," but also haunting and lovely ones that quickly became standards: "The Most Beautiful Girl In The World," "Little Girl Blue," "My Romance." The list goes on and on. During the late twenties when Broadway was treated to as many as thirty-odd musical shows a season, there were years when Rodgers and Hart accounted for as many as three. With sparkling musical-comedy gems in each one.

One Rodgers and Hart legend touched on the question "Where do you guys get your ideas for your songs?" The young songwriters were in Paris, riding in a taxi with two girls in 1926. Their cab skittered into a truck, and one of the girls blurted out, "Oh, my heart stood still!" From the floor of the cab, where the collision had thrown him, his hat jammed over his eyes, diminutive Larry Hart is supposed to have responded instantly, "Hey, there's a good title for a song!"

Even in those earliest years, Rodgers had difficulty in getting his partner to work. Rodgers's work pattern was fixed; he got up early, sharpened his pencils, and went to work. By that time Larry Hart had probably been asleep for only two hours, having finally ended an all-night party at his apartment. Ending a party at Larry's wasn't so easy. It meant throwing out a crowd: half of Paul Whiteman's band, an act from the Cotton Club, the bartender from Louie Bergin's midtown bar, and a dozen chorus girls from his latest show.

How does one paint a portrait in mere prose of the mercurial, witty Larry Hart, that diminutive, cigar-smoking genius whose generosity was

Mr. Hart and Mr. Rodgers caught in their remarkably productive early years. (Courtesy of The Rodgers & Hammerstein Organization)

as legendary as his bubbling wit? ("I never saw Larry let anybody else, even a complete stranger, pick up a check," remembers George Church, who danced in *On Your Toes* fifty-plus years ago.) Hart's profligacy extended not only to his wallet but also to his brilliant brain. Keenly sharp, ever deft, hair-trigger, Hart's agile wit functioned in rapid spurts. Mere alcohol could do nothing to dull it. Lyrics poured forth in torrents as if from an uncapped gusher. In his own book, *Lyrics*, Oscar Hammerstein, who had known Larry Hart all those years back to their Columbia University undergraduate days, paid his fellow lyricist the ultimate generous tribute. "If you would achieve the rhyming grace and facility of W. S. Gilbert, or Lorenz Hart," wrote Hammerstein, "my advice would be never to open a rhyming dictionary, or even to own one."

"I met Oscar before I met Larry," Dick Rodgers recalled years later in the *Dramatists Guild Quarterly*. "I was twelve and he was nineteen when my older brother Mortimer, a fraternity brother of Oscar's, took me backstage after a performance of a Columbia Varsity Show. Oscar played the comic lead in the production, and meeting this worldly college junior was pretty heady stuff for a stagestruck kid."

And Larry Hart? "I met him four years later," said Rodgers.

I was still in high school at the time, but I had already begun writing songs for amateur shows and I was determined even then to make composing my life's work. Although I had written words to some of my songs, I was anxious to team up with a full-fledged lyricist. A mutual friend, Philip Leavitt . . . introduced us one Saturday afternoon at Larry's house.

Larry came to the door of the brownstone, wearing house slippers, a pair of tuxedo trousers, and some kind of a shirt. It was a Sunday, so he needed a shave, but then Larry always needed a shave, except on state occasions. Larry was twenty-three. To me he was the old man of the mountain, and I was a naive child. But I wasn't so naive that I didn't know I was in the presence of talent. What Larry had to say about lyrics and the making of lyrics and the relationship of lyrics to the theatre was exciting and tremendously stimulating. In one afternoon I acquired a career, a partner, a best friend.

At the time the two met, young Hart was gainfully but gloomily employed translating German plays and musical comedy librettos for the all-powerful Shuberts. Rodgers and Hart shortly thereafter formed a working partnership with another Columbia alumnus, Herbert Fields, the son of the great Lew Fields, 50 percent of the legendary comedy team Weber and Fields. For a long time very little came of their efforts. Even with Herbie Fields supplying clever librettos it was, as it has always been and ever will be, tough for three aspiring writers to break down doors. Dorothy Fields, Herbie's younger sister, herself a great lyricist ("I Can't Give You Anything but Love, Baby," "On the Sunny Side of the Street," "Big Spender," to name but a sampling of her catalogue), remembered the feeling of frustration well. She was later to encounter it herself. "They had bright, fresh, wonderful ideas, but no one gave them an ear," she said. "Fields, Rodgers, and Hart peddled their wares to diverse producers, who fixed a baleful eye on brother Herbie and said, 'If you guys are as good as you think you are, how come your father isn't interested in producing your show?' " Fields *père* did interpolate one of their earliest songs, "Any Old Place with You," into a 1919 show of his called *A Lonely Romeo*. Hart's lyric contained the marvelous couplet

> I'll go to hell for ya,
> Or Philadelphia

but in general it was a long and frustrating period.

Herbie Fields went looking for jobs as a librettist. Rodgers and Hart then went to see diminutive Max Dreyfus, a major force in popular music who was then with the publishing firm of T. B. Harms. Dreyfus agreed that they had talent but felt they were too young for the business. His advice was that they go somewhere and study. Hart returned to his job with the Shuberts. Rodgers enrolled at the Institute of Musical Art to study classical music under Dr. Frank Damrosch. At the end of a year in that school he was selected to write the Institute's annual show; obviously his talents for popular music rather than classical were evident to his instructors.

But he and Hart continued working; they wrote no fewer than twenty amateur shows over the next two years, benefits for girls' schools, churches, and synagogues. It was work, certainly, but it was a dead end, and worst of all it brought in little if any money. One of Rodgers's family friends, a businessman in the garment district, had been lending the young composer small sums of money. By the time Rodgers owed his benefactor a hundred dollars he decided the onus of such a debt was overwhelming, and he decided to throw in the towel. He would take a job and earn a regular living. His friend led him across the hall to a Mr. Marcin, who was in the children's underwear business and was looking for a young man he could train to succeed him upon his retirement. He offered young Rodgers $50 a week to start immediately.

Rodgers asked for a day or so to think it over.

That evening, at home, he was called by Benjamin Kaye, the lawyer for the Theatre Guild, who offered Rodgers the task of writing *The Garrick Gaieties*. Rodgers suggested his partner Hart. Larry had recently spent most of his money trying to produce two shows that had been spectacular failures; he was also on his uppers. Luckily for the American musical theatre, the Guild agreed to employ both Rodgers and Hart, and the next day Rodgers passed up a possible career in childrens' underwear.

When the Guild opened the show in 1925 at the Garrick Theatre, the program note read, "*The Garrick Gaieties* believes in not only abolishing the star system, it believes in abolishing the stars. The members of *The Garrick Gaieties* were recruited, impressed, mobilized, or drafted from the ranks of *Caesar and Cleopatra*, *The Guardsman*, *Saint Joan*, *They Knew What They Wanted*, and other Theatre Guild productions." In the cast of that delightful and witty show were such future theatrical luminaries as Harold Clurman, Elsbeth Holman (who later changed her name to Libby and became not only a famous torch singer but the wife of a Reynolds tobacco heir), and Lee Strasberg. When the show opened critic Robert Benchley

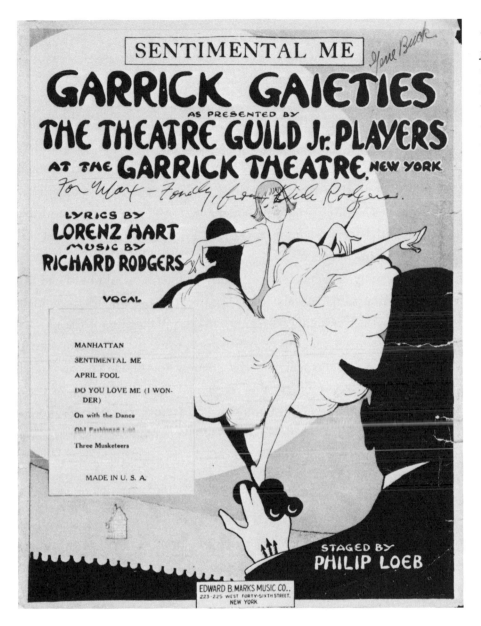

"Sentimental Me," from **The Garrick Gaieties,** *that brisk, clever revue which featured talented newcomers and was produced in 1925 for a limited run by the Guild at the Garrick Theatre, to raise funds for wall hangings at the new Guild Theatre. The Guild is no longer an active producing management, the wall hangings are long gone, the Guild Theatre is now the Virginia, but the young team that wrote the score for* **The Garrick Gaieties,** **Richard Rodgers** *and* **Lorenz Hart,** *will, happily, live on forever through their work.*

happily referred to it as "the most civilized show in town." (The fact that he had become enraptured with one of the singers in the cast, Betty Starbuck, may have somewhat affected his judgment.)

After their success at the Garrick Theatre, the young team of Rodgers and Hart were recognized. Reunited with Herbie Fields, they went to work for their early patron, Lew Fields, for whom they wrote a show called *Dearest Enemy* in 1925. Along with "Manhattan," they now had another song hit, "Here in My Arms." Then, in rapid succession, came the Fields production of *The Girl Friend*, which contained "The Blue Room," and the title song, and a second edition of *Garrick Gaieties*, which contained the lilting "Mountain Greenery."

For the ensuing decade or so the Broadway theatre would be the seedbed of great American musicals. To call the twenties and thirties the golden age of songwriting (certainly one cannot make a like claim for the libretti supplied by assorted gagwriters to fit the stars who twinkled in those shows) is no understatement. One has merely to run down the list of practitioners of the period: Irving Berlin; George and Ira Gershwin; Cole Porter; Jerome Kern; Sigmund Romberg; and Hammerstein. P. G. Wodehouse, B. G. DeSylva, Lew Brown and Ray Henderson. Bert Kalmar and Harry Ruby, young Harold Arlen. Vernon Duke, E. Y. Harburg, Harry Warren, Richard Whiting . . . on and on goes the roster of those major talents. Truly, Times Square and its environs were host to a movable, eight-performances-a-week musical feast.

And Rodgers and Hart quickly moved to the forefront during those happy, melodious years.

"The great thing about Larry," remarked Rodgers years later, "was that he was always growing, creatively if not physically. He was fascinated by the various techniques of rhyming, such as polysyllabic rhymes, interior rhymes, masculine and feminine rhymes, and the trick of rhyming one word with only part of another."

But Hart was no scholar. Once, when Margaret Case Harriman sought to probe his academic attitudes for a profile, she reported, "Stirred to some heat, Larry will wave his cigar dangerously, pull at his explosively patterned necktie, and yell, 'Why, I don't even know what onomatopoeia is, or a trope!'"

"Larry was intrigued by almost every facet of human emotion," Rodgers noted. "In 'Where or When' he dared to take up the psychic phenomenon of a person convinced that he has known someone before even though the two people are meeting for the first time. It should not be overlooked, however, that Larry was also attracted to the simple life. Remember his paean to rustic charm in 'There's a Small Hotel,' or to 'our blue room, far away upstairs'? Or his attitude in 'My Romance,' in which he dismissed as unnecessary all the conventional romantic props when two people find themselves really in love."

Innovation was Hart's mainstay, and he and Rodgers demonstrated it successfully over the years of their partnership before *Oklahoma!* Formulae were meant to be broken; in *Peggy-Ann* they abandoned the opening chorus in favor of fifteen minuts of spoken dialogue before the first song was sung. In 1926 it was a hit. *Chee Chee* in 1928 tried to meld songs and book into a single entity. It didn't succeed commercially, but it inspired the team to consider trying other significant rule-breaking. *Time* magazine summed up their attitude in 1938: "As Rodgers and Hart see it, what was killing musicomedy was its sameness, its tameness, its eternal rhyming of 'June' with 'moon.' They decided it was not enough to be just good at the job; they had to be constantly different also. The one possible formula was *Don't have a formula*; the one rule for success, *Don't follow it up*."

They had written no less than eleven hit shows before they ventured West in the early thirties to work at Paramount for director Rouben Mamoulian on *Love Me Tonight*, starring Maurice Chevalier and Jeanette MacDonald. Their score contained such brilliant work as "Isn't It Romantic?" "Lover," "Mimi," and the inevitable title song, "Love Me Tonight."

The year before they'd written several songs for a forgettable Warner

What can you say about Richard Rodgers and Lorenz Hart that they haven't already said for themselves? Well and truly launched by The Garrick Gaieties, they sang for their supper for almost a quarter of a century. Did you want a beautiful ballad? They could make your heart stand still. A sardonic comment on the life of a dance-hall hostess, one which still has a cutting edge? Try "Ten Cents a Dance."

Brothers film, *The Hot Heiress*, and came away justifiably convinced that talkies were not a medium they could function happily in, but the experience with Mamoulian was quite the opposite. He took their talents and ideas and embodied them in the Paramount film. The trio integrated story, music and lyrics, *and* film scenes into one rollicking, coherent structure. "We took numbers all over the place," said Rodgers. "In those days they used to plant the camera in front of the boy and girl and start to grind, and they'd sing, and that was it. But this was the first time that musical sound track was cut—dialogue and music interspersed. As a matter of fact, in the opening song, 'Isn't It Romantic?' we went from Chevalier's tailor shop in Paris to Jeanette MacDonald's castle, far away. Various people or groups sang the song, passed it along, so she heard it on the balcony of her castle and picked it up and learned it . . . all done through the use of music,

They journeyed
to London, where
Beatrice Lillie
needed numbers
for her latest show,
and British audi-
ences demanded
encores for "Morn-
ing Is Midnight."
And later on, when
the talented team
gave us the musical
Pal Joey, we were
treated to their
classic lament
of the lovelorn
lady, "Bewitched,
Bothered and
Bewildered."
   A remarkable
team. Has Broad-
way ever again
encountered such
a versatile pair?

sound track cutting, and so forth. Absolutely revolutionary for this period. But only because Mamoulian believed in this technique."

Despite this success, Rodgers and Hart were quickly characterized as far too sophisticated and high-toned by the musically illiterate studio heads. In 1933 their talents were utilized in a marvelously sophisticated film called *Hallelujah! I'm a Bum*, which starred Al Jolson and had a script by S. N. Behrman, but the film was a disaster at the box office.

Director Lewis Milestone told John Kobal, years later, "First time around it didn't make any money at all. . . . It was *too* far ahead of its time, especially in the songs and the lyrics. Larry Hart was a *real* genius, and I was always interested in the political changes happening in the country. . . . One time I remember we were in Tijuana when I said to Larry, 'You know, we ought to have a song for Al Jolson, for the hobo, which should be something like Chaliapin's famous song about the flea who lives in the king's coat.' This would be a plea for the rest of the hobos to understand him. Because the accusation was that he accepted a job, which is the worst crime in the world. We were in a car, going through the main thoroughfare of Tijuana. He yelled to the chauffeur to stop the car. He rushed out and I went after him, into a saloon and came up to the bar, and he said, 'Gimme a drink.' He got a drink and a paper and pencil to write on. He swallowed the drink, and the pencil flew across the paper, and he said, 'How would that be?' And he read me the lyrics. This is the plea the hobo makes during the kangaroo court . . . I think I can still remember the lyrics:

> Look, your honor, please take note,
> There are two little fleas on your honor's coat.
> Two little fleas, and we don't care whether
> The fleas are merry, they're just fleaing together.
> The way of the world is a he and she
> And if it's all right for a flea it's all right for me.

"This was done right there, with a drink, and I had to tell him it was marvelous."

Rodgers and Hart fled Hollywood. (Larry had written their exit lyric already, for Jolson to sing in *Hallelujah! I'm a Bum*—it was "I've Gotta Get Back to New York.")

Once back on their home turf they started in on Billy Rose's mammoth new spectacle for the Hippodrome Theatre, *Jumbo*. Their score would contain "The Most Beautiful Girl in the World," "Little Girl Blue," and "My Romance." They were truly back where they belonged; all through the runs of their next shows, *On Your Toes*, *Babes in Arms*, and the political satire *I'd Rather Be Right*, ticket buyers lined up at the box office, cheerfully plunked down their cash, and, when the show was over, ran out of the theatre, humming, to buy Rodgers and Hart sheet music and/or the recordings.

But beneath the charming lyrics, the sharp-edged wit, the laughter that his couplets induced, the lines that Hart could dash off to Rodgers' melodies, there was another, darker, and tortured Larry Hart.

"Larry was a night person," said one of the Broadway coterie who knew his habits well. "He never seemed to have any place to go. He'd hang around Louie Bergin's Tavern on Forty-fifth Street, stay there until closing time, buying everybody drinks. All he wanted to do was talk."

It began to be more and more difficult for Rodgers to persuade his partner to do the work he needed from him. "He had to have the music first," Rodgers related. "But Larry had to be trapped in a number of ways before he would work. Music was one of the ways. We had to work very closely in the same room, together. He wouldn't pick up a pencil unless I was there." Often, Hart would not be there at all. Once, defensively, in answer to a frown from Rodgers when he'd finally returned from some protracted absence from their work, he said, "Did Gilbert bawl out Sullivan for giving him the slip and writing 'Onward Christian Soldiers'?"

Hart's depressions, fueled by the self-hatred that had seeped into his soul, deepened. Once he said to Ted Fetter, another very talented lyricist (he wrote "Taking a Chance on Love" with John Latouche,), "I can't believe I make so much money. It's completely disproportionate for the work I do to earn it." He might have been able to come to terms with that lack of self-worth, but the other, far more deeply rooted angst which gnawed at Hart was his sexual appetite. Unlike his partner Rodgers, who was happily married to the lovely Dorothy and who lived an ordered life with his children, Hart was a homosexual. In the twenties and thirties, good Jewish boys from middle-class families who'd been properly educated at Columbia were supposed to go on to live a middle-class married life. Homosexuality was still "the love that dares not speak its name," as in Oscar Wilde's time. In England its practice was still an offense punishable by law, in America a powerful taboo. During the Jazz Age sexual license extended primarily to heterosexuals.

He was short, he wasn't very attractive, and inside the dark closet of his soul tiny Larry Hart must have sat and wept. Every so often his scribbling pencil would reveal the pain he constantly lived with each day. "Spring is here," he asked, "Why doesn't my heart go dancing?" And he finished that lament by saying "Maybe it's because nobody needs me." In 1926 one of his lyrics in a long-forgotten show called *Betsy* sighed:

> This funny world
> Makes fun of the things that you strive for . . .
> If you're beaten, conceal it,
> There's no pity for you.
> For the world cannot feel it,
> Just keep to yourself,
> Weep to yourself.

Later on, his complaint would be even sadder:

> Where's that rainbow we hear about?
> Where's that rainbow they cheer about?

Which ends with:

> It is easy to see all right,
> Everything's gonna be all right.
> Be just dandy for everybody, but me.

Even in his comic laments lay deeply imbedded self-pity.

> Two feet are ever cold,
> Four feet are never cold. . . .
> Nature is hard to deny.
> Everybody has someone,
> Why can't I?

Over the years of his enormously successful partnership with his steady and sober partner ("You know how he always calls me the high-school principal," Rodgers once reminded Josh Logan, their director on *By Jupiter* in 1942 when their working pattern was crumbling). Larry's bouts of self-hatred, his depressions, gnawed deeper and deeper into his psyche. Scotch had long since become his sustenance; all-night parties and monumental morning hangovers were his defense against despair . . . and they didn't help. It became harder and harder for him to address himself to lilting ballads that promised happy endings, or to provide the gaily insouciant couplets the performers needed up on stage, where everyone was play-acting.

In the year following *Pal Joey*, while Terry Helburn waited for Dick Rodgers to persuade Larry to join him on *Green Grow the Lilacs*, the two had been discussing the possibility of turning Edna Ferber's *Saratoga Trunk* into a musical. In July of 1941, Dick Rodgers had gotten in touch with Oscar Hammerstein, their old Columbia chum, about writing the libretto. But as often happens on Broadway, too many disparate elements were involved, and the project eventually was negotiated out of existence.

Shortly afterwards, Rodgers did something hitherto unheard of in their partnership. He took on a project without Larry. So frustrated was he at his partner's erratic work habits that in desperation he became George Abbott's silent producing partner in a new musical, *Best Foot Forward*, with a score by two extremely talented young writers, Hugh Martin and Ralph Blane.

After the show opened in Philadelphia, Rodgers took a day off and drove out to visit Hammerstein at his Doylestown farmhouse. There he explained to Hammerstein the predicament he now found himself in; he had taken on the Abbott project without any credit on the marquee or in the program, simply because he was afraid if Larry found out he was working without him it would cause his partner to go completely to pieces. But he and Larry also had a commitment to do the score of a proposed musical to be based on Ludwig Bemelmans's *Hotel Splendide* for which the screenwriter, Donald Ogden Stewart, was presently writing a book. And Dick had become convinced that Larry would be unable to do his share of the work. Would Oscar consider collaborating with them? That way, at least there was a guarantee of the project being finished. Hammerstein thought it over, and then he demurred. No, he could not, would not be a party to such an arrangement.

"I think you should keep working with Larry just as long as he is able to keep working with you," he told Rodgers. "It would kill him if you walked away while he was still able to function. But," he added, "if the time ever comes when he cannot function, call me. I'll be there." With that assurance, Rodgers returned to Philadelphia and his chores with *Best Foot Forward*, which came into New York and became a highly successful venture. *Hotel Splendide* was eventually abandoned.

By 1942 producer Dwight Deere Wiman had brought Rodgers and Hart into the production of a musical version of an old play, *The Warrior's Husband*. Starring dancer Ray Bolger, *By Jupiter* was prepared for rehearsals. But Hart's efforts were by now so haphazard and erratic that he had to be placed under a doctor's care. When Hart's physician had him hospitalized up at Doctors Hospital, Rodgers took the medico's advice and moved into the hospital; there he could work at a piano that had been installed in the interns' quarters when Cole Porter had been a patient. *By Jupiter* opened to enthusiastic notices and was a wartime hit.

DICK

Larry Hart had come to Dante's dark wood, but Dick Rodgers would not, could not follow. He turned to the *Green Grow the Lilacs* project in earnest. The Theatre Guild and Terry Helburn were waiting, not so patiently. It had been two years since Terry had conceived her plan; she and Lawrence Langner well understood what healthy box office grosses from a smash Rodgers and Hart show such as *By Jupiter* would bring into their depleted bank accounts. What they did not yet understand was that Rodgers could no longer work with his partner.

"Few people knew I was headed for the army," remembered Josh Logan, "so at a party given by the Theatre Guild, Theresa Helburn asked me to direct an old play . . . which was being turned into a musical for Rodgers and Hart. . . . I had to beg off because of my draft. I told Dick how sorry I was and asked that he and Larry think of me in the future.

"Dick said, 'Josh, I don't know how to put this, but Larry doesn't want to work any more. I don't know if it's some kind of boxed-up panic, or whether it's me. . . .'

" 'You mean, you'll work with some other lyricist?'

" 'I'll have to, Josh. Oh, I'll do something with Larry again. Maybe the only way to scare him out of this is to find someone else. What would you think of Oscar Hammerstein?'

"Just hearing the name made my heart beat faster. The *Show Boat* lyrics were one of my early enthusiasms.

"I said, 'Dick, you and Hammerstein would be unbeatable.'

" 'Can he do comedy songs? Larry was always able to get laughs. I don't know. I don't know.' "

Rodgers decided to make one last try, out of affection for his old and dear friend. He told Hart of his fondness for *Green Grow the Lilacs* and sent him a copy of the script. The two men met at the Chappell Music publishing offices, where Max Dreyfus, their friend and associate for all those successful years, reigned.

Even years later, Rodgers's memories of that day were painful.

A haggard and pale Larry walked in. He had obviously not had a good night's sleep in weeks, and I realized I could no longer avoid talking about what was on my mind—that if necessary I'd have to be brutal to make him understand what he was doing not only to himself but to our partnership. I began by telling him I wanted to get started on the new show right away but that he was obviously in no condition to work.

Standing at his antique desk in Doylestown, Pennsylvania, Oscar Hammerstein might well be pondering whether or not the very last couplet of "All the Things You Are" might possibly be rewritten to omit and replace that final word . . . "mine." Such are the problems that beset perfectionists. Their angst is our gain. (Courtesy of The Rodgers & Hammerstein Organization)

Larry admitted this and said that he needed a rest and was planning to leave soon for a vacation in Mexico. He was sure it would straighten him out and he'd return feeling much better.

This was nonsense; he knew it and I knew it.

"Larry," I said, "the only reason you're going to Mexico is to drink. When you come back, you'll be in worse shape than ever."

Larry looked as if I'd stabbed him. This was the first time in all the years we'd been together that I had ever spoken to him this way.

"We've got to work something out for the good of both of us," I continued. "I want you to have yourself admitted to a sanitarium, and I'll have myself admitted along with you. We'll be there together and we'll work together. The only way you're ever going to lick this thing is to get off the street."

Larry, who had been avoiding my eyes, looked at the floor and said, "I know, Dick, I'm sorry. But I want to go to Mexico. I have to."

I felt the blood rushing to my head. "This show means a lot to me," I told him. "If you walk out on me now, I'm going to do it with someone else."

"Anyone in mind?"

"Yes, Oscar Hammerstein."

Even the realization that I wasn't bluffing, that I actually had someone else waiting to take over, couldn't shake him. Still looking at the floor, all that Larry said was "Well, you couldn't pick a better man." Then for the first time he looked me in the eye. "You know, Dick," he said, "I've never understood why you've put up with me all these years. It's been crazy. The best thing for you to do is to forget about me."

There wasn't much more either of us could say. Larry could no more fight his compulsive drinking than I could have thrown aside my family and career. He got up to leave, and when he reached the door he turned around and said, "There's just one thing. I really don't think *Green Grow the Lilacs* can be turned into a good musical. I think you're making a mistake."

With that he was gone, and so was our partnership.

I walked out of the boardroom to tell Max Dreyfus, who was waiting in his office, what had happened. But I never got there. I simply broke down and cried.

Larry did go to Mexico. When he returned a month later, he had to be carried off the train on a stretcher.

By that time Rodgers had gotten in touch with Hammerstein. In July, four days after Oscar Hammerstein had finished the libretto and lyrics for a modern-day version of Bizet's *Carmen*, which he called *Carmen Jones*, Rodgers called.*

Rodgers and Hammerstein arranged lunch at the Barberry Room, where Rodgers came to the point even before the food was ordered. Letters, telegrams, and phone calls to Larry in Mexico had brought no response. The time had come when he had to be replaced. "The Guild wants me to do a musical based on one of their early plays," Rodgers told Hammerstein. "Terry Helburn approached me about doing it, and I think she's right. I wonder if we could get together? Why don't you read it and see how you like it."

"What's the play?" asked Hammerstein.

"*Green Grow the Lilacs*," said Rodgers.

"I don't have to read it," said Hammerstein. "I know it, and I'm crazy about it. I'd love to do it with you."

OSCAR

The fortyish burly gentleman who was shortly to go to work with Dick Rodgers as his new collaborator was a radically different personality from Larry Hart. Hart was mercurial, Hammerstein stable. He was also thoughtful, generous, and basically disciplined. He worked every day at the tall desk in his study, standing and writing. Both men were talented; comparing their work was as pointless as comparing apples and oranges. If Hart was the hare, Hammerstein was the tortoise. But Hammerstein had devel-

---

*According to Michael Feinstein, Ira Gershwin related to him how Rodgers, on a trip to California, had also approached Gershwin to offer him the task of writing lyrics for Riggs's play. But Ira had regretfully refused. It wasn't Riggs's play that bothered him; he liked it. But he simply did not feel himself the right talent for the job. "If I had written the lyrics," he mused years later, "they'd have been part of a completely different kind of show . . . and nowhere near as important as it became." While Ira certainly had the benefit of hindsight for his statement, he was probably correct.

oped the sort of determination best described in the lyrics of a popular song by his friend Dorothy Fields: he coped with failure by picking himself up, dusting himself off, and starting all over again. From his flops he accumulated scar tissue.

It began very early. Hammerstein wrote his first produced play in 1919, when he was twenty-four. *The Light* was tried out in New Haven. "After the first act, Dad knew he had a flop," recalls his son William. "In fact, later he always referred to it as 'The Light That Failed.' Well, he left the Shubert Theatre during the first intermission and went for a walk around the Yale Campus. He wasn't just going out for a depressed ramble; what he was doing was thinking what he would write for his *next* play."

That inner resilience would stand him well throughout his entire life. As would his keen social consciousness. Rodgers said of him, years later, "He was a joiner, a leader, a man willing to do battle for whatever causes he believed in. He was not naive. He knew full well that man is not all good and that nature is not all good; yet it was his sincere belief that someone had to keep reminding people of the vast amount of good things there are in the world."

His kindnesses to others in the business were legendary. He never forgot the old show-business adage, "Help people on the way up; you never know whom you'll meet on the way down." Edmund Hartmann, who later became a successful writer-producer in Hollywood, came to New York seeking his start in the theatre in the darkest gloom of 1932. A mutual friend sent the unknown young Hartmann to consult with Hammerstein, who'd already made a considerable career with Kern, Romberg, and Otto Harbach. "I went over to the theatre where he was in the midst of rehearsals for *Music in the Air*, a new show he'd written with Jerome Kern," remembers Hartmann. "Here I was, a total nobody, with an armful of material, hoping to get a break somewhere. Who needed to bother with me? But Oscar took time out from his hectic rehearsal, we went to the back of the theatre, he sat down with me, he read my stuff, and spent almost an entire hour telling me which of my things was commercial, which was funny, and why, and which wasn't. It was so helpful and generous—I've never forgotten it—a bigtime guy, the author of *Show Boat*, sitting down to consult with a bewildered kid!"

Oscar was a pragmatic teacher, not only a critic but willing to share what he'd learned. In the rough-and-tumble of show business, he was a rarity. He was also a perfectionist. "Even when songs were completed, they might not satisfy him," recalled his son William. "Take that final couplet of 'All the Things You Are,' from *Very Warm for May*, which he wrote with Kern; a song which everyone else considers near-perfect. Not Oscar. That next to last line—'To know that moment divine,'—he wanted to change that word *divine*. It always bothered him."

The song was written in 1939, and as late as 1949 his book *Lyrics* finds him complaining still: "Nothing served as well as that unwanted *divine*. I never could find a way out."

Hammerstein had grown up in a theatrical family. His grandfather, Oscar Hammerstein, was a major impresario of the 1890s and early 1900s. In 1906 he built the Manhattan Opera House on West Thirty-fourth Street, in an effort to give the Metropolitan a run for its money. Someone asked Hammerstein if there was any money in grand opera. "Yes," replied the impresario. "*My* money is in it." Under his management, the greatest singers of the day, Emma Calvé, Madame Tetrazzini, Mary Garden, and John McCormack, appeared on his stage.

His grandson Oscar entered Columbia in 1916. His family wanted him to become a lawyer, and for one year he dutifully studied law, but he gave it up soon after he began appearing in the Columbia varsity shows. In the 1917 show *Home, James!*, Oscar did a dance in a leopard-skin costume; he had also written most of the lyrics. The show was a success, and the young Columbia student, hopelessly infected with the family disease, left law behind. He went downtown and managed to persuade his uncle Arthur to put him to work as an assistant stage manager; similar jobs followed. While he worked backstage he kept on writing lyrics and concocting possible storylines for musical shows. Soon enough, in 1920, his uncle put him to work on two shows, *Always You* and *Tickle Me*.

Later Hammerstein recalled, "I was born into the theatrical world with two gold spoons in my mouth. One was my uncle Arthur, who took me into his producing organization and gave me wise guidance. It was he who supplied the second gold spoon, Otto Harbach. Harbach, at my uncle's persuasion, accepted me as a collaborator. His generosity in dividing credits and royalties with me was the least of his favors. Much more important were the things he taught me about writing for the theatre." He and Harbach began writing in 1922, and their first show was *Wildflower*. To the music supplied by Herbert Stothart and Vincent Youmans they produced two hits, "Bambalina" and the title song. In 1924 came *Rose-Marie*.

Years later Hammerstein wrote, "Like most young writers, I had an eagerness to get words down on paper. Harbach taught me to think a long time before actually writing. He taught me never to stop work on anything if you can think of one small improvement to make." Harbach's list of credits is formidable indeed. He also worked on *No, No, Nanette*, *Whoopee*, *Sunny*, *The Desert Song*, *The Cat and the Fiddle*, and *Roberta*. "It is almost unbelievable," mused Hammerstein, "that a man with this record of achievement received so little recognition."

Oscar became one of the most sought-after lyricists of the busy Broadway musical theatre in the twenties. Soon he began to collaborate with Sigmund Romberg, a prolific composer whose music was so easily appreciated that Broadway wits liked to quip, "His is the kind of music you hum as you go into the theatre." "Romberg got me into the habit of working hard," Hammerstein said. "In our first collaboration, *The Desert Song*, I used to visit him. I remember bringing up a finished lyric to him one day. He played it over and then he said, 'It fits.' Then he turned to me and asked, 'What else have you got?' I said that I didn't have anything more, but I would go away and set another melody. He persuaded me to stay right there and write it while he was working on something else. He put me in

Oscar Hammerstein's previous watershed work, which he wrote with Jerome Kern.

another room with a pad and pencil. Afraid to come out empty-handed, I finished another refrain that afternoon. I have written many plays and pictures with Rommy, and his highest praise has always been the same 'It fits.' Disappointed at first with such limited approval, I learned later that what he meant was not merely that the words fitted the notes, but that they matched the spirit of his music, and that he thought they were fine."

But it would be in collaboration with Jerome Kern that Hammerstein would reach the high-water mark of his early success. In 1927, when he was only thirty-two, Oscar wrote the lyrics and did the adaptation of Edna Ferber's novel *Show Boat*, with its indestructible classics "Can't Help Lovin' Dat Man," "Make Believe," "Why Do I Love You?" and the epic and powerful "Ol' Man River." *

Prior to the production by Florenz Ziegfeld of *Show Boat*, Broadway musicals were mostly assembly-line concoctions, arranged to show off a star comedian's talents or a leading lady's charms. Hammerstein summed up the state of the librettist's art years later. "The composer and the lyric-writer concentrated mainly on a few major efforts, a big dance number, a love ballad, a light comedy duet, and one or two songs for the comedians. In the latter, while the author would write the best jokes he could, the composer would write music which was not out of his top drawer— he did not want to waste a good melody on a comedy song. The librettist was kind of a stable boy. If the race was lost, he was blamed for giving the horse the wrong feed. For many years I read theatrical criticism and comment which contained the statement 'The book of a musical doesn't matter'; and yet, in the case of most failures it was pointed out that the book was so bad that it could not be survived."

In the years since Kern and Hammerstein created *Show Boat*, the show

*A classic Broadway story grew up about "Ol' Man River." Mrs. Kern and Mrs. Hammerstein arrived at a party, and their hostess introduced them. "This is Mrs. Jerome Kern," she began. "Her husband wrote 'Ol' Man River.'" "Not true," said Mrs. Hammerstein. "Mrs. Kern's husband wrote *dumdumdeedah, da dumdumdeedah*. My husband wrote 'Ol' man river, dat ol' man river!'"

has assumed its rightful status as an American classic. As important a watershed event in the theatre as *Oklahoma!* would be some fifteen years later, *Show Boat* was a truly remarkable meld of romantic story, drama, comedy, and emotion, plus spectacle, all of its elements deftly integrated and impelled for two acts by the music and lyrics.

Show Boat heralded a new era, one in which the musical's book and its lyrics would be treated by knowing producers with much more respect. The musical theatre began to mature. The Gershwins would provide scores to satirical books by sharp writers such as George S. Kaufman and Morrie Ryskind. Howard Lindsay and Russel Crouse could collaborate with Cole Porter, as could Moss Hart; Howard Dietz and Arthur Schwartz, E. Y. Harburg, Harold Arlen, and Vernon Duke would join in sophisticated revues, and eventually such a major operatic work as *Porgy and Bess* would find its place on a Broadway stage. But *Show Boat* had led the way.

Almost seven decades later, producer-director Hal Prince, who is preparing a revival of *Show Boat*, is lavish in his praise of Hammerstein's contribution to musical theatre. "His book is solidly constructed, like the very best play," he says. "What I find interesting is that if you analyze it, you find he still retains elements of past clichés—for instance, the two subsidiary comedy characters, male and female, who were played by Eva Puck and Sammy White out of vaudeville. They sang and danced and provided comedy relief—straight out of old musical comedies. But around them Hammerstein assembled this highly dramatic story which dealt with bigotry, race prejudice, tragedy—all sorts of elements nobody in those days had ever dared to touch.

"Funny about those two subsidiary comic characters," muses Prince. "They remained a fixture of musicals right up to *Oklahoma!*, where Hammerstein had them as Ado Annie and Will Parker. And even afterwards, if you look, you'll find them, even in Loesser's *The Most Happy Fella*. I think the first time we saw them gone for good was when Steve Sondheim began creating shows such as *Company*."

By the early thirties, Hammerstein would join with other dramatists who would migrate West to Hollywood, where the studios were rolling out all-talking, all-singing, all-dancing musicals on a monthly assembly line. "Everyone in those days was seduced by Hollywood," says Hammerstein's son William, who vividly remembers being transplanted to California when his father went to work in films. "They went out there to make money. Oh, some of them may have had noble thoughts about the art of the film, but I don't think in the early thirties it had reached that point yet. As everyone else did, my father succumbed to a big salary. Jerry Kern went out first, and that may have had a lot to do with it; they were always very close, not only in their work but socially."

During his years in Hollywood, Hammerstein continued writing lyrics. From a long-forgotten film, *The Night Is Young*, there is the haunting "When I Grow Too Old to Dream," set to Romberg's music, and for another lost Grace Moore musical he collaborated with Ben Oakland on "I'll Take Romance." But it was essentially a dry period. Every writer, even the usually industrious Irving Berlin, has to cope with such barren times. "He had nothing to worry him," says William Hammerstein. "Nothing, except if you were him. Money didn't satisfy him. He worried about what was happening to *him*. With all his capacity for enjoying life, it simply wasn't sufficient.

"Perhaps he wouldn't agree with this," he continues, "but I don't think Dad ever felt comfortable in movies. He understood the stage—he had a fantastic instinct for timing, for climactic construction of a play, how to deal with a live audience, how to fashion an entertainment for the people sitting in a legitimate theatre. But I don't think he ever really grasped the movie as a *form*."

In 1939 producer Max Gordon reunited Kern and Hammerstein for a show that would bring them both back to New York. The show was called *Very Warm for May*, and while its songs were brilliant, the book was tedious. Despite "All the Things You Are," which has become a standard, Broadway wags quickly retitled the show "Very Cold for Max." Then there

Sheet-music cover for Very Warm for May. The show itself vanished from sight, but this song Messrs. Kern and Hammerstein wrote for it remains one of the most beautiful ballads ever written.

ALL THE THINGS YOU ARE

MAX GORDON presents

VERY WARM FOR MAY

A MUSICAL COMEDY

music by JEROME KERN

book and lyrics by OSCAR HAMMERSTEIN, 2nd

production by VINCENT MINNELLI

PRICE 60¢

ALL IN FUN
HEAVEN IN MY ARMS
IN OTHER WORDS, SEVENTEEN
THAT LUCKY FELLOW
ALL THE THINGS YOU ARE
IN THE HEART OF THE DARK

T. B. HARMS COMPANY NEW YORK

were other misfortunes: a pair of quick flops in London, along with *Gentlemen Unafraid*, which played one week at the St. Louis Municipal Opera in 1938 and never got any further, despite the presence of a young Red Skelton in the cast. Somehow, Hammerstein could not get a project completed that would justify the effort, the hard work and the professional judgment which he always brought to his desk when he wrote and to the theatre when rehearsals began.

At one point he seriously considered retiring and moving out of the United States. Robert Russell Bennett, the great arranger, who had worked with Hammerstein since *Music in the Air*, recalled, "One time in 1938, when my wife and I were living in Paris, Oscar and his wife came to see us. He had had failures for quite some time, and at this dinner he said, 'Dorothy and I are going to live in a little place here in France, and she's going to cook and take care of the household, and I'm going to write poetry."

"And I told him then, 'Nothing on earth could ever make me happier than to hear that, because you have poetry in you—you have *great* poems in you! But if you always stay in show business, it'll never come out.' He said, 'Well, it's going to come out now. This is it.'" This Parisian evening, bittersweet in recollection, was, of course, before Hammerstein gave us not only *Oklahoma!* but also *Carmen Jones*, which amply demonstrate his enormous poetic gifts and prove that both he and Bennett were partially correct but basically wrong.*

Meanwhile, Hammerstein and Romberg had written yet another operetta, this one called *Sunny River*. It was given a summer tryout at the huge St. Louis Municipal Opera. Set in New Orleans in the early 1800s, certainly

---

* Fond thoughts of that dinner with the Bennetts in France before the war may have provided Hammerstein with one of his most memorable lyrics. In 1941, when Hitler's armies were marching into Paris, Oscar and his old friend Jerry Kern wrote "The Last Time I Saw Paris." This beautiful song often evokes tears, even if you've never been to the city. Simple, spare, but haunting, the song won an Academy Award that year for Best Song after Metro had bought it for the film *Lady Be Good*.

a reliable operetta background, the plot dealt with another sure-fire contrivance, two separated lovers. Producer Max Gordon came to St. Louis, saw it, and arranged sufficient backing to bring the show to New York. *Sunny River* arrived in December 1941, far from an auspicious time. Within three days after its opening, the United States would be at war. The New York critics found the show dated, boring, and hopeless. After thirty-six performances, *Sunny River* closed.

In a letter to Gordon, Hammerstein penned an epitaph to his past body of work. "Operetta," he said, "is a dead pigeon, and if it ever is revived, it won't be by me. . . . I have no plans, and at the moment I don't feel like making any."

But Hammerstein's resilience sustained him again, through the dreary winter following Pearl Harbor.

On a visit to Jerome Kern in 1942, Hammerstein broached the subject of the two men collaborating on another show, based on Lynn Riggs's *Green Grow the Lilacs*. Hammerstein explained to Kern that he was impressed with the vitality under the play's gentle surfaces and was attracted to those well-defined frontier characters. He was especially fond of Riggs's dialogue, which he considered "earthy and lyrical." Not so, thought Kern. After he read the play he demurred, finding Riggs's second act, with its climactic murder, completely hopeless. He pointed out that *Green Grow the Lilacs* hadn't exactly set New York afire back in 1931. Why should current-day audiences find it more interesting?

By spring, he had found a new project. Years before he'd attended a performance of Bizet's *Carmen* in the Hollywood Bowl. The opera, sung in French, was almost inaudible in that vast place, and the lyrics were lost to spectators behind the first few rows. And yet, as Hammerstein concluded, the music alone still told the story. Searching for an American equivalent of Bizet's Spanish gypsies, he would eventually decide that a close American approximation to the grace, fire, and humor of the Bizet characters could be found among American blacks. Thus to his fertile mind came the first notion to transpose Bizet's opera into what would become *Carmen Jones*.

Working from a translation of the original work, Hammerstein proceeded to write his own, without a contract or the slightest prospect of one. Standing at his desk, that waist-high sloped chest he always used, he spent his days working, totally on his own—a most remarkable venture for a man who'd worked on hundreds of published songs, forty produced shows. But doing it was typical of his attitude toward work. "If you're a writer, you write," he might have said if pressed. The project was worth the effort; if nobody was around to take a chance on it, or on him (he was hardly the hottest commodity around), then he would go it completely alone. Later, Oscar admitted that he had enjoyed this work more than any he had ever done.

As he worked, he decided to eliminate the operatic recitatives, those endless-words-and-music passages designed years ago primarily to get characters offstage or on, or up a flight of stairs, or down. The work he did was good. There was poetry and power in his lyrics. The "Seguidilla" became "Dere's A Café on de Corner," the "Flower Song" became "Dis Flower." Adapting Bizet's music to a new set of lyrics brought forth that essential gift in Hammerstein which Robert Russell Bennett was so certain existed—his poetry. Later, when *Carmen Jones* was produced by Billy Rose, Virgil Thompson would describe Oscar's work as "ingenious, neat, and wholly triumphant." The Broadway critics would be equally lavish in their praise.

But when Hammerstein finished, in the spring of 1942, he had reached a point where the future seemed cloudy. Even though faithful Max Gordon had taken an option on *Carmen Jones*, any immediate plan to go into rehearsals would have to go on hold until Gordon's bankroll was replenished. Meanwhile Hammerstein occupied himself with groups devoted to the war effort; he was always available to work with the Writers War Board, the Stage Door Canteen, and the American Theatre Wing. He had his duties at ASCAP, and at the Dramatists Guild, where he served on the board and took his chores very seriously. Out in California, Arthur Freed and the Metro executives were seriously discussing another contract with him, one which would take him back to Culver City and film work. Now that there was a war on, musicals were sure-fire winners. But Culver City wasn't Broadway, and Broadway was Hammerstein's turf.

Then Dick Rodgers called.

─────────

When Rodgers and Hammerstein finished their lunch at the Barberry Room, the musical version of *Green Grow the Lilacs* was a definite project. So delighted was Terry Helburn that Hammerstein would sign on with Rodgers that she promptly announced it to her staff, and to the press. And two years after that summer night in Westport, Helburn's Folly was finally on track.

THE WRITING

ery soon thereafter, Hammerstein and Rodgers sat
down beneath a tree at Dick Rodgers's pleasant Fairfield, Connecticut,
house, where the two men would begin to exchange their ideas for turning
Green Grow the Lilacs into a musical. A production that might, or might
not, eventually make it to Broadway under the auspices of the Theatre
Guild, which, as the word around town had it, was very close to closing
up shop.

"At the beginning of 1942," Helburn would remember, "we had about
forty thousand dollars in the bank. Lawrence was dividing his time between Washington and New York, immersed in work at the National
Inventors Council, which he'd initiated." Later, Langner would take a six-

week vacation from his work in Washington and join Helburn in helping to raise money for what he had already dubbed "Helburn's Folly."

"At that historic and uncertain period, serious interest in the theatre seemed like fiddling while Rome burned," said Helburn. "Because of the tremendous demands on capital, it was almost impossible to wheedle or beg any money for the stage from investors. As we only had that forty thousand, I was also in the new position of finding investors who would put up the estimated ninety to one hundred thousand to produce the show [and to provide the Guild with a reserve against losses], but I went ahead anyway."

Up in Fairfield, and down in Hammerstein's study in Doylestown, a great American partnership was being melded, one whose impact on the future of our musical theatre would be revolutionary. "It didn't seem great at the time, however," Helburn commented. "At least to the people whom I bombarded with pleas to invest. Hammerstein, they told me sourly, had had two successive flops since his big hit with *Show Boat*.

"Dick and Oscar, knowing the financial situation of the Guild," she says, "went to work without even asking for an advance." Years later, Helburn assessed their partnership's virtues most perceptively. "These two men have proved to be the most outstanding partners in their field, not merely financially, not even because of the magnificent work that has grown out of their collaboration. What has impressed me the most is the way in which two totally different personalities can complement one another so perfectly. Perhaps the only other comparable team was Gilbert and Sullivan . . . but that partnership was marred by personal hostility and bitterness."

Examined from a distance of fifty years, their masterpiece seems a simple, deceptively seamless piece of theatrical craftsmanship, not a bit complex and certainly unsophisticated. But it was and remains far more than that; it is a brilliantly imaginative integrated work, one which broke many of the established rules of its time. There is an old adage that in order to break the rules one must first learn them. Both Hammerstein and Rodgers had paid their dues over the years, while working with others. Together they applied everything they'd already learned to create a musical show that changed the form forever.

When audiences now watch and listen to *Oklahoma!*, it's familiar, as comfortable as anything we've grown up with. "People Will Say We're in Love" is a deft expression of young lovers' bashfulness. "Out of My Dreams" is a beautiful Rodgers waltz; he loved to write them, and it shows. "Kansas City," the Ado Annie–Will Parker comical duet "All Er Nothin'," and Annie's lament "I Cain't Say No" are witty and droll; Hammerstein certainly supplied all those laugh lines that Rodgers had worried so about when he lost Hart. "The Surrey with the Fringe on Top," is perfectly arranged to create the atmosphere of a young couple going courting, the trip, the rig itself, and the return ride home, all of it in one charming musical adventure. Jud Fry became far more than a stock villainous character when the pair supplied him with his solo lament, "Lonely Room," and his *angst* is brilliantly underscored with the sardonic asides of "Pore Jud." Then there is Laurey's lilting "Many a New Day." As for Curly's opening ballad, "Oh, What a Beautiful Mornin'," is that paean to the dawning of a bright new day not as pure and melodic as the best of Shubert's *leider*? And when it is ultimately transformed into a chorale for the ensemble of Oklahomans, has their rousing title song ever failed to bring down a house?

Years later, Stephen Sondheim most perceptively commented on the magic worked by Rodgers and Hammerstein when they wrote their first score, weaving together libretto with music and lyrics and always welding it all to the characters. "You can transpose songs from *Lady Be Good* to *Funny Face*," said Sondheim, "but you can't move songs from *Oklahoma!* to *Carousel*." Everything Rodgers and Hammerstein wrote that summer was of a piece, with the one exception of "Boys and Girls Like You and Me," a beautiful ballad which would be cut on the road because the director and the choreographer could not find a way to stage it. Translation: It had no relationship to any of the characters in the show.

Rodgers and Hammerstein had no insight that summer that this new musical they were working on would radically alter the existing forms. But fortunately, each of them would later recount how their day-to-day labors would bear such remarkable fruit, Hammerstein in his *Lyrics* and Rodgers in his *Musical Stages*.

Hammerstein

"The first serious problem that faced us involved a conflict of dramaturgy with showmanship. As we planned our version, the story we had to tell in the first part of the first act did not call for the use of a female ensemble. The traditions of musical comedy, however, demand that not too long after the rise of the curtain the audience should be treated to one of musical comedy's most attractive assets—the sight of pretty girls in pretty clothes moving about the stage, the sound of their vital young voices supporting the principals in their songs. Dick and I for several days sought ways and means of logically introducing a group of girls into the early action of the play. The boys were no problem. Here was a farm in Oklahoma with ranches nearby. Farmers and cowboys belonged there, but girls in groups? No. Strawberry festivals? Quilting parties? Corny devices! After

trying everything we could think of and rejecting each other's ideas as fast as they were submitted, after passing through phases during which we would stare silently at each other unable to think of anything at all, we came finally to an extraordinary decision. We agreed to start our story in the real and natural way in which it seemed to want to be told!"

Rodgers

"By opening the show with the woman alone onstage and the cowboy beginning his song offstage, we did more than set a mood; we were, in effect, warning the audience 'Watch out! This is a different kind of musical.' Everything in the production was made to conform to the simple open-air spirit of the story; this was essential and certainly a rarity in the musical theatre."

Hammerstein

"This decision meant that the first act would be half over before a female chorus would make its entrance. We realized that such a course was experimental, amounting almost to the breach of implied contract with a musical comedy audience. I cannot say truthfully that we were worried by the risk.

"Now, having met our difficulty by simply refusing to recognize its existence, we were ready to go ahead with the actual writing."

Rodgers

"For twenty-five years the only way I could get Larry to do anything was virtually to lock him in a room and stay with him until the job was finished. Oscar's working habits were entirely the opposite. I remember that when I first started to talk to him about our method of collaboration, he seemed surprised at my question.

" 'I'll write the words, and you'll write the music' was all he said.

" 'In that order?' I asked.

" 'If that's all right with you. I prefer it that way. You won't hear from me until I have a finished lyric.'

"And for ninety percent of the time, that's the way we worked together."

Hammerstein

"Searching for a subject for Curly to sing about, I recalled how deeply I had been impressed by Lynn Riggs's description at the start of his play.

> It is a radiant summer morning several years ago, the kind of morning which, enveloping the shapes of earth—men, cattle in the meadow, blades of the young corn, streams—makes them exist now for the first time, their images giving off a visible golden emanation that is partly true and partly a trick of the imagination, focusing to keep alive a loveliness that may pass away.

"On first reading these words I had thought what a pity it was to waste them on stage directions. Only readers could enjoy them. Yet, if they did, how quickly they would slip into the mood of the story. Remembering this reaction, I reread the description and determined to put it into song. 'Oh, What a Beautiful Mornin'' opens the play and creates an atmosphere of relaxation and peace and tenderness. It introduces the lighthearted young man who is the center of the story. My indebtedness to Mr. Riggs's description is obvious. The cattle and the corn and the golden haze on the meadow are all there. I added some observations of my own, based on my experience with beautiful mornings, and I brought the words down to the more primitive poetic level of Curly's character. He is, after all, just a cowboy and not a playwright."*

Rodgers

"Though Oscar was not a musician, he did possess a superb sense of form. He knew everything about the architecture of a song—its foundation, structure, embellishments—and because we always had thorough

---

*"For the first time since *Show Boat*, Oscar was aware of letting the material he was adapting dictate his course," writes Hugh Fordin in *Getting To Know Him*, his biography of Hammerstein.

discussions on the exact kind of music that was needed, this method of collaboration helped us enormously in creating songs that not only were right for the characters who sang them but also possessed a union of words and music that made them sound natural."

Hammerstein

" 'The corn is as high as a elephant's eye'—I first wrote 'cow pony's eye.' Then I walked over to my neighbor's cornfield and found that although it was only the end of August, the corn had grown much higher than that. 'Cow pony' was more indigenous to the western background, but I had reservations about it even before I gauged the height of the corn. It reads better than it sounds. Sing 'cow pony' to yourself and try to imagine hearing it for the first time in a song. It would be hard for the ear to catch.

" 'All the cattle are standing like statues.' This picture had come into my brain several years before I wrote the song, and it had stayed there, quietly waiting to be used. When I came to the second verse of 'Oh, What a Beautiful Mornin',' I remembered it. I remembered sitting on a porch in Pennsylvania one summer's day, watching a herd of cows standing on a hillside about half a mile away. It was very hot and there was no motion in the world. I suddenly found myself doing what I had never done before and have never done since. I was thinking up lines for a poem to describe what I saw. It was not to be used in a play, not to be set to music. I got this far with it:

> The breeze steps aside
> To let the day pass.
> The cows on the hill
> Are as still as the grass.

I never wrote the lines on paper, nor did I ever do any work to polish them, nor did I extend the poem any further. Perhaps I was called to the phone, or perhaps I was infected with the laziness of an inactive landscape. But those cows on the hill 'as still as the grass' were crystallized in my memory by the words I had quite idly and casually composed, and up they came several years later to inspire me when I needed them."

Rodgers

"I was a little sick with joy because it was so lovely and so right. When you're given words like that you get something to say musically. You'd really have to be made of cement not to spark to that."*

Hammerstein

"Almost all composers have a reservoir of melodies which come to them at different times and which they write down in what they call a sketch-book. When they start work on a new musical play, they play over these previously written melodies for their collaborator, and it is decided which ones can be used in this particular score. Dick Rodgers, however, does not work in this way. He writes music only for a specific purpose. Ideas for tunes seldom come to him while he is walking down the street or riding in taxicabs, and he doesn't rush to his piano very often to write a tune just for the sake of writing a tune."

Rodgers

"I remember that shortly before beginning the score Oscar sent me an impressively thick book of songs of the American Southwest which he thought might be of help; I opened the book, played through the music of one song, closed the book, and never looked at it again. If my melodies were going to be authentic, they'd have to be authentic on my own terms. . . . This is the way I have always worked, no matter what the setting of the story. It was true of my 'Chinese' music for *Chee-Chee*, of my 'French' music for *Love Me Tonight*, and later of my 'Siamese' music for *The King and I*. Had I attempted to duplicate the real thing, it would never

*Observes Fordin: "Completed in ten minutes, the music had all the simple, sweet charm of a folk song and a poetic lyricism that was different from Rodgers's previous work."

have sounded genuine, for the obvious reason that I am neither Chinese, French, Siamese, nor from the Southwest. All a composer—any composer—can do is to make an audience believe it is hearing an authentic sound without losing his own musical identity."

Hammerstein

"The problem of a duet for the lovers in *Oklahoma!* seemed insurmountable. While it is obvious almost from the rise of the curtain that Curly and Laurey are in love with each other, there is also a violent antagonism between them, caused mainly by Laurey's youthful shyness, which she disguises by pretending not to care for Curly. This does not go down very well with him, and he fights back. Since this mood was to dominate their scenes down into the second act, it seemed impossible for us to write a song that said 'I love you' and remain consistent with the attitude they had adopted toward each other."

Rodgers

"Oscar hit on the notion of having the young lovers warn each other against showing any signs of affection so that people won't realize they're in love. (Larry and I had already written a different song of this kind in 'This Can't Be Love,' and later Oscar and I would try another variation on the theme with 'If I Loved You.')

"This song also demonstrates another familiar problem, especially for lyric writers. There are, after all, only so many rhymes for the word 'love,' and when Oscar decided to call the duet 'People Will Say We're in Love,' he was determined to avoid using any of the more obvious ones. After spending days thinking about this one rhyme, he called me up exultantly to announce that he'd solved the problem. His solution: The girl ends the refrain by admonishing the boy:

> Don't start collecting things,
> Give me my rose and my glove:

Sweetheart, they're suspecting things—
People will say we're in love."

Hammerstein

"It takes me a week, and sometimes three weeks, to write the words of a song. After I give them to him, it takes him an hour or two and his work is over. He responds remarkably to words, and when he likes them, they immediately suggest tunes to him."

Rodgers

"When the lyrics are right, it's easier to write a tune than to bend over and tie your shoe laces. Notes come more spontaneously than words."

The next song would be "The Surrey with the Fringe on Top," which would also be derived from Lynn Riggs's original play. In the scene as it was written, Curly tries to lure Laurey into going to the box social with him and proceeds to describe the carriage in which they'll travel. "A bran' new surrey with fringe on the top four inches long—and *yeller*! And two white horses a-raring and faunching to go! You'd shore ride like a queen . . . and this here rig has got four fine side-curtains, case of a rain. And isinglass winders to look out of! And a red and green lamp set on the dashboard, winkin' like a lightnin' bug!"

Rodgers

"Oscar's lyric suggested both a clip-clop rhythm and a melody in which the straight, flat country road could be musically conveyed through a repetition of the straight, flat sound of the D note, followed by a sharp upward flick as fowl scurry to avoid being hit by the moving wheels."

Hammerstein went back to his home in Doylestown, leaving Rodgers in Fairfield, where he spent that evening working on what Hammerstein had already written, the beginning verse and the end. Rodgers had set it to the rhythm of a carriage-wheel turning over and over, over and over, but he had no middle part. So he sat, not so patiently waiting for his new partner to provide one.

The following day Hammerstein arrived with lyrics that included a middle verse which would give Rodgers the exact meter.

> The wheels are yeller, the upholstery's brown,
> The dashboard's genuine leather.
> With isinglass curtains you can roll right down,
> In case there's a change in the weather.

That was all Rodgers needed to complete the song melodically forthwith.

Rodgers

"Oscar was so moved by this song that just listening to it made him cry. He once explained that he never cried at sadness in the theatre, only at naive happiness, and the idea of two boneheaded young people looking forward to nothing more than a ride in a surrey struck an emotional chord that affected him deeply."

Hammerstein

"Jud Fry worried us. A sulky farmhand, a 'bullet-colored growly man,' a collector of dirty pictures, he frightened Laurey by walking in the shadow of a tree beneath her window every night. He was heavy fare for a musical play. Yet his elimination was not to be considered because the drama he provided was the element that prevented this light lyric idyll from being so lyric and so idyllic that a modern theater audience might have been made sleepy, if not nauseous, by it. It was quite obvious that Jud was the bass fiddle that gave body to the orchestration of the story. The question was how to make him acceptable, not too much a deep-dyed villain, a scenery-chewer, an unmotivated purveyr of arbitrary evil. We didn't want to resort to the boring device of having two other characters discuss him and give the audience a psychological analysis. Even if this were dramatically desirable, there are no characters in this story who are bright enough or well-educated enough to do this. So we solved the problem with two songs, 'Pore Jud' and 'Lonely Room.' They are both sung in the smokehouse set, the dingy hole where Jud lives with no companions but a mouse who nibbles on a broom and a gallery of 'Police Gazette' pictures on the wall—a most uncompromising background from a musical standpoint.

"In 'Pore Jud,' Curly, after suggesting to him how easy it would be for Jud to hang himself by a lasso from a rafter, goes on to describe what his funeral would be like. Unwelcome as the idea seems at first, Jud finds some features not unattractive to speculate on—the excitement he would cause by the gesture of suicide, the people who would come from miles around to weep and moan, especially the 'womern' what had 'tuk a shine' to Jud when he was alive. Jud is incredulous about these, but Curly points out that they 'never come right out and show you how they feel, less'n you die first,' and Jud allows that there's something in that theory. He becomes then, for a while, not just wicked, but a comic figure flattered by the attentions he might receive if he were dead. He becomes also a pathetic figure, pathetically lonely for attentions he has never received while alive. The audience begins to feel some sympathy for him, some understanding of him as a man.

"In the second song, 'Lonely Room,' he paints a savage picture of his solitary life, his hatred of Curly, and his mad desire for Laurey. This is a self-analysis, but it is emotional and not cerebral. No dialogue could do this dramatic job as vividly and quickly as does the song. When Lynn Riggs attended a rehearsal of *Oklahoma!* for the first time, I asked him if he approved of this number. He said 'I certainly do. It will scare hell out of the audience.' That is exactly what it was designed to do."

Rodgers

"Oscar and I made a few changes in the basic plot and the characters. We added the part of Will Parker, Ado Annie's girlfriend, and we made her a more physically attractive girl. For the ending, we tied the strands together a bit more neatly than in the play by having Curly being found innocent of murdering Jud Fry, rather than being given his freedom for one night to spend with his bride."

Long after the fact, a friend once asked Rodgers how long he had taken to compose the entire score of *Oklahoma!*

"Do you mean 'flying time' or 'elapsed time'?" asked Rodgers. When pressed for a definition, he explained: "Counting everything—overture, ballet music, all the songs, the most I could make it come to was about five hours—'flying time.' But the total 'elapsed time' covered months of discussion and planning."

Finished, the script went to the Guild offices.

It was now more than two years since Elaine Steinbeck had been present in Westport at the revival of *Green Grow the Lilacs*, and she'd worked on several other shows, becoming a full stage manager. "John Haggott, who'd directed it up in Westport, said, 'The script of that musical we're going to be working on is on your desk.' And I picked it up and I started reading.

"Aunt Eller is sitting, churning and silent, and after the curtain goes up, there's silence. Dead silence. Then it said we were supposed to hear Curly's voice offstage singing, and I started reading:

> There's a bright golden haze on the meadow,
> There's a bright golden haze on the meadow.

> The corn is as high as a elephant's eye,
> And it looks like it's climbin' clear up to the sky.

and I said, 'Haggott, are you *kidding!*' " It went on to:

> All the cattle are standin' like statues,
> All the cattle are standin' like statues.
> They don't turn their heads when they see me ride by,
> But a little brown maverick is winkin' her eye.

'Haggott,' I said, 'You've *got* to be kidding!' Shows how little imagination I had!"

Casting for the new production hadn't yet officially begun, but an actor named Alfred Drake was called by the Guild. Very soon there would be auditions for backers; could he come in to discuss being part of them?

"It was Dick Rodgers who suggested me," Drake remembered. "He knew me all the way back to *Babes in Arms*, in which I was one of the kid singers. I'd worked for the Guild the year before in *Yesterday's Magic*, and they were sure I could act. I'd missed out on Rodgers and Hart's *By Jupiter* because the Guild had no understudy for me in *Yesterday's Magic* and I couldn't leave it. The Guild had told me it was going to continue, so I stayed in that play instead of going with *Jupiter*. Then Paul Muni left *Magic*, after six weeks, and we closed—and there I was, waiting for the phone to ring.

"Oscar didn't know me, so he asked if I'd come up and read for him. I went up and I read the part of Curly, with Oscar reading the other parts; he read very well. They were both still working on their score, but his libretto was finished.

"I'd read about a page, and he stopped me and said, 'Let me tell you what this is going to be.' And he began to tell me about what he intended to do with the speech in which Curly describes the surrey to Laurey—

he was going to make that into a song. He was charming, as always, and very enthusiastic. When he finished, *I* was as enthusiastic as he was; I was looking forward to it.

"Then, a little while later, Richard Rodgers asked me to meet him at Steinway Hall, in one of the studios. He wanted to play me some of the music and lyrics because they were going to do auditions for backers and I'd been asked to sing at them. So this was the first time I'd heard the score, and I was mad about it. It wasn't all written at this point, but I was terribly excited by what I'd heard. . . . But this is the strangest thing. If you knew Richard Rodgers, it's hard to think of him as being insecure. 'Well, tell me,' he asked, 'do you really *mean* it?' 'Yes, of course, I mean it!' I told him. 'It's wonderful!'

" 'Well, you know,' he said, thoughtfully, 'this *is* the first time I've written with anybody excepting Larry . . .'

"Then he gave me copies of the sheet music—the very first lead sheets, and I went home and learned them. That private audition for me was pretty exciting; not only was the score beautiful, but he played so beautifully. Oh, yes, I remember something else about that first day up at Steinway. When Richard played the music for me, and he did 'Oh, What a Beautiful Mornin',' and I told him how much I loved it, it was so charming—he said, 'Alfred, I must warn you, this is really only to set the scene. Don't expect much applause at the end of this number—it's *not* an applause getter.' "

BROADWAY, BACKERS, AND 1042

t the Theatre Guild offices, an aspiring playwright named Helene Hanff, who would later achieve considerable success with her book *84 Charing Cross Road*, had managed to land a job.

" 'Joe Heidt needs an assistant,' Terry Helburn said to me. 'He's our press agent. Run up and tell him I said you need the job and you're very bright.' So we found a typewriter for me, and I was assistant to the Theatre Guild press agent," Hanff recalled years later in her memoir *Underfoot in Show Business*. "The first show I assisted on was *Hope for a Harvest* by Sophie Treadwell, which flopped so badly that the stars, Fredric March and his wife, Florence Eldridge, took an ad in the papers the next day depicting a trapeze artist missing connections with his flying partner in mid-air, with a caption underneath that read, 'Oops, sorry!'

"Subsequent Guild accidents included *Papa Is All*, which was Pennsylvania Dutch,* *Mr. Sycamore*, in which Stuart Erwin became a tree in the second act [that is not a misprint and you did not read it wrong], and *Yesterday's Magic*, in which Paul Muni[†] as an alcoholic ex-star flung himself out the window at the end. There had been a couple of ill-fated revivals of classics (*Ah, Wilderness!* and *The Rivals*), a limp comedy called *Without Love*, which not even Katharine Hepburn had been able to prop up for long, and now there was *The Russian People*, a ponderous bore about the Nazis and the Russian front."

Prior to Miss Hanff's arrival there had been eight more Guild accidents, including a Philip Barry allegory called *Liberty Jones* and a dramatic version of Richard Hughes's novel *The Innocent Voyage*. By now the Guild was teetering on the brink. Hanff describes the mood in 1942:

> Looming up, according to the brochure we had sent out to Guild subscribers in nineteen subscription cities, was a new American Folk Opera. Like *Porgy and Bess*, we assured everybody. It was to be based on a flop the Guild had produced in the 1930s, and in true operatic tradition it was to have not only a murder committed onstage but a bona fide ballet.
>
> Considering our track record on even the most standard fare, this proposed epic had given everybody the jimjams. But it was budgeted at $100,000, and the rumors that reached us on the bleak December morning after *The Russian People* opened put an end to our worries about a $100,000 folk opera. The rumor was that after sixteen flops the Guild was bankrupt. By noon the next day word had spread from floor to floor that Terry and Lawrence were selling the Guild Theatre and

---

*And whose cast contained an actress named Celeste Holm.
[†]Supported by Alfred Drake and an aspiring actress named Jessica Tandy.

building to pay their debts. When the sale was completed, the Theatre Guild would go out of existence.

People from the other departments wandered morosely into our office all day, to indulge in the usual morning-after castigation of the management. Our top floor was ideal for this, since it was the one place where Terry and Lawrence could be counted on not to set foot, especially in December.

On this particular day, the tone was especially bitter. Not just because December is a very cold month to be thrown out of work in, but because for all their talk, nobody who worked there was terribly anxious to see the Theatre Guild close down. Most of them could remember the great days: the Lunts, and the Shaw openings, and the five-hour O'Neill drama which one doorman was said to have to referred to innocently throughout its run as "Strange Intercourse."

Joe and I made up the ads in a thick gloom. . . . Then Joe went down to get Lawrence's OK on the ads, and I went down to get Terry's.

She was in her office, in an armchair, having tea. Her fluffy white hair was rinsed a deep cerulean blue that season, and her toy-bulldog face was as cheerful as ever

"Well, dear," she said, "we seem to be having a run of bad luck!" . . . glancing at the bad reviews now and then to check a quote against the ad and murmuring, "I don't know what the boys want!"

As I reached the door she said, patting her hair casually, "I notice Lawrence was first on the program, dear. That's twice in a row, isn't it?"

If the program for one show read "Produced by Lawrence Langner and Theresa Helburn," the program for the next show had to read "Produced by Theresa Helburn and Lawrence Langner."

I said I was sure Mr. Langner hadn't been first twice in a row, because Joe was always careful to rotate and always had me check the last program before he made up the new one.

"All right," she said agreeably. "Just remind him; I'm first on the new show."

My gloom evaporated. *The Russian People* hadn't been the one-flop-too-many after all. We were going to do another one.

We read about it the next day in one of the gossip columns. Joe came in with the afternoon papers and said resignedly: "Terry scooped her own press department again."

She was always scooping us. . . . It now turned out that between acts of *The Russian People* she had told a columnist—in strictest confidence—that the composer and librettist had finished the new Theatre Guild operetta and that it was to be called *Away We Go!*

Down the hall, Jack, the auditor, floating on a sea of unpaid bills, screamed at anybody who went past, "What the hell do they think they'll produce a musical with? What are they using for money?" And the question was indeed pertinent.

Terry Helburn herself confirmed Jack the auditor's outcry. "I don't think I've ever worked harder than I did on trying to wrest and beguile that hundred thousand dollars from reluctant and frankly skeptical investors," she said with feeling. She'd certainly picked a dreadful time to try to raise money. The summer and fall of 1942 were far and away the darkest times of World War II. Americans, still smarting from the astonishing defeat at Pearl Harbor, gritted their teeth at the loss of the Bataan peninsula, with the ensuing dreadful Death March of General Wainwright's troops. In Europe, the Axis reigned unchallenged and triumphant; only England still withstood its military force. General Doolittle and his bombers raided Tokyo in April, and in May our fleet had defeated the Japanese navy in the Battle of the Coral Sea; in June we'd win at Midway, but we were a long, long way from breaking the Japanese grip on the Pacific.

People were learning to do without. Consumer goods were temporarily set aside until the war was over (who knew when?). So a new car was a fond dream, and even if you had wheels, where could you go on severely rationed gas? Cigarettes, Scotch whisky, new tires, sirloins and porterhouses, nylons, all of them were suddenly unavailable, except on the black

Theresa Helburn
and
Lawrence Langner

This sketch by Irma Selz from Theatre Arts Monthly of Helburn and Langner wearing the classic masks of comedy suggests that the Theatre Guild producers had a season to smile about.

market. Which, of course, was nothing new to Manhattan theatregoers. For years they'd known how to get two good seats to Broadway's latest hit. You simply slipped the cash into the scalper's open hand and presto, you and your lady were down front, in third row center.

Sardi's Restaurant on West Forty-fourth Street served cottage cheese instead of scarce butter; since old Mr. Sardi vehemently refused to deal in the black market, his patrons did without meat. Ergo, one plowed through piles of spaghetti with tomato sauce, and/or endless servings of canneloni stuffed with cheese, and left Sardi's feeling virtuous, if a bit gassy.

Tallulah Bankhead publicly vowed she would not touch another drop of alcohol until her idol Winston Churchill and his new American allies opened the Second Front by landing in Europe. (What she switched to she kept to herself.)

There were very few problems, believe it or not, parking in New York streets; nobody drove except buses and trucks. Taxis, as time went on and they ran up thousands of miles, began to resemble war casualties.

Leaf through these sample advertisements depicted in the Broadway theatre programs circa 1942–43—an era in which home-front Americans lived with rationing and short-ages—and you will be left with the distinct impression that wartime advertisers had nothing to sell the public—except liquor, brassieres for Madam, and emphysema for future generations.

They were being patched together with odds and ends of parts scraped out of junkyards by ingenious mechanics. So frail would the New York cabs eventually become that one would often be greeted by a sign inside which cautioned DO NOT SLAM DOOR! The inference was clear—the door could fall off.

In Manhattan's theatre district, and everywhere else in town, there was a nightly brownout to save energy. Restaurant signs, movie-house electrics, theatre marquees, and those old reliable Times Square advertising displays were dimmed or totally put out. But the crowds kept coming to the theatres. They'd saved cooking fat, had their shoes repaired (or half-soled) to save leather, gone without sugar, cut down on cigarettes, given to the USO and knitted sweaters and socks for the boys overseas, bought War Savings Stamps, and done without practically everything . . . except amusement. That was a necessity.

These would be boom-times for the movie houses, and for the West Coast studios that were cranking out films on their own assembly lines. More ticket buyers than ever jammed the picture palaces (which in some towns across the land were staying open twenty-four hours, featuring 4 A.M. double-feature bills called "swing-shift matinees"). Film cans were being shipped out to GI's wherever they were, so that our boys could bask in the sexual aura of buxom Betty Grable, gorgeous Dorothy Lamour in her sarong, and sensuous Rita Hayworth in anything. They smiled down from the screen and blew kisses and promised they'd walk alone until you returned, even on Saturday night, the loneliest night of the week; they were keeping themselves only for you, and you, and you. The Andrews Sisters wouldn't sit under the apple tree with anyone else but a few 4-F dancing boys, and since most of the younger leading men had gone off to war, the only ones left behind we could rely on to win our soundstage battles were John Wayne or Gary Cooper, and the ever-reliable Errol Flynn.

People hurried down city streets, finding their way in the gloom by memory or with the help of sympathetic New York mounted police, who

Broadway in 1942 specialized in marketing one very profitable commodity to avid wartime theatregoers: escape. It provided the people who were coping with problems a smorgasbord of song and dance, belly laughs, beautiful girls, bright lights, and excitement, eight performances a week. Ticket buyers flocked to a welcome couple of hours' enjoyment with the reliable assistance of brassy Ethel Merman in **Something for the Boys,** *or the Lunts*

in **The Pirate,**
Danny Kaye ca-
vorting through
Let's Face It! *or*
Ray Bolger leaping
like a demented
gazelle in **By**
Jupiter. *And if you*
wanted your laughs
a bit more raucous,
Mike Todd would
oblige you by sell-
ing you a pair of
tickets to his show
Star and Garter,
a high-priced,
glorified bur-
lesque bill in which
hilarious Bobby
Clark proved the
perfect foil for
that delectable
high-class strip-
per Miss Gypsy
Rose Lee. (Cour-
tesy of Vandamm
Photography)

could point their way to the theatres, where the sign above was dark but the light still gleamed from behind the box office window.

Once inside the theatre doors, thank heaven, there were still all the old reliables. Warmth and energy, bright lights and beautiful girls, and best of all the reassuring glow of love and lovers who conquered all for a happy ending. Plus laughs.

That brand of escapist entertainment kept the orchestra seats in New York's legitimate theatres filled nightly with tired businessmen and their customers, fresh-faced soldiers and sailors in town for a hurried two or three-day pass, and homefront citizens taking a few hours off, all of them seeking a couple of hours of release.

Laughter was vital, and in the midtown theatres the jokes came in all shapes and sizes, classy or vulgar, hoary or quasisophisticated, usually set to music. Bobby Clark, in *Star and Garter*, leered at the show girls and waved his cigar at naughty Gypsy Rose Lee, who had turned stripping into a polished art. Willie and Eugene Howard still broke up audiences with such hoary vaudeville classics as "Pay the Two Dollars." Cavorting up and down, tearing the theatre apart with manic gusto, was the indefatigable Jimmy Durante; Joe E. Lewis chanted his risqué ditties "Can't Get the Merchandise (It's Tough to Get Stuff)" or "The Groom Couldn't Get In." Milton Berle fired off salvos of one-liners like some demented machine-gunner, and Sophie Tucker and Georgie Jessel put on a vulgar exhibit called *High Kickers*, which contained the memorable Tucker lyric dedicated to her sailor-boyfriend, "He may not know much about Cape Hatteras, but he sure knows his way round my mattress."

Creativity wasn't needed; audiences wanted it luxurious, loud, and lewd. And, of course, draped in red-white-and-blue. Danny Kaye, starring in *Let's Face It*, was a happy soldier boy surrounded by willing ladies trying to seduce him to Cole Porter's songs. No female sacrifice was too much for our boys, correct? But real, solid, patriotic socko entertainment came marching up Broadway like some unstoppable tank when three hundred GI's, most of them show business veterans now enrolled with their Uncle

Sam, paraded in precision behind a band and into the stage door of the Broadway Theatre to present a musical revue written by Irving Berlin. He'd done exactly the same thing back in 1918 and shrewdly figured a soldier show had to work again. He was absolutely right.

On the night of July 4th the orchestra struck up the overture; up went the glittering curtain to reveal a huge cast in khaki singing out "This Is the Army, Mr. Jones!" The audience cheered and stamped its feet, roaring its approval of the ensuing two hours' worth of song-and-dance-with-laughs; but the ultimate magic moment would arrive in the next-to-closing eleven o'clock spot.

There, diminutive Mr. Berlin himself, beaming shyly, stepped forth from his 1918 tent wearing his original 1918 uniform from *Yip, Yip, Yaphank!* and began to sing that same song he'd written all those years before, "Oh, How I Hate to Get Up in the Morning." It was unforgettable— an American genius providing his countrymen with the massive bolt of sentimental electricity they needed, at precisely the right time and place. When that audience roared and stood up, it was clear that Berlin had once again, as he had for all these years, touched the American nerve.

Audiences needed hope—served up with bright lights, laughter, and foot-tapping songs— the same prescription that had sold tickets to our grandparents in World War I. *It's a mess over there, but we'll come out of it winners, you bet we will!* That was what show business could assure us.

The weekly grosses recorded in *Variety* were remarkable. Every producer in Hollywood or New York was in search of another profitable bundle of escape to peddle to eager audiences at top prices. Patriotism may be the last refuge of scoundrels, but it's a surefire moneymaker.

When the Theatre Guild came knocking on doors and making phone calls, searching for potential backers for this new Rodgers and Hammerstein musical version of Riggs's play, the response was negative. Not passively negative, but aggressively so. For openers, this Guild venture had no stars. Helburn made a valiant try to do something tangible about that. Despite Rodgers and Hammerstein's initial disapproval, she suggested box-office names. Since her debut in *Leave It to Me*, the brightest young leading lady in town was sparkling Mary Martin. Unfortunately, Miss Martin was already booked for a new musical called *Dancing in the Streets*, a venture that would make it to Boston, where it would close, ironically enough, while *Oklahoma!* was running at the Colonial.

Shirley Temple for Laurey? Miss Temple's parents did not feel the part was right for their daughter. Deanna Durbin was suggested, but Universal's president, Nate Blumberg, refused to release his star to appear in a chancy Broadway show. (After the show opened and became a hit he jovially told Helburn, "You should be happy. Look at all the money you saved by not having to pay Deanna!")

For the part of Ali Hakim, the peddler, Helburn thought of Groucho Marx. When Marx turned her down, she began to waver. Rodgers and Hammerstein were certain they were right: No "stars"; let their work stand or fall on its own merit.

But when Helburn conceded to them, she was back to square one— where and how to raise the necessary funds to get this show produced. "Lawrence and I put our heads together, did some figuring. We decided to put in $25,000 of the Guild's own capital. That left us $15,000 for 'emergencies.' A private pool of regular backers [among them Lee Shubert and the American Theatre Society] came in with an additional $15,000. So we started with $40,000, knowing we must double it to raise the curtain."

Going out to unknown investors was a new experience for the Guild. Helburn began a series of auditions. Oscar Hammerstein read aloud from the book and did Aunt Eller. Alfred Drake had agreed to sing Curly, and a pert young leading lady, Joan Roberts, who'd recently been in Hammerstein's last failure, *Sunny River*, sang Laurey. The two pianos that accompanied the singers were manned by Dick Rodgers and his faithful rehearsal pianist, Margot Hopkins. (Helburn chafed at the $25 extra rehearsal rental for the second piano but reluctantly agreed.)

The tiny troupe began a tour of what Rodgers later referred to as "the penthouse circuit." Affluent upper-echelon Park Avenue audiences sat and listened, drinks in hand, while the script was read and the two young singers performed the lovely score. The reactions were polite. But night after night the Guild came away empty. "It's ironic," said Helburn later, "to think of the difficulty we had in promoting thousands for a show which was to gross millions."

To such society audiences, nothing about this new show was attractive. "I remember the flat, empty feeling I had when a woman for whom we put on this performance, our hostess at a particularly splendid apartment, all white-and-gold and filled with chic people, all her friends, said, in a chilly voice, 'I don't like plays about farmhands,'" remembered Helburn in her autobiography.

"Then came those Broadway regulars, 'angels,'" she continued. "Their response was universal. 'Helburn's Folly' began to be known on Broadway as the Guild's 'No-play.'"

One of those old Broadway hands was Howard S. Cullman, a dapper, successful businessman who thrived on investing in plays and musicals produced by his many theatrical pals A good friend of Dick Rodgers, he'd invested over many years in Rodgers and Hart musicals, with excellent returns. When Helburn approached him he read the script she sent and passed, sending her a polite demurral. Years later, Cullman asked for his letter back. He framed it and hung it on his office wall, to remind himself of his own fallibility. Ten years after the fact he ruefully remarked, "That letter must have cost me $970,000."

Since MGM had the screen rights to *Green Grow the Lilacs*, Helburn hurried over to see J. Robert Rubin, the head of the east coast offices. Mr. Rubin cooperatively offered to forward Hammerstein's new libretto to his boss, L. B. Mayer, to ascertain whether MGM would consider investing in the show. It was a fairly straightforward proposal: Miss Helburn suggested MGM put up $69,000 in return for 50 percent of the show's eventual profit and an additional $75,000 if it wished to acquire the screen rights to the musical version. (MGM owned only the rights to Riggs's play, which it had purchased from RKO, who bought them back in 1931.)

Should the show be a success, MGM would certainly recoup its original investment, and if it were to fail, the studio would have lost a mere $69,000, which, for the Culver City studio at least, was petty cash.

Back came an abrupt Mayer turndown. MGM, it seemed, was "not interested in backing Western musicals."

But Helburn did not quit. As Rodgers fondly remarked to her, "Your name is Terry, but it should be Terrier." She returned to MGM with another proposal. What about the eventual film rights to this new Hammerstein libretto? Since MGM wasn't investing, and owned the underlying rights to the play, how could the Guild interest any other prospective backers, whose lawyers would (rightly enough) point out that should the show succeed the backers would have no future share in any film rights?

This time out Oscar Hammerstein pulled a few strings. He'd been negotiating a contract with MGM to function as Arthur Freed's associate producer at the studio (insurance lest this current venture flop). Freed was a Hammerstein fan, as was L. B. Mayer. Hammerstein pleaded Helburn's case. The Guild desperately need such an option from MGM on the film rights in order to lure backers. Could Mayer see his way clear to granting the Guild such an option? If the show flopped it would cost MGM nothing.

The request seemed fair enough, and a deal was arranged. MGM granted the Guild an option to exercise the purchase of the film rights to Riggs's original play for $40,000 within thirty days after the opening of the Guild's new musical play version of said show. The MGM people reasoned that this show wouldn't get on, and if it did it couldn't be a hit—hadn't L. B. Mayer already passed on it? Which meant that Hammerstein would eventually have to show up for work at Freed's MGM unit after it flopped. So why not do Oscar this favor? Some day he'd be called on to pay it back. Meanwhile it cost MGM nothing.

Helburn and the Guild got their option on the film rights. (It would be exercised within twenty-four hours after the successful opening of the show in March by a triumphant Helburn and her creative associates.)

Meanwhile, raising the nonexistent backing continued, with nightly auditions.

"All those auditions that we held never raised a penny," commented Alfred Drake years later. "And believe me, we did quite a few."

"Then I turned to rival producers," said Helburn. "They usually bought a slice of each other's productions. They looked over the book. 'Too clean,' they declared. 'It hasn't a chance.' When you're raising money, people reminded me, you ought to offer them a surefire success, not a play that hasn't done so well in the past. Musicals, they told me with disgust, don't have murders in the second act."

But the diminutive lady never wavered. "I became almost demented in my attempts to get investors," she said. "For the first time since the Guild had really got into its stride, years ago, we had no business manager. Warren Munsell, our staff of strength, had been called into the army. For one dark period Dick Rodgers expected to get a commission in the air force, and Oscar wondered if perhaps he'd be wiser to call it quits and go out to MGM in California."

Harry Cohn had been invited to the Park Avenue audition in that white-and-gold apartment. But the gruff, outspoken boss of Columbia Pictures (about whom one Hollywood wit remarked, "He was a great friend, and a great enemy") hadn't shown up; he'd been busy. The following night Langner and Helburn had dinner at a restaurant where, remarkably enough, they found themselves seated (at the adjoining banquette) to Cohn, who was dining with Columbia executive Nate Spingold and one of his stars, Grace Moore.

"Harry was somewhat apologetic," said Helburn. "He came over to our table, put his arm around me. 'You know, folks,' he said, 'I'm not really interested in the theatre. I'm a picture man. If I go in, then I must take less of the play but more of the picture rights for Columbia.'

"If you're really serious," we said, "there'll be a special audition for you."

It was arranged for the following Saturday afternoon at Steinway Hall.

Cohn had begun his career years back as a "song-plugger" along with songwriter Harry Ruby, going from café to saloon, to vaudeville houses and to beer gardens demonstrating the latest wares of his bosses—music publishers—to prospective buyers and performers. He had never lost his affinity for songwriters. The prospect of having such talents as Richard Rodgers and Oscar Hammerstein demonstrate their newest work for him, and for him alone, must have gratified Cohn's ego mightily.

On Saturday afternoon Hammerstein read, Drake and Roberts sang, and Rodgers and Hopkins played to a small but powerful audience.

"As we came to the end of Act One," remembered Helburn, "I said, 'At this point, the ballet takes over.'

"Cohn grimaced. 'Ballet? In a musical show? One of *these*?' He stood on his toes, hands flipped over his head in an airy circle, and all but pirouetted.

"My story-telling couldn't compete, so I stopped. Harry listened to the music for a while; then he jumped up impetuously.

"'I like it!' he'd decided. 'Dick's songs. Oscar's book. The whole idea! If you'll all come out to the studio and make the picture, I'll put up all the money!'

"It was a typical offer, but one we all felt was impossible to accept. Finally, the offer was withdrawn, and Cohn suggested Columbia merely invest."

It seemed a fait accompli. But remarkably Columbia's board of directors balked. They would not go along with their boss's own enthusiasm. Once again, despite the enthusiastic reaction from Cohn and from his New York associate, producer Max Gordon, the Guild was back to square one.

Until, at Gordon's urging, Cohn agreed to invest $15,000 of his own money, provided Max Gordon would join him for an additional sum. Other monies trickled in. Terry Helburn doggedly continued nagging, arguing, and persuading. Playwright S. N. Behrman, who'd had many successes with the Guild, was approached (or perhaps a better word would be "sandbagged") by the diminutive Terry. When she finished twisting his arm and reminding him of the Guild's loyalty to him, he conceded and wrote his check for $5,000. At the time he thought he was lending Helburn the money. Happily for Behrman, he was a limited partner, and his $5,000 would net him thousands of dollars return over the years as well as a reputation for theatrical astuteness. Through little fault of his own. Behrman would later, somewhat wryly, point out, "I now have a reputation as the most discriminating of investors."

As the backing arrived slowly and none too lavishly, Helburn was faced with another calculation. The Guild might be able to put *Green Grow the Lilacs* into production in that dark and dreary fall of 1942, but could they proceed without the full capitalization of $100,000? No matter how she and Langner skimped on production costs, pinching pennies here and there, they still faced an out-of-town tryout. In New Haven and Boston they would play the show to audiences that might or might not buy tickets under a starless marquee, even if the reviews were good. Many a previous show had foundered on such reefs and sunk out-of-town without a trace. One of the last of the Rodgers and Hart collaborations, *By Jupiter*, starring Ray Bolger, an established "draw," had lost $17,000 on its road tryout the previous year. Producer Dwight Deere Wiman had brought it to New York where it had become a success and recouped those losses eventually. But Wiman had money in the bank. The Guild had little reserves. The cost of this show hadn't been raised. Could it withstand any future disasters?

"In reserve," said Helburn, "we had the slender fund of $15,000. Lawrence said to me one day, 'This is how it is. If we lose five thousand dollars a week during the three weeks we're out of town, and we use our own money now as an investment to cover that, then the Guild treasury can be wiped out.' So, to my later regret, we went out and raised additional funds, as a safeguard." Had the Guild used its own capital, the eventual profits derived from that $15,000 would have accrued not to those lucky backers whom they finally persuaded to invest but to the Guild itself!

You are looking at a truly historic document. From the perspective of 1993, the Guild's cost figures for the production of Away We Go! seem ridiculously low. Optimistic as well, when one considers the difficulty Terry Helburn had raising even that much. A full-scale Broadway musical to cost $68,763? (Plus a reserve for loss, plus bonds to cover cast salaries, for $30,200?) In this era when musical comedies open on Forty-fifth Street staggering beneath the load of a $6 million budget, and the smallest theatrical venture—say, a two-character play, sans stars— arrives in an off-Broadway theatre requiring the capitalization of $400,000, who can deny that our

live theatre has, in a half century, gone from popular entertainment,

available to most people on a regular basis, to, alas, a very expensive

luxury, costing as much as $130 a pair for seats?

```
March 5, 1943.
                        AWAY WE GO!
                      PRODUCTION SCHEDULE

Scenery:  Designing                         3100.
          Building                          6300.
          Extras:  Traveler - 823.
                   Drapes   - 650.
              Extra Set     - 590.
              Extra Border  - 225.          2288.
          Painting                          4500
          Labor                              400:    16,588.

Props:    Purchase                          1500.
          Labor                              425.     1,925.

Electrics:  Purchase                        700.
            Labor                           850.      1,550.

Cartage                                                650.

Costumes:  Design                           2000.
           Purchase                        15000.
           Shoes                            1760.
           Labor                             130.    18,890.

Rehearsal:  Stage Labor                     2500.
            Musicians                       3000.
            Producing Dir.                  3500.
            Dance Director                  1500.
            Cast Salaries                   5500.
            Theatre Rental                  1000.
            Piano Rental                     125.    17,125.

Press:   Agent's salary                     350.
         Newspaper                          500.
         Signs, printing                    750.
         Photos                             700.
         Press, other                       150.     2,450.

Auditions                                   725.
Scripts                                     150.
Insurance                                    50.
Author's Expenses                           800.
Director's   "                              400.
Board's      "                              500.
Orchestration                             5,000.
Transportation                             350.
  Social Security                           300.
Office Expense                            1,250.
Audit                                       60.      9,585.
                                    SUB-TOTAL$68,763.
Bonds:                  15,200.
Loss Provision:         15,000.                     30,200.
                                                   $98,963
```

It would take Terry Helburn more time to dragoon the rest of the $100,000. For the record, the entire capitalization of what would eventually be *Oklahoma!* came from a small list of twenty-eight hardy investors who put their money where their mouths were. And while she pursed them, Helburn had many more problems confronting her. Foremost was the vital question—who should direct this show?

Not *if* it went into production (no one could deter her from achieving that) but *when*.

PUTTING IT TOGETHER

he search for the director for the musical version of *Green Grow the Lilacs* had begun as early as June 1942, when Dick Rodgers got in touch with Josh Logan; both were fresh from their successful experience with *By Jupiter*.

Logan would have been delighted to work with Rodgers, especially now that it would give him a chance to join forces with Hammerstein, but that would have to wait until after the war. Logan had also had a call from his next employer, Uncle Sam; in fact, he was in the process of finishing up a whirlwind last-minute job. At Irving Berlin's behest he was pitching in on the sketches and musical numbers of *This Is the Army*. His future association with Rodgers and Hammerstein would come some years later when he'd direct their production of *Annie Get Your Gun*.

Mr. Rodgers is setting some of Mr. Hammerstein's words to music. (Courtesy of The Rodgers & Hammerstein Organization)

Terry Helburn then suggested Bretaigne Windust, a director who'd done *Arsenic and Old Lace*, *Life with Father*, *Idiot's Delight*, and *Amphitryon 38*, a string of solid legitimate hits. But his background as far as musicals went was limited to a rag-tag exhibit called *Strip for Action*. By mutual agreement with her partners Helburn moved on, and she decided to try for the brilliant Elia Kazan, who had just directed the highly successful produc-

Mr. Rodgers in pursuit of Mr. Logan.

June 15, 1942

Dear Josh:

Will you please read this script as soon as you possibly can. Terry Helburn and I have ideas for it. I'll talk to you about it the first time I see you.

Sincerely,

Dick Rodgers

Mr. Josh Logan
Hotel Gorham
New York City

tion of Thornton Wilder's play *The Skin of Our Teeth*. On November 21st she sent him a wire at the Plymouth Theatre suggesting he pick up a copy of Hammerstein's script at the Guild Theatre box office. "Please keep confidential," cautioned her message.

"I reread *Green Grow* carefully," said Kazan's return wire, "and I just don't click with it. I'm afraid I'd do a very mediocre job and neither of us would benefit. I'd feel so proud and honored to do a show for you, but this had better not be it. Best always, Gadget."

Then, in December, Rouben Mamoulian came to town.

The Guild's association with that talented director had begun long years back when Mamoulian won the critics' ovations for his staging of DuBose Heyward's play *Porgy* in 1927. In the following years the Armenian-born Mamoulian had done considerable work for the Guild, staging Eugene O'Neill's *Marco Millions*, Karel Čapek's *R.U.R.*, and Turgenev's *A Month in the Country*. In 1929 Mamoulian made the crossover from the Broad-

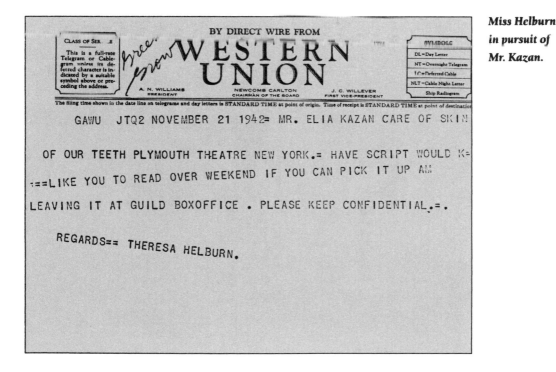

Miss Helburn in pursuit of Mr. Kazan.

Mr. Kazan, unlike Ado Annie, can say no.

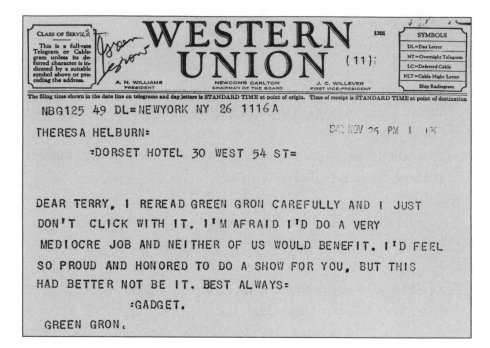

WESTERN UNION

1201

CLASS OF SERVICE

This is a full-rate Telegram or Cablegram unless its deferred character is indicated by a suitable symbol above or preceding the address.

A. N. WILLIAMS
PRESIDENT

NEWCOMB CARLTON
CHAIRMAN OF THE BOARD

J. C. WILLEVER
FIRST VICE-PRESIDENT

SYMBOLS

DL=Day Letter
NT=Overnight Telegram
LC=Deferred Cable
NLT=Cable Night Letter
Ship Radiogram

The filing time shown in the date line on telegrams and day letters is STANDARD TIME at point of origin. Time of receipt is STANDARD TIME at point of destination

NBG125 49 DL=NEWYORK NY 26 1116A

THERESA HELBURN=

    =DORSET HOTEL 30 WEST 54 ST=

1942 NOV 26 PM 1 18

DEAR TERRY, I REREAD GREEN GRON CAREFULLY AND I JUST
DON'T CLICK WITH IT. I'M AFRAID I'D DO A VERY
MEDIOCRE JOB AND NEITHER OF US WOULD BENEFIT. I'D FEEL
SO PROUD AND HONORED TO DO A SHOW FOR YOU, BUT THIS
HAD BETTER NOT BE IT. BEST ALWAYS=

        =GADGET.

GREEN GRON.

Miss Helburn indefatigably goes in pursuit of Mr. Mamoulian.

December 2, 1942.

Dear Mr. Mamoulian,

    Miss Helburn asked me to
send you the enclosed script and
printed version of GREEN GROW.

      Sincerely,

      Secretary to Miss Helburn.

Mr. Rouben Mamoulian,
Gotham Hotel,
New York City.

way theatre to the Paramount Astoria studios, where talking pictures were being produced with New York legitimate theatre talents. Producer Walter Wanger assigned Mamoulian to direct singer Helen Morgan in a remarkable musical called *Applause*. The film was a trailblazing example of how a creative imagination could actually make use of this new invention of talking films; before him the process through which screen actors now miraculously talked had been strictly in the hands of the sound engineers. Mamoulian elbowed away their technical shibboleths and began to create on film.

He went to Hollywood and made a remarkable version of *Dr. Jekyll and Mr. Hyde*, with Fredric March and Miriam Hopkins. Then, in 1932, he directed *Love Me Tonight* starring Maurice Chevalier and Jeanette MacDonald and a Rodgers and Hart score. This joyful amalgam of talents produced a movie regularly revived for appreciative audiences on TV and art houses six decades after the fact, one that is memorable for its innovative use of music and lyrics to create character and further the high-comedy story line. *Love Me Tonight* hasn't aged at all, only improved, like rare wine. Its importance is even more telling when one compares it with other musicals of that same period. In 1932 the studios cranked out endless static reproductions of creaky old theatre productions made by directors who placed the cameras in front of the actors and the chorus and shot them all head on while they sang or danced.

Mamoulian changed all that; he boldly suggested to Rodgers and Hart that their story be told as inventively as possible using every clever device and keeping the mixture afloat with music and lyrics that furthered the plot. There are even passages of rhymed couplets by Hart that illuminate character; amazingly, the laughs haven't become dated.

"At that time," Rodgers later remarked, "all of that depended on the skill and daring of the director. Mamoulian was God at Paramount. Whatever he wanted to do, he did. He believed in Larry and me, and we believed in him, and we got along beautifully."

Mr. Mamoulian and Ethel Merman studying the script for Sadie Thompson. Miss Merman shortly withdrew from the lead, to be replaced by June Havoc. The Vernon Duke–Howard Dietz musical was a quick failure.

Mamoulian then made the first feature film in Technicolor, *Becky Sharp*, again with Miriam Hopkins. He returned to the Guild and Broadway in 1936, when he staged the Heyward-Gershwin opera *Porgy and Bess*. Once again in that landmark production he demonstrated his virtuosity, this time with the great libretto and score that has become an American classic.

But these were the thirties, and the theatre was unable to lure talent away from those high-salaried Hollywood assignments that had long-term studio contracts attached to them. Mamoulian went back West to do more films. One was the Paramount operetta *High, Wide and Handsome*, written by Hammerstein and Kern. If that film wasn't a massive financial success, it was a salubrious experience for those who'd worked on it, and it also meant that both Hammerstein and Rodgers, separately and from direct experience, had a high opinion of Mamoulian's abilities.

Thus, Helburn went ahead and sent a script of *Green Grow the Lilacs* to Mamoulian's Gotham Hotel suite in December 1942. Mamoulian had been occupied the past years making *The Mark of Zorro* and *Blood and Sand* for Twentieth Century-Fox. Profitable work, but hardly challenging. The story of Curly and Laurey's romance on the prairie at the turn of the century, set to the simple and beautiful Rodgers and Hammerstein score that moved the story so well and constantly illuminated the characters, struck a responsive chord in Mamoulian.

"When I laid the story down," he told Helburn, "I knew I was on my way back to Broadway and the theatre."

Mamoulian had always gambled on challenges; wartime Hollywood wasn't in the challenge business. It backed only sure things. Armenians, especially talented ones, enjoy gambling. Rodgers and Hammerstein had crafted something rare, completely different, a true challenge for anyone who would stage it. The Theatre Guild had finally reached the right man.

Compared with his customary Hollywood salary, the terms Mamoulian agreed to with Helburn and Langner were minuscule. His fee would be $3,000, to be paid at $500 per week for five weeks and $250 for the two weeks after opening out of town—plus a weekly royalty of 1 percent of the weekly box-office gross after the show opened in New York.

Certainly Mamoulian had gambled before, but never would he end up with such a jackpot as that 1 percent of the show's gross would eventually provide him week after week, year after year.

Now that Helburn finally had her director to stage the show when and if the rehearsals began, she needed a choreographer.

When one was finally hired it would be the Guild that was gambling. Earlier that fall, Langner had written to Dick Rodgers.

Sept. 30, 1942

Dear Dickie:

Agnes de Mille, who is an old friend of mine, asked me if I would speak to you about the possibility of her working on the dancing for *Green Grow the Lilacs*. She has done some very good comedy ballets as well as aesthetic ones. She is doing a Wild West Rodeo Ballet at the opening of the Metropolitan Ballet season, and you really should go and see this because it shows her ability to handle Western material.

Please give this your usual kind consideration.

Sincerely,

Lawrence Langner

"Dickie" and his partner, Oscar Hammerstein, accompanied Theresa Helburn to the opening night of Miss de Mille's ballet, which she had choreographed to the music of Aaron Copland. Hammerstein had known of de Mille's work for many years. He had, by coincidence, attended her first recital, in California in 1930, and in Miss de Mille's own recollection, "stood by the side of his handsome wife and gazed with benevolence and kindly enthusiasm." Hammerstein had been certain that this young daughter of film producer William de Mille had talent. His only reservation was the question of how she might channel it.

Twelve years passed, filled with constant struggle and study; Agnes soon learned it was not yet the time when an American choreographer

could make a place for herself in ballet. De Mille's uncle, the powerful Cecil B. DeMille, gave her a chance with the dances for his epic *Cleopatra*, but not many such opportunities presented themselves, nepotistic or otherwise. She was hired by Irving Thalberg to create the dances for George Cukor's film *Romeo and Juliet*, and customarily she might have remained in her native California, continuing to do such work in the studios, but de Mille was determined to make a place for herself in ballet.

In New York she was hired by the Shuberts in 1937 to work with Vincente Minnelli on the tryout of a musical starring Ed Wynn, *Hooray for What!* but she was fired during the out-of-town tryout. She went to England and studied, and worked in London until the beginning of World War II, when she returned to New York. Finally she was commissioned to create a ballet called *Rodeo* for the Ballet Theatre.

Opening night of *Rodeo* was October 16, 1942. "This was not a great performance," de Mille said. "We gave better, later. Neither was it a great ballet. . . . But it was the first of its kind, and the moment was quick with birth." The approving audience granted young Miss de Mille, her choreography, and her dancers twenty-two curtain calls.

The next day she received a telegram from Theresa Helburn: "We think your work is enchanting. Come talk to us Monday."

At the Guild offices there was no question that de Mille had talent, but Dick Rodgers wasn't certain she could make the crossover from ballet to the Broadway stage. He understood well what was involved; he had been one of the first Broadway composers to tackle original ballets. In *On Your Toes* he'd created the first act "Princesse Zenobia" ballet, a sly take-off of Rimsky-Korsakovian opulence, and he'd followed it with the climactic "Slaughter on Tenth Avenue," in which Ray Bolger, Tamara Geva, and George Church danced to George Balanchine's choreography. But that show had been strictly a musical in which the ballets were appended to the story of a hoofer from a vaudeville family trying to make it in the ballet.

In *Green Grow the Lilacs* the choreography would be integral to the story. The dances were planned to reveal character and to further the story. There was no precedent for this; it was all new. Could this woman, who hadn't really done anything in the theatre before, be relied upon to carry out such a major task? Rodgers had a right to worry. Even de Mille understood the problem. "He recognized clearly the crucial difference between the two media," Agnes remarked later.

Langner and Helburn both felt certain that de Mille would provide an excitingly fresh and new element to Helburn's Folly, but the final decision was slow in coming. "Even after the success of *Rodeo* I just barely succeeded in getting the show," de Mille wrote in her memoirs. "Indeed, I heard nothing official until I met Oscar Hammerstein, by chance, in a New York drugstore, and knocked a plate off the counter in my haste to speak to him. Dick had qualms, he said. I continued pressing until Dick capitulated."

When de Mille's deal was negotiated she would receive $1,500 for six weeks' work and thereafter $50 a week for ten weeks after the production cost of the show was paid off. Hardly munificent, but it was de Mille's big chance. The terms agreed upon, she went on her scheduled Ballet Russe de Monte Carlo tour. Before she left, Rodgers played her his score so she would be familiar with the work she had to do. "When I heard it the first time," she remembered, "I was just open-mouthed, and I said to him, 'Why that's like Schubert, some of that.'"

"On my tour went a blank copybook labeled 'Lilacs,' with pages entitled 'Ballet—Many a New Day,' 'Cowman and the Farmer,' 'Kansas City,' 'Jud's Postcards,' and as I sat happily in hotel bedrooms, I made my notes." She toured California and then returned to New York, ready to go to work on *Green Grow the Lilacs*.

"I went for my first interview very firm and determined," she remembered. "Hammerstein seemed understanding, but as I had found out, one could never tell. First, I informed him, I must insist that there be no one in the chorus I didn't approve. 'Oh, pshaw!' he murmured. He was sorry to hear I was going to take that attitude—there was his regular girl, and Lawrence Langner had two, and Dick Rodgers always counted on some.

For one beat I took him literally, there being no trace of anything except earnestness on his face, and then I relaxed on that score for the rest of my life."

But Hammerstein would soon enough discover that de Mille was ready to lock horns on more basic problems. She'd been doing her homework on their script and already had basic questions for him and Rodgers. She didn't agree with Hammerstein's first-act closer. "The ballet that was outlined by Hammerstein was to be a circus," she said. "And I was the one who said it didn't make any sense. Oscar said, 'You've got to have a light ballet to end our Act One with, you can't send them out into the lobby with gloom.' I said, 'Why not? Just depress the hell out of them.' And I did my spiel, and they listened. Now this was so because they were very gifted men. But I absolutely threw out that circus ballet." De Mille's brilliant solution would be another ballet, "Laurey Makes Up Her Mind."

In between her steady badgering and arm-twisting of potential investors, for the final backing was not yet all in place, Helburn went on assembling a creative cadre for the show.

"The locale of the show, the Oklahoma Territory at the turn of the century, was an ugly period for clothes," she recalled. "The choice of a costume designer was of vital importance for this reason. At the Guild we'd been impressed by the brilliant color and flair two young men had provided for Alfred Lunt and Lynn Fontanne, in our previous production of S. N. Behrman's *The Pirate*. One was Miles White, who'd designed the lavish costumes. I told him I was worried about the 'period.' Those high, tight little collars on our chorus youngsters? The white shirtwaists, long skirts hiding pretty legs? The hats in those days seemed so unwieldy. Would the effect of all those birds' wings, ruffles, and flounces be comic? We certainly didn't want the costumes to have a dated charm, but instead be lovely to remember."

Green Grow the Lilacs must have been a decided challenge for young White, who'd come to New York from California and spent his first years in the theatre doing costumes for traditional musicals like *Best Foot Forward* and the newest edition of *Ziegfeld Follies*, both shows light years away from turn-of-the-century prairie Oklahoma. But he went to his studio and returned with designs for this off-the-beaten-track venture. "Laurey's wedding gown, . . ." exulted Helburn, "Ado Annie's gay pink flounces . . . the checkerboard suit of Ali Hakim, the peddler . . . all those warm blends of color and grace which would cause such gasps of delighted comment when the ballet swept onstage."

White's inspiration? "I borrowed a 1904–5 Montgomery Ward catalogue from Dazian's—that was the fabric house where Emil Friedlander supplied us with all the various materials. When I went through those pages I found out exactly how the people dressed in that period, both men and women—it was all there, even the hats. And I knew that even if they didn't buy them, or couldn't afford those outfits in the catalogue, people in Oklahoma would *copy* them . . . so that's where I got all my 'inspiration,'" says White.

The scenery was designed by the other young man from *The Pirate*, Lem Ayers, who would go on to become the coproducer of Cole Porter's 1948 smash musical *Kiss Me Kate*. Ayers's challenge was to evoke the broad Oklahoma plains but to keep it simple, not only aesthetically but also—and most important, considering the present state of the Guild's bank account—financially.

"Lem tried for a spare and vivid look," Miles White says, "based on Grandma Moses images." Against sweeping vistas Ayers placed a few minimal stage props. A chair, a table, here a butter churn, there a piece of fencing. "He caught at once the clear blue blaze of sky we wanted," said Helburn. "The hot yellow sunshine of Oklahoma, the shades of wheat and tall corn." Ayers's designs had the simplicity of genre painting, but on a stage they became most evocative. For *Green Grow the Lilacs*, they would be perfect.

"What we also needed, as supervisor of the overall production," said Helburn, "was a top stage manager. Someone thoroughly skilled in the routine of stage details. Dick Rodgers got hold of Jerry Whyte, who'd been so efficient on several of Rodgers and Hart's previous musicals, most recently *Pal Joey* and *By Jupiter*. A big, tough 'sergeant-major' type of a man, Jerry Whyte knew his Broadway. Over at the Guild, we hadn't met him before."

Costume designer Miles White's definitive source of style for his work on Oklahoma! was his precious copy of the 1901 Montgomery Ward catalog. Its pages provided the prototypes not only for the women's costumes, hats, and accessories, but also for Curly's surrey with the fringe on top!

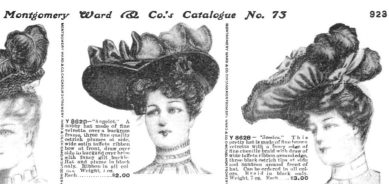

Y 8612—"Lottie." A medium size hat made of fancy felt braid, cloth brim and adorned velvetta crown with large gilt buckle at back, two ostrich tips at side with knot of ribbon under brim. Colors, navy, brown, castor or black. Weight, 5 oz. Each $1.70

Y 8620—"Angelot." A nobby hat made of fine velvetta over a buckram frame, three fine quality ostrich plumes at side, wide satin taffeta ribbon bow at front, draw over side to back and over brim with fancy gilt buckle. Hat and plume in black only. Ribbon in all colors. Weight, 7 oz. Each $2.00

Y 8628—"Jessica." This pretty hat is made of fine brown velvetta with a fancy edge of fine chenille braid with draw of wide taffeta ribbon around edge, three black ostrich tips at side and bandeau around front of hat. Can be ordered in all colors. Braid in black only. Weight, 7 oz. Each $3.00

X 3542

X 3530

X 3536

X 3548

X 3554

At the turn of the century, cigarette packs came with cards that featured provocative females. It was designer Miles White's happy inspiration to use these as the basis for his ballet costumes. (Courtesy of Miles White)

ADMIRAL CIGARETTES.

A surviving costume drawing done by Miles White for Oklahoma! Others, alas, were lost in a warehouse fire, along with some of designer Lem Ayers's drops. (Courtesy of the Museum of the City of New York)

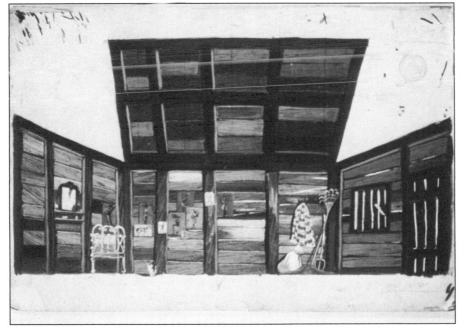

Lemuel Ayers's colorful set drawings. Pay close attention to the details of rural living at the turn of the century. For the old smokehouse, home to the menacing Jud Fry, Ayers provided an especially dismal, desolate, and disturbing environment. Where better to execrate "Pore Jud"? (Courtesy of the Museum of the City of New York)

"'Go around and drop in on the Guild directors,' Dick told him. 'Stop in and ask for Terry Helburn.'

"I found out later how Mr. Whyte first expected he'd be meeting some burly Irish type named 'Terry.' I am probably the shortest living producer in town," remarked Helburn. "Five feet one in my nylons. Billy Rose tops me by an inch or two. My office desk is large; that day, it was piled high. Behind scripts and contracts I had my nose well down in a cup of tea. Big Jerry Whyte peered down at me; he was looking for somebody named Terry. Could I help him? I could. 'How about stage managing this show for us?' I asked.

"'Us?' he asked.

"'Me, and Lawrence Langner, here at the Guild,' I explained.

"Jerry quickly got the message. Out came his large hand with a firm tingle of good will attached."

Elaine Steinbeck, who'd been present two years before when the whole project sparked into life, was already on the Guild's staff, and now she would work with Jerry Whyte.

Robert Russell Bennett would do the orchestrations for Rodgers's music. To conduct, Rodgers wanted young Johnny Green. A successful songwriter in his own right ("Body and Soul," "Out of Nowhere," and many others), Green had conducted *By Jupiter*, and that venture had so pleased Rodgers that he proposed to Green that he assume that task for the Guild.

"I had already signed," Green remembered, "and I was particularly happy about that because Dick had teamed up with Oscar, whom I adored. But Arthur Freed of MGM insisted, 'You've got to come to Metro!' The contractual offers made by Metro got to the point where it was too good to turn down. I was a New Yorker, lock, stock, and barrel, and I didn't want to go to Hollywood; I was not in love with Hollywood, nor even liked it very much."

Green departed for Culver City, which left an opening for some other conductor.

Designer Lem Ayers, who would go on to produce the great **Kiss Me Kate** *with Saint-Subber.*

Elaine Scott Steinbeck, who stage-managed **Oklahoma!** *from Westport down to the St. James Theatre.*

Oscar Hammerstein had another young man in mind, a talented new-comer who'd been at the St. Louis Municipal Opera for six years working for producer Dick Berger on the seasons of musical shows. His name was Jacob Schwartzdorf, he was newly married, and he had conducted Hammerstein's operetta *Sunny River* previously. But Schwartzdorf, who would shortly change his name to Blackton, was not at all certain he wished to commit his future to *Green Grow the Lilacs*. "In my pocket I had a contract for a seventh summer in St. Louis, a firm commitment," he says. "I was also coaching at the Juilliard School. To me, the gamble of being on Broadway was a little more than I was willing to accept." Blackton had firm ambitions to become an opera conductor. This new venture of Rodgers and Hammerstein's did not seem all that promising. So he hesitated, unable to decide. Give up a permanent summer season to gamble on this untested venture, which could flop and leave him stranded?

The first meeting of the cast, at which Rodgers and Hammerstein would demonstrate their score, was imminent. Blackton was invited; would he at least come and listen?

"I reluctantly came," he says, now. "I wanted to be there, but I didn't want them to feel in any way that I'd committed myself. I'd spoken to Dick and told him my problem; he appreciated it, he understood. Oscar was a little firmer in trying to push me into making up my mind . . . he'd urge me. So, here I was, sitting there, while they went through their score for the first time.

"They started off with the first song, which was 'Oh, What a Beautiful Mornin'.' When the song was over, I was filled with emotion at the beauty and the simplicity of this work, which had such a wonderful lyric! It sparkled, as the morning sun sparkles! I was overcome with it. I leaned over, and I very boldly whispered in Rodgers's ear, in the most affectionate manner . . . I just blurted out . . . *'You son of a bitch!'*"

CASTING

hen it came time to assemble a cast for *Green Grow the Lilacs* there arose an entirely different set of problems. Each of the creative minds on Helburn's crew had a different set of images in mind for the performers who'd be populating Riggs's story. "Auditioning was no bed of roses," remembered Helburn, who quickly discovered she'd opened a Pandora's box of complex priorities. "Oscar wanted people who could speak his lines. Dick wanted people who could sing. . . . So we held auditions for a long time, hearing every one we could."

In rugged circumstances.

Vivian Smith, who would shortly become one of Agnes de Mille's most reliable ballerinas, shudders a half-century later at the memory. "Oh, those auditions at the Guild Theatre. I remember Dick and Oscar were sitting

Audition? Rehearsal? Whatever is happening up on that Guild Theatre stage, one cannot tell how it is succeeding from the faces of Mr. Hammerstein, Miss Helburn, Mr. Rodgers, and Mr. Langner.

out front, all bundled up in their overcoats, in that cold barn. Remember, the Guild was about to sell the theatre, and they were so short of money, nobody could afford to turn on the heat!"

Day after day they sat, watching and listening. "Our intent was to discover *actors* who could *sing,*" said Helburn. "The leading parts must be played by actors with dramatic talent, plus the unusual combination of an attractive singing voice. That's how we ended up with a cast of people most of whom were fresh to musical comedy!"

Alfred Drake had earlier been cast for Curly, and Joan Roberts, who had joined him in all those fund-raising auditions that so far hadn't raised much funds, would be Laurey. As the auditions continued, other talents joined the cast list. Lee Dixon, a jovial young song-and-dance man who'd had a modest success in Warner Brothers musicals in Hollywood, was the ideal choice for Will Parker, who'd pursue Ado Annie as well as chronicle in song and dance the amazing virtues of up-to-date Kansas City.

Betty Garde, a leading New York radio actress for many years, seemed right for Aunt Eller and was promptly signed. (Alas, after rehearsals began her part would be subject to constant cutting. Trouper that she was, Miss Garde swallowed her disappointment and pride and stayed with the show.)

Joseph Buloff, a star with considerable experience at the Yiddish Art Theatre, had the correct comic sense to play Ali Hakim, the peddler, and Howard Da Silva, who had shuttled between Broadway's Group Theatre and Hollywood for the past decade, was the choice to play the dark and menacing Jud Fry. Ralph Riggs and Owen Martin were two seasoned character actors.

The real controversy began when it came to the dance ensemble.

The young dancers whom de Mille brought in for auditions were far different from what the producers expected. "Agnes," said Helburn, "wanted people who could *dance*." Whether or not the dancers fit the acceptable Broadway dancing-girl mold was of no interest to the choreographer. "Why, I kept asking, can't we have girls who can dance and *also* have pretty legs? It seemed reasonable to me. It seemed unreasonable to Agnes."

"I knew these girls," de Mille recalled later. "I'd studied with them and we'd had classes together. I'd seen them grow up from brats to mature sixteen-year olds, and they were extravagantly gorgeous. Bambi Linn, Diana Adams, and Joanie McCracken. These were personalities, and they were soloists, and they had big, strong techniques. But when Bambi came to a rehearsal, with braces on her teeth, and she looked like hell, she had a fur hat on that made her look like a rabbit in a tea cozy, I'd never seen such goings on." Neither, it is safe to say, had Messrs. Rodgers, Hammerstein, and Mamoulian.

"McCracken was just starting," said de Mille, "and she had a little tiny mouth and she had very big legs, piano legs. But what she could do with them, that was something else. And that face! . . . Well, you know, magic. . . . The thing was, these girls were all individuals, and I cast them as such, and Dick Rodgers was very, very concerned with who was in the chorus."

Bambi Linn was a remarkable blend of talent and naiveté, even though she'd been dancing most of her years:

> I started dancing when I was six, in little schools, and then I left Brooklyn and went to Manhattan, when I was around eleven; my mother took me to Michael Mordkin's studio in Carnegie Hall. I studied with him for a while, and I began to investigate the other studios; there was one down the hall where Edward Caton taught, and I'd peek in; Miss Lee, who ran the class, would say, "Come on in," and let me watch. Finally, I got to meet Mr. Caton, and when I was about thirteen, I ended up studying there. . . . That's where I met Agnes, when she began teaching a class called "Acting for Beginners."
>
> I'd never been in show business. I didn't know any of the people. Rodgers and Hammerstein were just names to me; they wrote songs, that was all I knew. I was so green—when Agnes brought me up to audition, and I saw John Haggott, the stage manager, with his pipe, I thought *he* was Dick Rodgers! I even developed a crush on Haggott, I guess it was the pipe, my father used to smoke one. . . . For a long time, I didn't realize Haggott wasn't Rodgers at all. When I finally found out, I was so surprised and shocked. That round little stubby man who was playing the piano for us—*he* was Rodgers? I was overwhelmed. That's how amateurish *I* was!

An amateur in the world of show business Bambi may have been, but not when dancing. "I'd say to Bambi, 'Jump!' and she'd spring like Baryshnikov," says de Mille. "She had the jump of a deer—it was simply amazing. But then, I knew a great reservoir of talent had been gathering in the dance studios around town, waiting for some sort of a chance, and I had been watching the young dancers mature in daily practice, so the lineup I put together was accordingly without any parallel."

The arguments continued, the old show business veterans insisting on some representation of sheer beauty in the ensemble, whether such women were dancers or not. "Just for appearance' sake," says de Mille, "we took in two chorus girls. They seemed terrified at the vigorous company they found themselves suddenly in, and sat or stood, locked close together from pure loneliness."

For the lead in her ballet "Laurey Makes Up Her Mind," which would close Act One, de Mille cast her good friend the beautiful Katharine (Katya) Sergava, late of the Ballet Theatre. "And then I brought in Diana Adams," she says, "who had extraordinary techniques; I mean, she could do anything you asked for."

Young Miss Adams was a demure beauty. "She could be the typical showgirl type that Rodgers was used to," comments Linn. She pleased Hammerstein as well. "She's like everybody's little sister," he remarked, fondly.

"But Joanie McCracken and I, we were little girls with piano legs," says Linn. "And Rodgers took one look at us, and he said to Agnes, 'Uh-uh. No.' Agnes started bargaining. She said, 'Well, let me have one of those, and you can have two of yours.' That's how she bargained. I remember that so well; my life was on the line, so how could I forget it? And Agnes was furious that she had to bargain that way."

Originally, de Mille had thought of young Bambi to be her Laurey in that first-act closing ballet. But eventually, when Sergava was cast, Bambi's characterization had to be changed; she would be a very young girl in the same scene. "So whenever I appeared in the ballets, my skirts were shorter, I had pigtails, and that's why you noticed me," she says. "Not that I had that much to do—I stood out because I was *the* little girl."

Another of de Mille's choices was Kate Friedlich. She was a longtime friend of the choreographer who'd been dancing professionally for many years. The two had originally met in Des Moines, where Friedlich lived. "[Agnes] was doing a concert; she used humor with dance," says Friedlich today. "Years later I met her at the American Ballet School; her partner there was Paul Draper. Then she asked me to do a concert with her; I was delighted, and I really enjoyed it. She so obviously had gifts as a choreographer." Next came a small revue, which de Mille choreographed with two of the dancers from the American Ballet School. "It was called *Hell on Wheels*, and Agnes explained she was exploring some dance material that would be used later in *Oklahoma!* The show was really charming, and it got excellent reviews."

Meanwhile, Friedlich had begun her Broadway career, dancing in various Broadway shows. "I'd been in *I'd Rather Be Right*, *Very Warm for May*, a terrible flop called *Hiya, Gentlemen*, and *Banjo Eyes*, with Eddie Cantor. Agnes invited me to be in this new Rodgers and Hammerstein show, and since Dick Rodgers knew my work, he agreed with her, so I was spared the dance audition.

"I was also asked by Agnes if I'd put in some rehearsal time before the actual rehearsals began," says Friedlich. "Sometimes a choreographer will work with a few dancers for several weeks, in order to get a running start on the choreography."

The Guild was also looking for understudies to the cast members. Friedlich was asked to read one of the parts. "I had the script in one hand; I clamped it with the other, to keep down the shaking! I was that nervous. I probably read very badly."

But she had been hired, and when it came to a discussion of Miss Friedlich's salary, the young dancer was far removed from the starry-eyed amateur who'd begun in Des Moines. "I knew the Guild was notoriously chintzy, so I asked the stage manager of the show I'd just been in, *Star and Garter*, how to go about getting a decent salary. He was a lovely man named Frank Hall; he told me, 'Take your current salary and almost double it. The Guild will cut you down, and they will be pleased with themselves. You'll be earning more than you are now, and you'll be happy.'"

Hall's strategy, albeit elementary, worked. "I ended up making more than most of the dancers!" chortles Friedlich. "Of course," she adds, a bit ruefully, "later on, after I'd been injured on opening night in New York and I was out of the show, I asked if I could see the matinee from out front. I'd never seen the show as a spectator. They agreed, and got me an orchestra seat. Six weeks later, when I finally came back into the cast, I found the Guild had docked me $6 for my matinee ticket!"

The grueling audition process continued.

"I wanted talent and personality," says de Mille. "Rodgers wanted faces, but he was inclined to stand by me on many occasions. His idea and my idea of a face, I found, had frequently to do with the character in it. Oscar wasn't around. Lawrence Langner was down in Washington, doing important war work with the patent office, top secret. So we finally chose all but three."

The ultimate decision brought on an explosion, resulting not from arrogance and ego, as is usually the case in such creative arguments, but from de Mille's own frustration.

Years later Celeste Holm would remember that scene with exactitude.

Agnes had them all lined up, and she brought Mr. Mamoulian down, he always had that cigar with him, and he said "Agnes, they're certainly not pretty. They're useless to me."

Then he looked at the one on the end, with the tiny head and a great long neck, and those big legs, not fat, but solid, and he shook his head.

She said, "You know what I'm going to do."

He said, "No, what?"

She said, "You'll see. They're not chorus girls, they're dancers."

"Well," he said, "That little girl, though, with the braces in her teeth, and the tiny head, and those big legs . . ."

Agnes picked up her purse and threw it against the back wall of the theatre, and she said, "If she goes, I go! *I quit the show!*"

The detonator of the explosion, young Bambi Linn, stood by, nervously watching.

De Mille never forgot Mamoulian's reaction.

"He shrugged, and then said, 'Just keep them out of my way.' "

"Later on," she added, "Dick Rodgers looked at my ballet dancers and remarked, 'I don't know—they're sort of *endearing.*' "

Marc Platt had been dancing with the Ballet Russe for almost six years, under the name of Marc Platoff. In those days American ballet dancers needed the cachet of Russian auspices in order to be taken seriously by audiences.

I was a soloist. I'd done a lot of good work for them and I was well known in the dance ballet. I was making $325 a month; I wanted $400. They refused. George Balanchine came to do a couple of ballets with the company and I asked, "George, can you get me into a musical comedy where I can earn some real money? It won't happen here." George said, "Let me think. I vill call you."

A week later he called me up and said, "Here, you vant vork in a Broadway show? Get here quick, right away. I have show for you." So I went over with a girl named Luba Rostova, and we did a comedy ballet

for George. The show was *My Dear Public*. Total bomb. From there I went into something called *The Lady Comes Across*, with the British star Jessie Matthews. Closed in less than a week. Now I was out of work, didn't have any money, had to get a job. Third show, *Beat The Band*. Also a flop. Now I was really in trouble.

Danny Kaye was playing in *Let's Face It*, and I went backstage to see one of the dancers; as I was coming downstairs, I met Dick Rodgers coming up. I knew him from the ballet *Ghost Town* he'd written for the Ballet Russe. So I said, "Dick, do you have anything coming up? I'm here in New York, and I want to work." "Do you know Agnes de Mille?" he asked. Well, I certainly did. "Why don't you call my office, get her number, and get in touch with her?" said Dick.

Next morning, I did it. Called Agnes. We met, we talked, I had a job!

Rodgers had worked with many other dancers in the past few seasons, among them George Church, a strapping chap who'd appeared in Rodgers and Hart's *On Your Toes*, where he'd danced the "Slaughter on Tenth Avenue" ballet. "I was the villain who threatened Tamara Geva, the leading dancer," he recalls. But after that success, Church was also job hunting. "I'd been in two flops, and I already knew that in this new show Dick was doing they'd decided to find ballet dancers who could double for the actors in the dream ballets." Around Broadway theatres such information traveled fast, especially among out-of-work dancers.

"I'd already heard how Marc Platt had just been hired to double for Curly in the dream ballet. There was another story going around that the Guild had offered the part of Curly to Dennis Morgan, the movie star, who turned it down. Weren't the Guild and Alfred Drake lucky Morgan did so? I also knew they had to find a ballet dancer to double for Jud Fry—for that part they'd already hired Howard Da Silva, who was six feet tall and weighed over two hundred."

Armed with such information, Church called Rodgers, and was asked to dinner at Sardi's, for a friendly chat.

During dinner, Dick explained how Jud, in the ballet, would be called on to choke Curly, and then he said, "Now, who do we know that's six feet tall, weighs two hundred, and is a ballet dancer?"

I laughed. I knew what Dick was getting at, but I waited.

Dick said, "Agnes de Mille saw you dancing the Big Boss in "Slaughter on Tenth Avenue" in *On Your Toes*. She says there's no one else alive who can do Jud. I say there isn't, the Theatre Guild agrees there isn't, and Mamoulian says there isn't. What do *you* say?"

I sat there in silence, thinking this over. This show looked like a sure loser. No stars. Based on a flop play. Dick had just lost his longtime partner, Larry Hart, and the Guild hadn't raised all their backing. And compared to what I'd been making, I knew the salary they'd pay would be small.

"We need you, George," Dick continued. He waited for me.

"Okay, Dick," I said. "*If* I can have a two-week cancellation clause in my contract, I'll do it." What I'd figured out was that if the show, and my part in it, turned out badly in the out-of-town tryout, I could give my notice and not be embarrassed on Broadway. [It was as it turned out, shrewd enough reasoning on Church's part, especially since, changes were made in Boston that eliminated Church's second-act solo.] Dick went right to the phone and called the Guild, and told them they could make out a contract for me.

Between de Mille and Church there would develop an immediate rapport. "I found her to be the most dance-loving, hardworking person I'd ever met!" recalls Church with admiration. "Her choreography was based on both ballet and modern dance, and it fitted *Away We Go!* like a glove. I don't know if Agnes ever played a musical instrument, but she has a great knowledge of music as it pertains to the dance. She was made to order for that show!"

Simultaneous with the casting auditions were the endless backer auditions. The indefatigable Terry Helburn was everywhere, consulting, conferring, and moving the crew of her Folly forward. Oscar Hammerstein would later describe her fondly as "a very small sheepdog, always pushing you relentlessly to some pasture that she felt would be good for you"—as she would do one particular night while she and her faithful pair of performers, Alfred Drake and Joan Roberts, accompanied Rodgers and Hammerstein uptown to a fund-raising hour or so at the home of Jules Glaenzer, the head of Cartier's.

On the way, Helburn murmured to Hammerstein, "I wish you and Dick would write a song about the earth."

Somewhat surprised by this suggestion, which had dropped so abruptly into their conversation, Hammerstein asked her what she meant.

"Oh, I don't know," said Helburn. "Just a song about the earth—the land . . ."

Hammerstein was somewhat nonplussed by the vagueness of Helburn's suggestion, intuitive though it certainly was. But according to his biographer, Hugh Fordin, two days later Hammerstein found himself writing a lyric he had never intended to write, a lyric describing a "brand new state" that would provide "barley, carrots and pertaters, pasture for the cattle." He wrote of the wind sweeping down the plain, and how sweet the waving wheat smelled when the wind came right behind the rain. It was a song about a young couple expressing their happiness that they belonged to the land, and that the land they belonged to was grand. Helburn had seeded what would become one of the show's major hit songs and almost an American anthem.

The new song became part of the second act, as a next-to-closing number. De Mille choreographed it with a small ensemble of Oklahomans singing the song blithely; in the middle of the number George Church, wearing boots, did a character tap dance, one which he choreographed for himself.

"George and I were both hired as soloists," recalls Marc Platt. "But later on, when we started rehearsals, Mamoulian began to put us into every scene in the show, because he wanted everybody to act as his chorus. We resented that; we were *soloists*. So every time they called the entire ensemble onstage we would go back and hide behind some flats, or back of the house, or behind the curtains. And finally the stage managers became disgusted. They said, 'Forget it, they're gone.' And we were never bothered again."

"But we were wrong, of course, and Mamoulian was absolutely right," says Church. "The play *was* the thing, and when they took out those speciality numbers, one of which was mine and the other of which was danced by Eric Victor up in Boston, the show went much, much better!"

And what was that long-gone second solo spot?

"I can remember that," says Paul Shiers, another mainstay of de Mille's original ensemble, a reliable performer who was often called on to substitute for others, especially Lee Dixon. "It was a little solo for Eric Victor, who did it with Bambi. He did a tap step, not a conventional one, and Bambi caught on to the sound he was making. It was that sound which fascinated her, so she followed him around as if he were the Pied Piper. Charming number; it was a show-stopper. But once we had opened in New Haven, they realized this number wasn't advancing the plot at all. Even though the audience responded to it, out it went.

Eric Victor's response was immediate. He took a settlement of his contract and left the show.

One major character was as yet uncast during those frigid audition sessions at the Guild Theatre: Ado Annie, the acquiescent lady-friend of Will Parker, whose flirtation with Aly Hakim, the peddler, would induce the second-act comedy climax. The role, which would eventually prove to be a passport to stardom, needed someone special. There had been numerous casting suggestions, but so far no one had been set for the character.

"Celeste Holm was a prime example of how we unearthed unexpected musical comedy talent," recalled Helburn. "She was a talented young actress who'd appeared for us in the Pennsylvania Dutch comedy *Papa Is All*. She then did a short, fragile scene in William Saroyan's *The Time of*

Your Life. Now she was appearing in a new straight play called *The Damask Cheek* by John Van Druten. Then she came over to audition for us."

Elaine Steinbeck had been stage-managing at all the auditions. "The day Celeste came, I walked down to the footlights and I leaned over and said to Dick and whomever else was out there, 'I think I'm going to apologize first. I'm going to bring on somebody you all know. I can't imagine she can possibly sing, but she *says* she can.' I was embarrassed about bringing her out, can you imagine?" she chuckles today.

"And they asked me, 'Who is it?' and I said, 'Celeste Holm.'

" 'Hey,' said a voice, 'If she can sing, she'd be great for you-know-what.'

" 'Ado Annie?'

" 'That's it!' "

Elaine returned to the waiting Celeste.

"She thumped me on the back and said, 'Be great! It's only the best part in the show!' " remembers Celeste.

In my excitement, I didn't notice the three steps leading down onto the stage. I couldn't see over my music, which I was hugging to my chest like school books. I fell flat on my face, with the music skating out in front of me.

"That's pretty funny," said a voice. "Could you do it again?"

"I'd rather not," I said, fishing for my belt, which had popped with the impact.

The voice said, "I'm Richard Rodgers."

And I said, "Hello."

"And what are you going to sing?"

"*Who Is Sylvia?*" I answered.

"Oh, good," he said. "I haven't heard that this year." He let me sing all three choruses. When I finished there was a stunned silence, and then he said, rather disappointedly, "But you have a trained voice. Could you sing as if you'd never had a lesson in your life?"

"You mean I've studied for three years for that?"

"Oh, you have to know how to in order to know how *not* to," he said.

"I want a loud, unedited sound, like a farm girl."

"I can call a hog,"

"I dare you," he said."

I leaned back and let fly. *"Sooeee!"* None came.

"Okay," he said. "That's loud enough. Come on down here." I jumped down off the stage and we shook hands. "But aren't you in a hit? I don't steal actors," Dick Rodgers said. I *was* in a hit. I was playing in *The Damask Cheek*, and it had been voted the most literate play of the season by the critics.

"Well, it's before Christmas," I said, "and business is okay now, but I don't know how solid we'll be later."

"You'll hear from me." He smiled. And when I left the theatre I didn't mind the rain at all.

A week passed, and then Miss Holm was called back to repeat her performance, complete with hog-calling. "It was for the Theatre Guild people and Oscar Hammerstein. Meeting him was like meeting an old friend. He was big and kind and comfortable. Then I was asked to read a scene from the new show. They seemed pleased, but when I left that day there was no decision. It was all rather vague. On the corner of 48th Street and Sixth Avenue there was a Gypsy Tea Kettle on the second floor. Wouldn't it be fun, somehow, magically, to know the future? My gypsy wore just what you'd expect; a chiffon scarf with bangles on the edge, and all those flowered skirts. When she 'read my leaves,' I tried not to show my disbelief."

" 'Do the initials "RR" mean anything to you?' "

" 'No,' I said, not thinking of Richard Rodgers. We'd barely met!"

" 'They will,' she said seriously. "I see you surrounded by dancing cowboys. And there will be a tremendous change in your life.'

"I thanked her for what I thought was complete nonsense and left."

Shortly afterward, Flora Robson, the star of *The Damask Cheek*, became ill, and the play promptly closed. But Miss Holm would not be out of work for long.

"When I got the call to come to the Theatre Guild, to talk contract," she says, "I didn't have an agent, so I called Edith Van Cleve at MCA. I told her about my auditions. She thought I was crazy. I was coming along nicely as a serious actress, she insisted, and what did I know about musical comedy?

"Would she please negotiate a contract? I asked. Against her better judgment, she did. I was to receive $250 a week to play Ado Annie, and I was to receive fourth featured billing.

"But it wasn't until we actually opened in New Haven, and I'd gotten a big hand for 'I Cain't Say No,' that I remember Jo Healy, who was the guardian of the Theatre Guild switchboard, admitting, 'Well now, I guess it's all right to tell you, but all during rehearsals they had me calling Hollywood to get someone to replace you—mostly Judy Canova and Shirley Booth.'"

And as for young Jay Blackton, the as-yet undecided conductor? The Guild drew a contract for his services with the show and sent it to him. As deeply moved as he had been by the Rodgers and Hammerstein score, he still hesitated. However, as if drawn by an irresistible magnetic force, each day he would return to the Guild Theatre to sit in on the conferences and early preparations for *Green Grow the Lilacs*.

Which by now could no longer be called that. MGM owned the title to Lynn Riggs's play, along with the film rights. Therefore, under the terms of their new agreement with L. B. Mayer's corps of lawyers, the Guild could only acquire those rights, as well as the title to same, if and when they exercised their option. *After* the show opened. Ergo, a new title for Hammerstein's libretto was in order forthwith.

Ideas were tossed back and forth (see pages 196–197). Helburn, Langner, and Rodgers proffered suggestions that would lead to the final choice. Final, at least, for New Haven and Boston.

REHEARSALS

hey began on February 8, 1943.

"That afternoon," says Celeste Holm, "on the stage of the Guild Theatre, Richard Rodgers played, and Oscar Hammerstein sort of sang the songs. That moment is particularly memorable to me. Those two men, who were to become the titans of our musical theatre, presented their work so unpretentiously. No matter how many ways the work has been sung and played since then, I'll always remember Oscar and Dick's version for us."

George Irving, later to become a Broadway star, was a singer cast in his first show. "The lowest of the low" is how he defines his status. "When Dick came out to play for us," he says, "I remember noticing that there was

The color and spirit of Agnes de Mille's dance numbers for Okla-homa! echoed her choreography for Rodeo, *a show the reviews called a "thoroughly American piece" when she performed in it at the Ballet Theatre of New York in October 1942. The ballet firmly established de Mille as both choreographer and dancer. (Maurice Seymour/Courtesy of Photofest)*

no music on the piano at all. He played everything from memory, and not only was it a wonderful score, but his performance was very impressive."

Before rehearsals began there was a moment when Lawrence Langner made a brief speech to the assembled cast. Obviously moved by the circumstances that had forced the Guild to sell its theatre, he told them, "This is the last time that Guild thespians will tread these boards."

Rouben Mamoulian was also moved by the moment. "I remember him looking at the bare back wall," says George Irving, "with all those steam pipes running up from the floor, and he made a very touching speech, almost a monologue, totally extemporaneous, about how much those pipes reminded him of the interior of a cathedral . . . that they were like organ pipes. 'For me, this theatre is a holy place,' he said to us, 'and this work here in which we're involved is a noble, holy thing.' We were all very moved."

Then the work began.

According to Actors Equity rules, the Guild had five days to decide which members of the cast would be kept on permanently, after which the contracts would be formally issued. Thus, Bambi Linn, who kept a diary, could note, ". . . was told today we are in the show for sure." The following day's entry reads, "Signed my contract today. I was hoping it would be white, but it was pink. We get $45 on the road, and $40 in town, less than other shows, I'm told. . . ."

"There wasn't an inch of the theatre that wasn't being used by chorus, principals, dancers," reported Helburn. "Mamoulian, who integrated drama and song and dance, sweated at his task. Agnes drilled her dancers relentlessly. Dick sat at his keyboard, watching, listening. I bit my nails and scurried around and wondered if I had made the most fatal mistake of my life. Everyone else thought so."

During those weeks Helene Hanff remained at her post in the Guild press department offices working for Joe Heidt. "People from other floors drifted into our office with progress reports," she remembered. "This was, they informed us, the damndest musical comedy anybody'd ever hatched for a sophisticated Broadway audience. It opened with a middle-aged farm woman sitting alone on a bare stage churning butter, and from then on it got cleaner. They did not feel a long sequence of arty dancing was likely to improve matters on the farm."

Downstairs in the drafty lobby, on rugs that had not been vacuumed in months, Agnes de Mille worked at top speed. "Since Mamoulian took the stage," she recalled, "I worked below in what had been the foyer and way above in what had been costume and rehearsal rooms." ("That deserted and badly lit box room, which was way upstairs, was filled with cartons," says Bambi Linn, "and we placed them all in one corner, and then the dust began to come up. There was no way of opening a window to let the dust out, and you didn't want to open the window because it was very chilly. So sooner or later, we would all get sick.")

"With the assistance of Marc Platt and Ray Harrison, another dancer, I kept three rehearsals going at once," said de Mille. "I was like a pitcher that had been overfilled; the dances simply spilled out of me. I had boys and girls in every spare corner of the theatre sliding, riding, tapping, ruffling skirts, kicking. We worked with enormous excitement, but always under great strain. For the first three days, Richard Rodgers never left my side. He sat with fixed surgical attention, watching everything. This made the dancers nervous, but it was I who really sweated. He did not relax until the third afternoon, when smiling and patting me on the shoulder he gave the first intimation that I would not be fired."

"Agnes did tremendous homework," says Bambi Linn. "She does it in her mind first, then she gets up and she walks it, and then she'd call us together and say 'try this,' and we worked that way. Then she'd suggest a movement to us, say 'Sweep across the floor,' so you'd sweep across the floor, each of us would try it, and she'd say, 'Okay, try this arm movement,' and she would evolve it into a movement, or something that was usable, and she'd say, 'Okay, let's do that, that's what I want you to try here.' And she never even stopped you if you'd ask 'Could I try this?' She'd let you explore it for yourself, and if she didn't like it, she'd say *no* and you'd go on. It was wonderful. . . . You know, a lot of people I think were crushed when she would throw out something they'd suggested, but it never bothered me, because I was so used to that process from working with her in her class."

Jay Blackton had still not made up his mind to sign a contract to conduct the show, but he came the first day, and whenever he was free he'd drop by the Guild Theatre to watch the rehearsals.

I'd sit there, watching Mamoulian on the main stage, as he rehearsed with his actors. Every time I was there, Rodgers would urge Oscar to talk to me. He told me that later. So Oscar would ask, "Well, what about it, are you with us or not?" I was torn. I liked what I was seeing, but I was afraid to give up my steady job in St. Louis at the Municipal Opera in order to commit to this untested new show. After all, I had responsibilities to my wife; she was expecting our first child, plus I had my job, coaching up at Juilliard; it would be a real gamble to go with them. A tough decision.

But one time, when Mamoulian declared a break and everybody left to go get coffee, Hammerstein nailed me. He took me out on the bare stage, backed me into a corner, and gave me a tongue lashing I have never forgotten. I've never seen Oscar that disturbed, before or after. Berating me! He said, "You've got to make up your mind! You're a man who's got to be on Broadway. That's where you *belong*!" He kept on urging me—*"Make up your mind!"*

That more or less did the trick. I left him with my tail between my legs. I was really desolate because I knew I had to make up my mind. And I went home, and Louise and I decided I had to do this show, whether or not I lost the St. Louis job. Believe me, it was a big step.

Dick Berger, who ran the Municipal Opera, was great. He said he'd try to hold off hiring anybody else for my job until this new show opened in New Haven. I went back to the rehearsals, and now I went downstairs to the lobby, where Agnes de Mille was working out her

In the spirit of the frontier, May Gadd of the American Country Dance Society came to the aid of Agnes de Mille and her "farmers" and "cowmen." Soon all of Oklahoma would learn the proper square-dance etiquette of how to honor one's partner, bow to one's corner, promenade, and do-si-do. (Courtesy of Photofest)

choreography. She had a fine pianist working with her; he turned out to be Buddy Lewis, a pretty damned good songwriter in his own right.*

Now that I was the musical director, I became her liaison with what was going on upstairs. It was fascinating to watch her at work. What amazed me was how she took Dick and Oscar's lyrical songs and used them as the framework, the roots, the sperm of her choreographic devices.

As the frenetic days passed, the only available heat in the soon-to-be-sold Guild Theatre was that of creativity. "It was February, and frigid," recalled Kate Friedlich. "I got a wicked cold. Missed two days of rehearsals. I came back to find that Joan McCracken had been given the part of 'the girl who falls down' in the 'Many a New Day' ballet, which de Mille had already begun to choreograph for me, and so I was steamed."

To add to the misfortunes, the youngest dancer in the show, Kenneth

---

* Morgan (Buddy) Lewis, who wrote "The Old Soft Shoe" and "How High the Moon" with Nancy Hamilton.

LeRoy, came down with German measles and had to retire temporarily from rehearsals. But, alas, not before he had infected many of his confreres. So while the rehearsals continued at a furious pace, the dancers, unaware they were now in an incubation period, went on taking direction from de Mille, who herself had developed a dreadful cough and would have to spend a valuable day at home recuperating.

Meanwhile, Mamoulian sat upstairs in the drafty theatre, puffing incessantly on his cigars and staging scenes from Hammerstein's libretto. "He never relinquished that stage to Agnes," said Alfred Drake. "And he insisted on having everybody up there on the stage while he was rehearsing the scenes. That meant a lot of people were playing poker on the sides of the stage, and we were all most unhappy about that. It could be that he'd be rehearsing a simple scene between the two of us, but everybody else had to be there!"

"He was very autocratic," says de Mille. "Very wary of me, and when he saw what I was doing downstairs he became warier. Every time he saw one of my song settings, or a dance routine, or anything, I would later find he had helped himself to some of my tricks in *his* settings of the actors, in the lead-ins preceding my dances. He was without shame. But Rodgers protected me from him. I would have been absolutely obliterated because nobody at the Guild did so, but Rodgers actually ran the body interference between the two of us."

"I can remember the first day of really tremendous excitement," said Drake. "It was the day Agnes brought the dancers upstairs and had them go through the ballet."

"It was on a Sunday," says Elaine Steinbeck, "and Rouben said, 'I think it would be nice to put a few things together today.' Oscar wasn't there, he was at home in Bucks County, and Dick was with his family, here in town at a hotel. Rouben said, 'Elaine, go down and see if Agnes would come and bring up a number or two and we'll run them just to try them—a little bit together.'

"Without an audience, without anything, with just the rehearsal piano and her dancers on that bare cold stage, she ran some numbers for us, and I suddenly thought, 'Uh-oh!' and without asking or telling anybody, I ran to the phone and called Dick up at his hotel where he was with Dorothy, and I said, 'Can you come?' He asked, 'What's the matter?' I just said, 'Something here looks awfully good, and it looks so different from anything, and please *come!*'

"And Dick came, and he sat in the orchestra, and when he saw what had been put together he grinned and said, 'Oh, *that* was worth making a Sunday trip for!'"

"Rodgers is not only a great songwriter," commented de Mille, years later. "He is one of the most astute theatre men in the world. He concerns himself relentlessly with every detail of production. Nothing escapes his attention, and he takes vigorous and instant action. This might be interfering if he were not sensitive, sensible, and greatly experienced. . . . Mamoulian and the Guild frequently said 'It can't be done.' It was always Rodgers who urged 'Let's see.'"

There were more than the usual crises, some of which were due to the problem of finances. Terry Helburn was still indefatigably hunting for more badly needed backers. "By now," she said later, "it was so bad that Dick Rodgers used to say to me, 'There's even a Chinese gentleman in Shanghai who's turned us down!'"

"We all got increasingly nervous," recalled de Mille, "and when Terry Helburn started interrupting rehearsals to show unfinished work to prospective backers in her frantic efforts to raise money, I blew every fuse I had. Hurling my pocketbook at her head, I shouted and flounced and was dragged off screaming by Marc Platt and held under a faucet of cold water until I quieted down."

According to de Mille's journal, she accomplished an enormous amount of work in the first two weeks of the rehearsals; she set *all* the dances in the show, including "Boys and Girls Like You and Me," a ballad that would eventually be cut.

= FGA GA   JTQ1===3 FEBRUARY 8 1943 DAYLETTER = MR. LEE

SHUBERT VERSAILLES HOTEL MIAMI BEACH FLORIDA= FIRST REHEARSAL

TODAY PLAY AND MUSIC GREEN GROW PERFECTLY ENCHANTING. WE WANT TO

PUT IT INTO ST JAMES THEATRE BUT FEEL THE VERY DIRTY SEAT COVERS

WILL HURT THE SHOW. WE HAVE PUT TSO===TWO HIT SHOWS IN THIS

THEATRE ALREADY SO WONT YOU PLEASE TELEGRAPH NEWYORK AND

AUTHORIZE NEW SLIP COVERS AND WE WILL SIGN CONTRACTS. HOPE YOU ARE

HAVING FINE REST.= THERESA HELBURN.

Mr. Lee Shubert was one of the two brothers—the other being J. J. (Jake)—who controlled a vast theatre operation that stretched from Manhattan across the United States. Through their United Booking Office the Shuberts had a lock on legitimate theatres in most major cities. The Shuberts needed shows to fill their theatres; in order to assure bookings it was their practice to invest in the productions of independent managers, thus collecting from both ends and giving their organization absolute power. They invested in the Guild's new musical, with the understanding that Away We Go! would be booked into their St. James Theatre.

Here, on the first day of rehearsals, Terry Helburn reports to her backer and future landlord. Note the bargain being struck: new seat covers at the St. James and then the signed contract! Certainly this is not the type of musical comedy history show biz fans expect, is it?

Miles White's cigarette-card girls brought to vivid life as the dance-hall girls of Jud Fry's dreams. In de Mille's famous ballet the dancers were (left to right) Joan McCracken, Kate Friedlich, Vivian Smith, Margit DeKova, and Barbara Barrington.

"I'm well again," she reported, in the third week. "I never worked so fast in my life. I've set forty minutes of straight dancing in less than three weeks. The company raves. Rodgers put his head on my shoulder this afternoon and said, 'Oh, Aggie, you're such a comfort in my old age.' And Marc Platt said this evening, 'In all soberness, I've never worked with any-one I respected more.'"

"We live in the basement," she continued. "I see sunlight only twenty minutes a day. The dust from the unvacuumed Guild rugs has made us all sick, and I put away three thermos bottles of coffee an afternoon. I look awful."

De Mille can still look back on her work of almost a half century ago and reflect on its impact on the final production. "It was that first-act bal-let which changed the quality of the show," she says today. "Once Laurey realizes that she's really frightened of Jud, and why she's frightened, you can see the change. Up till then it's been an innocuous gingham-aprony Sunday-school sort of a show. That first act, there was nothing in it, no threat, no suspense, no sex, no nothing. And I told this to Oscar, who said, 'No sex?' 'No, Mr. Hammerstein,' I said. 'None. What have we done with those postcards of Jud Fry's?' And he looked at me, and then he went to the phone and called Dick. 'Dick, get over here immediately.'"

Jud Fry's French postcards, which he kept hidden in his lonely barn lodgings, would come to life in costumes by Miles White, who would draw his inspiration for their images from turn-of-the-century cigarette cards, those same ephemeral tiny photos that showed the buxom belles of the early twentieth century, so favored by the young "sports" who puffed on the "coffin-nails" of the day. Now they would be danced by de Mille's ballerinas.

"I put them on the stage, and that was the first big belly laugh," de Mille says. "And then, when I also introduced the dramatic motif that Laurey was scared of the violence inherent in Jud, the danger in that man, I let the act curtain come down on that, which introduced a dark, suspenseful, ominous note, which the show hadn't had. And it made everything else more real."

"With those ballets," commented Helburn, "created out of so much travail and turmoil, nerve strain and confusion, Agnes came into her own as one of America's leading choreographers. If she was sometimes annoyed past endurance with me during the exhausting weeks while the show went into production, she had some justification for it."

Ten days before the crew was scheduled to leave for New Haven the first run-through was held.

"We came back after supper to find the stage newly marked off with laths to indicate walls and openings for gates or doors," remembered Celeste Holm.

*　　*　　*

The Theatre Guild people arrived. They were followed by a most un-expected group; well-dressed gentlemen and ladies, wearing hats—looking as though they had just come from "21."

The strangers walked down the steps from the stage and took seats out front. They all looked at us in that odd way civilians look at per-formers; through a glass wall, with gentle, phony smiles.

"Who are they?" I asked Terry Helburn.

"Just think of them as friends," she said sweetly.

How could we have known that the Guild *still* needed money for the show? When we started our first complete run-through, those "strangers" were thirty prospective backers, scattered lumpily out front.

. . . The rehearsal piano began, and so did an over-controlled night-mare! As I was about to make an entrance, a whole ballet came on, and I got out of its way just in time. Cues were missed, actors tripped over the laths and forgot their lyrics, and no one out front laughed at all. I watched the civilians leave. The phony smiles were still there, frozen on. And not one of that bunch had a dime's worth of confidence in us.

We rehearsed all day; and at night, from then on, there'd be more of those well-dressed people, picking their way across the stage, taking seats in the orchestra. We made them laugh on subsequent nights, but not one backer ever emerged from those groups.

One day de Mille brought in her friend, May Gadd, the head of the American Country Dance Society, who spent the entire rehearsal session instructing the boys in square-dancing. "How to offer their hands to the women, to bow to them, to pass in and out of the groups, courteously, gal-lantly, as if they cared about them, a point of view," de Mille commented, and then added dryly, "in which many of the boys could afford to take instruction."

As the day loomed closer on which the company was to leave for New Haven, there were the customary outbreaks of tension and temperament.

"I had trouble with Joe Buloff," recalled Celeste Holm, whose character Ado Annie would be romantically involved with Buloff's Ali Hakim.

The first day we did our scene he came on eating a banana. Well, the chorus girls thought that was the funniest thing they'd ever seen. The next day he came on with a cane, with which he began hitting me on the ass. He seemed to have no sense of the other actor's responsibilities, or his needs. . . . You see, as far as I'm concerned, a scene is a covenant. I promise to be standing in the same spot every night, so you can do what you have to do, and I can do what I have to do, and then we get the play on. If you start doing something that I don't know about, out goes the show!

One day Joe stood on my foot; didn't even *know* he was standing on my foot! So I went to Mamoulian and I explained very quietly that I'd have to get this scene set, one way or the other. I said, "I'm his partner in this scene and I want to know what he's going to do!"

So Mamoulian went to Joe Buloff, and in front of the entire company he said to him, "Joe, you carry one more prop on this stage which I have not seen before and I come back and break every tooth in your head. I have seen you in show after show, always you get good notices, always you steal the show, and the show closes. You've never been in a hit in your life. This time I want you to be in a *hit!*"

I hadn't realized I was reaping a whirlwind. . . . But you know something? From then on, Joe behaved himself. He was very good, and he *was* in a hit! And years later, a quarter of a century after we opened, we met at a party and he said to me, "Oh, I love you so much, I love you!"

I said, "You never told me, you never let me know."

He said, "I *couldn't.*" But he was now eighty or so, and he finally could say it!

"However ruffled temperaments became, we had our lighter moments," said Helburn. "Mamoulian wanted more atmosphere of the Oklahoma farm when the curtain rose. 'How about a donkey, or a goat?' he asked.

But we couldn't travel with a barnyard on the road." Langner thereupon suggested a cow, to be tethered by Aunt Eller as she churned the butter in the opening scene. The cow never made it to the stage.

Mamoulian had other ideas. "One morning, during the third week of rehearsals," remembers George Church, "Moo-Moo, that was our name for him, declared, 'What we need is spectacle—to build up the last scene of the show! Max Reinhardt was right—go out and find some agent who has some specialty acts we can audition—find us *spectacle!*'"

The next afternoon brought on the auditioners. The first to arrive in the theatre was an honest-to-goodness cowboy from Oklahoma, an authentic roper. "He spun his ropes in spectacular fashion," says Church, "and Moo-Moo jumped up, ecstatic! 'Now, we're getting somewhere!' he said, and proceeded to improvise a moment onstage in which Alfred Drake and Joan Roberts would sit together with the cowboy standing behind them. He ordered the roper to spin the rope around all three, and then suggested that Drake and Roberts, on cue, would sing 'Oklahoma!'

"The cowboy promptly began spinning his rope above his head, paying it out until he had a huge circle some fifteen feet in diameter, and then he lowered it on himself and the two performers. '*Sing!*' shouted Mamoulian. Drake and Roberts began, but that rope kept whipping around them, often coming dangerously close. They were scared silly," says Church, "and they were right. Suddenly that rope scraped Alfred's face and gave him a pretty good rope burn! He grabbed the rope and threw it to the floor! Neither he nor Joan Roberts would permit themselves to be roped a second time.

"Moo-Moo shouted, 'There's no danger! I'll show you how to do it.' He sat down and the roper started again. This time with only himself and Mamoulian in the circle. 'Faster, faster!' cried Moo-Moo. The roper revved it up until you could hear the whine of his rope. Suddenly the rope came near Moo-Moo's face; it sideswiped Mamoulian's ever-present cigar. The hot ashes ended up in Moo-Moo's ear . . . and that Oklahoma roper ended up out in the Guild Theatre alley, his opportunity to become part of the Reinhardtian 'spectacle' forever terminated."

Unfazed, Mamoulian continued searching for "spectacle." His quest would continue through the New Haven tryout. Could there perhaps be pigeons in that Oklahoma barnyard? "A flash of white wings, sweeping across that blue sky?" That suggestion took flight. A trainer for pigeons was located, along with his troupe of birds, and plans were made for his journey to New Haven. At a given cue the birds would flash across Lem Ayers's blue backdrop, then fly back and perch on a fence until the curtain came down.

Downstairs in the theatre lobby, Agnes de Mille went on ceaselessly creating her ballets. "I had coughed and cursed and quarreled," she wrote later. "I had run from the stage to the basement and back to the roof." Everyone was worried about the future, none more so than Celeste Holm.

"I'd ask Mamoulian for some idea of how to play Ado Annie; each day I tried something a little different and each day I awaited some disagreement or corroboration, but Mr. Mamoulian would just say, 'Fine, darling,' and puff on his cigar. So it wasn't until we saw Miles White's wonderfully vivid costume sketches that I began to feel Ado Annie take shape. Big pink polka dots and all those ruffles—and a parasol!

"Next day I spoke to Agnes. I need something . . . reassurance, criticism, a response of some kind. 'You're fine,' she told me, 'but your performance is too small. It's a big stage. Oklahoma was a big, wide-open territory. Think of Ado Annie that way and everything you do will be all right.' "

That satisfied Celeste for the moment and would carry her through opening night in New Haven.

But even de Mille couldn't be certain all the work she'd been doing on this show was correct. Inevitably, after those endless hours of creating she'd lost all perspective. "We worried and groused and fretted," she wrote. "I knew the show had possibilities of greatness, but it was being wrecked, wrecked, wrecked. It could be nothing else, since I was composing so fast and easily. There was only one man who rode the froth quietly and failed to turn a hair." That was the composer.

"He was standing in the shadows listening to all of us—there wasn't anything formal about this, we were just saying what we thought was wrong with the show. And he very quietly came out and said, 'Would you like me to tell you what I think is wrong with the show?' And we told him of course we would. He said, 'Nothing. I think it's simply wonderful. It's extraordinary. You have no idea how extraordinary it is.' And he listed all the things he liked. 'Now, why don't you all quiet down?' And we went home chastened and quiet."

Just before the company packed up and left that drafty theatre there would be a run-through for an invited audience. No sets, no costumes, merely the bare stage with one work light.

Mary Hunter Wolf remembers that night well.

"I was invited by Lynn Riggs," she says. "He'd gone into the army, but I was in New York and we stayed in touch. He called me up and asked if I'd go with Garret Leverton, his agent at Samuel French, to the Guild Theatre, I believe it was a Saturday night, and see the run-through so we could let him know what they'd done with his play and what we thought of it."

The theatre, that night, was far from filled. "Each of the Guild people sat far apart from the others," she says. "Terry Helburn sat in one section with her secretary, who was there to take down Terry's notes. Armina Marshall sat in another area with her secretary. Lawrence was separated from both of them, and he had *two* secretaries. Afterwards, when it was over, they'd get together and pool their notes into one report."

With music supplied by the rehearsal pianist, the run-through began.

"Right off, from the very beginning, I found it very exciting," says Mrs. Wolf. "They'd caught the spirit and the flavor of Lynn's play so marvelously. From that moment when Alfred strolled on singing his opening song, it all went so well. It was lovely. I also remember that when Alfred and Howard Da Silva did their duet, 'Pore Jud Is Daid,' it struck me as being so funny I began to chortle out loud. The Guild people turned around to me very sternly and went 'Shhhh!' "

Mrs. Dorothy Rodgers was also there that night. "Afterwards, everyone got together to discuss what they thought. Dick put me in a cab. I went home and wrote a note which I put on his pillow. It said, 'Darling, this is the best musical show I have ever seen in my life.' "

The post-run-through conference went on for some time. "I remember there was a big argument," says Mrs. Wolf. "Mamoulian was quite upset. He told Helburn and Langner, 'This first-act ballet of Agnes's is beautiful—a wonderful theatre piece—I admire her work, it's remarkable to see Laurey in her dream of her future and how she makes up her mind. But when it's over we have told the entire story of the *second* act! What does that leave *me* to do? The play is over.' "

"He was correct, of course," says Mrs. Wolf. "He was telling them the truth, and there was a large controversy over this. Finally, he was told the ballet had to stay."

"Who prevailed that night?"

"Oh, it had to be Terry Helburn," confirms Elaine Steinbeck. "She stood up to Mamoulian, and Agnes's work was left exactly the way it was."

But Mamoulian's appraisal was right on the mark. The second act would provide the problems out of town. And when they arose, in New Haven and Boston, could they be solved?

Then it was time to pack up and leave the dusty, miserably chilly Guild Theatre, which would now pass on to another owner. The *Away We Go!* troupe left on Sunday morning, March 5th, for the New Haven opening of a show that everyone hoped would be successful enough to justify the Guild's faith and to restore the producers to their former solvent status. For the Guild it was a make-or-break situation.

Agnes de Mille and her dancers (plus some invisible measles germs that were incubating in many of the troupe), Rodgers and Hammerstein, the singers, Mamoulian, the actors, and the rest packed their bags and headed

for Grand Central Station. Some of the troupe were already ill. "Dorothea MacFarland was the first one in our group who got sick," remembered Vivian Smith. "And then I got it, and the doctor didn't want me to leave New York. But I went anyway. That was my training. You go."

Along with the performers went the Lem Ayers backdrops and the scenery; all of Miles White's costumes, as yet unseen on a stage; Jay Blackton and his key musicians (the rest of the orchestra would be recruited in New Haven); Robert Russell Bennett and his copyists, some still racing the clock to finish the parts of Bennett's arrangements for the pit orchestra; Jerry Whyte and his backstage assistants; Elaine Steinbeck and John Haggott; Helburn, Langner, and his wife, Armina Marshall; office assistants;

plus the latest members of the *Away We Go!* troupe, that flock of white pigeons and their trainer.

Did the cast think they might have a hit?

"At that point," said Alfred Drake, "I don't know that anybody thought much of anything, except that it was a good show and we were very happy to be working."

"Just before I got to New Haven," adds Bambi Linn, "I said to Joanie McCracken—she was my source of everything worldly—'Joanie, what do you think, is this going to be a successful show or what?' And she said, 'Are you serious? This is going to be the dud of all duds. We're not going to make it, so enjoy yourself *now*!'

"But to me it didn't matter, because I didn't know what a success *was*, and I was having a ball. I was away from home, we were dancing, it was the best fun I'd ever had in my life! I mean, I was only sixteen," she says now. "And what *was* all this business of a career, anyway?"*

* By turning seventeen on the 26th of February, Linn was legally permitted to play on stage in the state of Connecticut by the narrow margin of ten days.

way We Go! had been scheduled by the United Booking Office (the arm of the Shuberts, who were the Theatre Guild's partners in the show) to open at the Shubert on March 11th and play until Saturday night, the 13th. Four performances, three evenings and one matinee—known in the trade as a "split-week."

An accurate appraisal of a 1943 New Haven split-week of a new show would be "trial by fire." An obstacle course. A crucible. Behind this simple, noncommittal word "split-week" lay terrors for all who entered the Shubert stage door. Inside those walls lurked a Pandora's box of insanities, a grueling nonstop six days' worth of mounting tension, usually sans regular meals and/or sleep for any and all of the hapless souls consigned to open a brand-new, untried show on Thursday night at 8:30 P.M. and play four performances, ending on Saturday, with luck, by 11:30 P.M. (Anything that lasted onstage past that magic hour meant overtime for the stagehands and the musicians.)

Today, merely to attempt such a three-day booking with a full-scale musical like *Away We Go!* would be financially disastrous. Based on 1992 running costs, a touring show needs at least a full week in a theatre, usually with subscription audiences, in order to turn some sort of profit. As for taking a *new* musical from New York anywhere out of town to try it out, such a venture these days would be hideously expensive, even disastrous. A 1990s musical costs so many millions to mount that its producers can afford only to spend three or four weeks in a Manhattan theatre, in "previews," until that fateful day when Frank Rich of the *Times* comes in to decide whether this project will get his thumbs-up and live, or his thumbs-down and die.

But in 1943 there was still a supply of masochists, such as those Helburn and Langner had assembled, willing to run the grueling New Haven tryout track. For years now theatrical entrepreneurs had considered the Shubert their regular jumping-off place. Season after season they ascended the ladder to the diving board, held their noses, and Thursday evening at 8:30 P.M., ready or not, they jumped.

Into uncharted seas, complete with attendant crises, temper tantrums, glitches, errors and omissions, gags that didn't get laughs, songs that didn't get applause, nervous actors going up in their lines or missing cues, scenery that might or might not work or even might fall down on performers, costume changes that held up the show's action—name a crisis, it was guaranteed to happen during that hideous New Haven split-week. Is it any wonder that anyone who ever ran that gauntlet would fervently tell you: "If you haven't died in New Haven, you've never died at all!"

Some shows emerged triumphantly from the Shubert and rode the fast track to glory. Others limped up to Boston and Philadelphia, headed for major repairs. And some sank without a trace on Saturday night, never to be heard from again.

```
                        AWAY WE GO!
                        PRODUCTION SCHEDULE          Feb. 21, 1943.

Thursday, March 4       - Dress parade at Brooks

Saturday      "    6    - Load out
Sunday        "    7    - Crew travel, New Haven
Monday        "    8    - Haul in and set up, New Haven

Tuesday       "    9    - Finish set up and do preliminary lighting
                       - Company travel to New Haven
                       - 10 a.m. - Reading rehearsal
                       - Evening - Walk-through rehearsal on set

Wednesday     "    10   - 10 a.m.-6 p.m. - Orchestra and Company rehearsal
                       - 7 p.m. - Dress rehearsal without orchestra

Thursday      "    11   - Finish lighting in morning
                       - 12 noon to 3 p.m. - Company rehearsal with orchestra
                       - First Public Performance
```

For *Away We Go!* it was six days of angst at the Shubert. On Monday the 8th, the technical staff arrived from New York. Inside the theatre stagehands and truckers worked feverishly to "load in" the freshly painted backdrops and scenery. Then the designer and his technical people set up everything for the first time. Spots and kliegs had to be hung, focused, and cued to the backstage lighting board. Not the state-of-the-art nineties electronic marvel, with its capability of programming hundreds of cues that function automatically throughout each performance; in the forties every individual lighting cue had to be switched on or off by hand.

Amplification? Blessedly, in the forties there was none to install. Performers relied on their vocal chords.

The costumes had been brought up from New York. They'd been seen at a dress parade at Brooks Costume the previous week, but now White's creations would be distributed by the wardrobe mistress to the various dressing rooms, to be worn for the first time by the cast.

Tuesday the cast and the rest of the company arrived from New York. With luck the set and the lighting were ready. At 10 A.M. there would

D Day for Away We Go! Here are the Guild's official marching orders to New Haven. As we know, the financing was not yet all in place for the show, but Helburn and Langner were damning the torpedoes—full speed ahead!

be a reading rehearsal onstage of the entire show; for the first time the cast could familiarize itself with the actual set. For the rest of the day there would be rehearsals at which frenetic last-minute changes and "fixes" would be put into the show under the eye of the director and the choreographer.

Wednesday the musical score, which had heretofore been heard only on a rehearsal piano, had to be distributed in all its individual parts to be ready for a 10 A.M. orchestra reading by musicians who had heretofore not seen a single note. Freshly copied by a corps of expert copyists, many of whom might still be down in the basement finishing up the last pieces of the arranger's work, the score would arrive on the conductor's stand.

Then in came the New Haven musicians, to be led by the conductor through the orchestra reading from overture to finale. At the conductor's side the composer, guarding his music like an anguished mother hen, screamed in pain at errors, missed notes, and nuances of interpretation.

Backstage there was still last-minute hammering and banging, plus occasional cursing and complaints.

The company would rehearse with the orchestra until 6 P.M., then take a brief break for supper, with attendant conferences, arguments and crises, temper tantrums and urgent last-minute decisions. At 7 P.M. a weary company reassembled, now in costume, ready for a "dress"—followed by more explosions: Why was this outfit so garish? Who'd picked this color? Why didn't this goddamned skirt fit properly, and more important, why did the chorus girls' outfits in the big second-act number look better than the star's outfit?

Inexorably the clock ticked on, and the dress rehearsal finally began. Still glitches: missed entrances; blown cues; scenery that didn't work properly; light cues that missed by beats, leaving performers in the dark or revealed at the exact wrong time! Anger. Frustration. On and on it went, into the wee hours of the morning, and one could be certain of only one truth this ghastly night: everything that could possibly go wrong would.

The clock kept on ticking. Frazzled nerves. Thursday morning, a final lighting rehearsal to eliminate any more mistakes. Should something not be ready for tonight, too damn bad! Forge ahead, damn the torpedoes. Tonight's curtain loomed above everyone's head like some implacable Damoclean sword. From noon to three or so a full company rehearsal with orchestra.

Zombies by now, the cast dragged itself to Kaysey's across the street or to a nearby coffee shop to take in some nourishment, perhaps even 86-proof liquid restorative. Then back to the Shubert and into the dressing room to put on the makeup and get into one's costume, cross oneself, tell one's beads, or mutter a brief prayer, run down stairs and yell "Break a leg!" to the rest of the doomed souls on this journey, and psych oneself up for whatever would take place on this opening night.

A vanguard of customers was already filing into the Shubert lobby. Ready or not, there they came. Tonight was the night.

The wonderful thing about actors and actresses is that in spite of all the disasters that had gone on in the past, they were willing to climb up the ladder, to the diving board, and now, at 8:30 on Thursday night, take the plunge.

Such was the madness of a split-week in New Haven, circa 1943. Seen in retrospect, it seems to be a totally improbable procedure. That any musical show, any cast, any creative crew, any producer would venture it, nay any backer would invest cash into such an incredible process without being consigned to a sanitarium (and who is to say some were not?) is hard to believe.

When Larry Gelbart, who has been there often himself, quipped "Hitler should have had to go out of town to try out a new musical," he must have meant New Haven.

"Joe Heidt, the press agent, went up a few days before the opening to 'beat the drum' for it," wrote Helene Hanff in *Underfoot in Show Business*. "He was very worried. Not about the show. Joe admitted frankly that there was

Photographer Eileen Darby recorded the various reactions as performers appeared in Miles White's costumes for the first time, in New Haven.

Joan McCracken is not completely certain this outfit is appropriate.

Richard Rodgers is enjoying one of Miles White's hats, done in 1901 style.

Alfred Drake appearing in front of Aunt Eller (Betty Garde) in his cowboy duds for the first time. She is obviously impressed.

Bambi Linn and her costume make a marvelous pair.

Joan Roberts, Alfred Drake, and Celeste Holm.

Joan Roberts and the ensemble in White's dresses, whose style was derived from a turn-of-the-century Montgomery Ward catalog.

A very young George Irving watches as Joan Roberts offers a morsel to an even younger Kenneth LeRoy.

still some work to be done on it, but he believed that by the time it opened in New York it would be the greatest show since *Hamlet*. What worried him was that some drama editor or some columnist's assistant like Winchell's Rose would sneak up to New Haven and see the show before it was Ready. As of now, Joe did not feel it was Ready.

"It was always a producer's worry that somebody in a newspaper's drama department would sneak out of town to a pre-Broadway tryout and write a report that would kill the show before it ever opened. But no drama department editor scared them half as much as Winchell's Rose. Walter Winchell's column appeared in cities across the country, including all the Guild's subscription cities, and was immensely influential. If Winchell's Rose—she must have had a last name but I never heard her called anything but 'Winchell's Rose'—snuck out of town to see the tryout, the effect might be devastating."

Heidt's fears were right on the mark.

Just prior to the troupe's departure for New Haven on March 4th there had been a "dress parade" at Brooks Costume, where Miles White and his assistant, Kermit Love, had tried out all their costumes on the cast members. "I learned something that day about temperament in the theatre from Joan McCracken," says Kate Friedlich. "We were up at Brooks, where each costume was being checked out. I disliked a hat assigned to me, and so did McCracken. I said so. But McCracken put hers on the floor, took aim, and jumped on it! Absolutely smashing it beyond repair. She got a hat to her liking, and I stuck with mine. You know, we learn something from this, don't we?" White's costumes had already been fitted in New York, but they had not yet been worn by the cast on a stage, in Lem Ayers's settings, under stage lighting.

When the final dress parade took place at the New Haven Shubert it was late at night. "It was a real event," says Bambi Linn. "All the boys came out in their yellow, pink, and blue shirts, and the costume people had spent days hand embroidering circles into polka dots—these weren't printed on, mind you, but they were *sewn*! So out came the 'cowboys,' all polka-dotted, and they had chaps on, and boots on, they had big hats, they had gloves with fringes on, I mean, they looked like the typical Hollywood cowboys!

"Well, everybody looked at that, and each one of the producers starting picking away, and if I remember correctly, it was Agnes who said, 'Well, let's get rid of the polka dots!' "

One can readily imagine the ensuing scene; a determined director and a distraught designer, both determined to defend their creative work. "Once they got rid of the polka dots and they were down to a solid color, then they told Miles White, 'Let's get rid of those chaps,' except for a couple of the cowboys who could wear them—Alfred Drake could because he was the lead, but not everybody else—they wanted him highlighted. Then Agnes and Helburn went to work on the gloves, to get rid of those fringes, and then they changed the boots, so the boys could dance in them—they certainly couldn't dance with those high heels . . . and then the hats— well, it was 'Let's keep them all simple, all uniform!' "

"Poor Miles!" said Bambi. "I thought he was going to *die*. . . . Then, they started on the girls. They had shawls and lots of flowers and things. But Agnes said, 'Okay, let's strip!' and I think Joanie McCracken ended up with *one* flower. Away went the shawls. And then they were down to basically silhouettes and color, which was beautified by being seen in front of Lem Ayers's settings. Agnes was absolutely right; each scene ended up looking like a painting."

White argued, pleaded, but to no avail. Both de Mille and Helburn had definite ideas. Helburn stressed simplicity; de Mille wanted authentic designs in which her people could dance.

"We saw this man moaning and groaning, he was obviously fighting for his own concepts," Friedlich recalls, "but it had to be. His costumes were delightful, with wonderful colors, but remember, they were also *heavy*. During most of the show we wore camisoles, great long bloomers, petticoats, bustles, high suede shoes, and sometimes gloves. Dancers have to work through all these yard goods. It makes it a whole lot harder. If you

*Everything's up to
date in "Kansas
City." (Courtesy
of The Rodgers &
Hammerstein
Organization)*

have a real wispy chiffony thing, with a leotard underneath, you're absolutely free. But I remember the fright when we had to start moving in those costumes in New Haven. It felt as if you were moving yourself *and* a Mack truck around!"

Helene Hanff was also present at the New Haven dress parade. "As the girls walked across the stage in their period farm dresses, not an ankle nor an upper arm was visible. I don't even remember seeing a neck. As I left the theatre I heard Lawrence suggesting to the costumer that the dresses might be cut a little lower, here and there, without spoiling their authenticity!"

Almost half a century after that disastrous session in New Haven, Miles White chuckles at the memory. "Oh, I learned my lesson on that show," he says. "The next show I did with Agnes and Terry was *Carousel.* I knew they'd be after my costumes, cutting here and trimming there, the way they had in *Oklahoma!* . . . so, I purposely put all sorts of additional stuff on my costumes. . . . And sure enough, when I'd go downstairs into the basement of the theatre, backstage, I'd find them by my racks, cutting away! But this time I was ready for them!"

In the Shubert pit the New Haven musicians were ready to play the first orchestral reading of the score. "We had in all about thirty men, which was unusual," says Blackton. "But Dick Rodgers felt we should have more strings than usual. *Ten* violins! Unheard of . . . In those days New Haven was such a regular stopping-off place for musicals that there was a sort of bank of local musical talent on which we could draw, so we had about twenty-five from New Haven. They were very good, they had to be, because working on brand-new orchestrations is a very ticklish job. If there are mistakes, and let me first say that with Robert Russell Bennett doing the orchestrations there were not—but there always is *something* to correct, a printing mistake, a copyist's mistake, and while we're running through the score, the conductor has to have cat's ears in order to hear those errors and to try and correct them during those precious musical rehearsals. Which cost *money*—musicians do not come cheap—even in those 1940s!"

"So you want to do them and get through as quickly and as efficiently as possible. That particular day I said to the musicians as I was rehearsing, 'I can't take too much time on this.' And it was Dick Rodgers, sitting behind me, who leaned over and whispered into my ear, 'Jacob, take all the time in the world!' "

But tryouts are filled with improvisations as well. "Things were so tight, rehearsals with the cast and doing the final dress, that we still hadn't had time to prepare a proper overture for Thursday night's opening," says Blackton. "So we had to use a little improvised thing that Robert Russell Bennett pasted together in time for that first performance. It was later, when we got to Boston, that we had the time to prepare a full overture. By that time it was easy. We opened with 'The Farmer and the Cowman' and we ended with 'Oklahoma'—one started it, the other ended it. It's the usual vaudeville gimmick—no matter what you do in the middle, get on and get off *right*."

"Things were very, very tight that week," says Linn. "I remember a second-act number with Lee Dixon and Celeste, and Katie and Joanie were both in it, it was 'All Er Nothin' ' . . . that was done at the very last minute. I don't think they even had a chance to try it out. . . . They realized that song needed something, like a tag . . . and it was done in one—out in front of the audience, because backstage, behind the drop, they needed time for a change."

"Agnes had to do that very fast," said Vivian Smith. "When she did it that day she had gotten sick and was bedridden in New Haven, in her hotel room, there were three of us there, maybe four, and we were working between the foot of her bed and the hotel room wall!"

"We're working around the clock now," de Mille wrote in her diary on March 10th. "Thursday we open. Dick Rodgers took my hand in his yesterday and said, 'I want to thank you for doing a distinguished job.' . . . There's hell ahead, and unless we pull the show up very quick we're sunk."

On went the feverish preparations. Coffee in paper cups. Ayers and White supervising the lighting of the show. Arguments. Tantrums. Exhaustion. "All Broadway shows are simply fierce during rehearsals," de Mille wrote on the 13th, "but this one has been insanity. . . . And only Dick Rodgers has kept me from flouncing out.

"Everybody's temper went absolutely to pot," she recalled. "I began to become aware of Oscar Hammerstein, who had stayed up to this point almost exclusively in the book rehearsals. He sat through the endless nights, quietly giving off intelligence like a stove. He never got angry, or nasty, or excited, but when people were beating their heads on the orchestra rail he made the one common-sense suggestion that any genius might think of if he was not at the moment consuming himself. . . . Lawrence Langner expounded. Terry Helburn snapped and badgered and barked at our heels with a housekeeper's insistence on detail. Mamoulian created, in spite of the hour and other peoples' nerves. But Oscar just quietly pointed the way."

"He was always around," says Linn. "Quiet. Listening, like some sort of a gentle giant. We always felt this *giving* coming from him."

Just before the first dress rehearsal the "spectacle" second-act closing pigeons that Mamoulian had called for arrived at the theatre.

"Out on the stage of the Shubert," remembers George Church, "there came this old vaudevillian carrying his special cage of white birds, which cooed and fluttered. 'I vill now show you how mine pigeons do vat I tell zem,' he announced, with a decided Teutonic accent.

"He then opened the top of the birdcage and the birds obediently emerged from the opening, fluttered onto the top. Then he held up a stick, about three feet long, and he proclaimed 'Zis is mine magic vand.' He swung the stick in a circle above his head and the birds took off and flew in formation in a huge circle around the Shubert orchestra. It was a beautiful sight," says Church. "And then, just outside the theatre doors in the street, a truck backfired with a resounding *bang!* Whereupon those birds scattered in every direction and in complete panic they flew away, to disappear into the far reaches of the Shubert backstage loft, high up in the flies!"

The distraught trainer waved his wand, called and whistled to his birds, trying to get them back to where they could assume their proper role in the second-act finale.

No use. The pigeons were obviously no troupers. They stayed up in the flies, cooing and grooming and steadily dropping little messages on the busy scene below.

"The hell with them!" came the collective decision. "Let 'em stay there—we've got a show to do!"

"And there they remained," said Alfred Drake. "When we left for Boston they were still flying around up there in the flies."

No one seems to know what became of the bird trainer, but the second-act finale of *Away We Go!* went on without Mamoulian's touch of "spectacle."

―――――――――――――

And then, suddenly, it was time to do the first performance for a paying audience.

"I sat in my ruffles and polka dots cut to there—no, even lower," remembers Celeste Holm. "I put on my mouth three times because my right hand trembled. There was a knock on my door. Lawrence Langner came in.

"He said, 'Just remember the Chaplinesque quality of the part. The fact that she can't say no is a terrible problem to her.'

" 'All the time?' I asked.

" 'That's the spine of the part,' he said, and left, like Hamlet following his father's ghost.

"Terry Helburn came in. 'Up, up, up!' she twinkled. 'We're counting on you for the comedy. Lift every scene you're in.'

" 'Oh, God!' I thought fervently. Have they been seeing the same rehearsals?'

"Then Armina Marshall came in. She kissed me and said, 'I suppose I shouldn't say this, I think you're absolutely wrong for the part, but good luck!' "

In another dressing room in the Shubert backstage, Bambi Linn was preparing to make her theatrical debut. "We hadn't put makeup on before," she says. "This was opening night, and I discovered I didn't know how to put makeup on! I'd never been to school for that. I was sitting next to Katherine Sergava in the dressing room, so I asked her if I could copy what she was doing, and she said I should, and to use her makeup. When I finished copying—I didn't realize her makeup was the typical Russian ballet makeup, with the dark eyes and all that so out I went, with a Russian ballet makeup!

"Then I went downstairs to the costume department, run by a wonderful old lady named Hallye Clogg, who'd been at it for years and years, and she gave us stockings which went halfway up our thighs and gave us both belts that came down, so we could hook on the stockings—but there were no pants! I had these short skirts, and my legs were flying all over, and I said, 'I can't go onstage without some kind of knickers, I need bloomers— I need *something!*

"That's when I saw that Sergava had knickers, white, with lace and all, and I saw there were two pair—there was a second pair for another performance—so I went and stole those. . . . I don't know if Hallye Clogg found out, but I did tell Agnes. I said, 'You know, I stole these pants.' And she said, 'You did good. I don't have to worry about you, you'll be all right!'

"I felt guilty about stealing Sergava's extra pants, but at that point I realized that it was everyone trying to protect oneself—and at that point we were just trying to get this show going!"

The house lights went down.

The audience was in place, save for the inevitable latecomers pushing their way into the rows past the impatient theatregoers already in place. The New Yorkers (Hammerstein referred to them as "grave-diggers" or "smarties") who had made the trip in order to pass judgment on this new work sat back and stared at the curtain.

Jay Blackton raised his baton, and his orchestra went into the first improvised "overture."

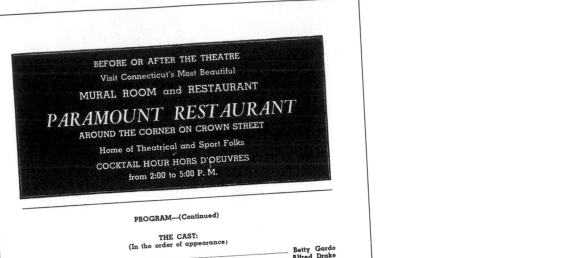
PROGRAM—(Continued)

THE CAST:
(In the order of appearance)

Aunt Eller	Betty Garde
Curly	Alfred Drake
Laurey	Joan Roberts
Ike Skidmore	Barry Kelley
Fred	Edwin Clay
Slim	Herbert Rissman
Will Parker	Lee Dixon
Jud Fry	Howard da Silva
Ado Annie Carnes	Celeste Holm
Ali Hakim	Joseph Buloff
Gertie Cummings	Jane Lawrence
Ellen	Ellen Love
Andrew Carnes	Ralph Riggs
Cord Elam	Owen Martin
Mike	Paul Schierz
Joe	George Irving
Cowboy	Jack Harwood

9

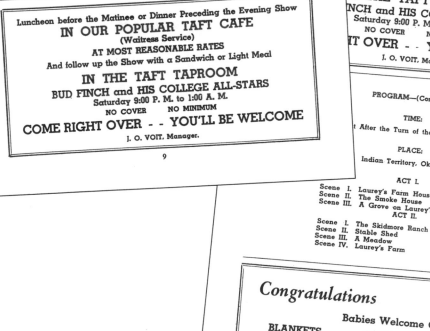

re the Matinee or Dinner Preceding the Evening Show
OUR POPULAR TAFT CAFE
(Waitress Service)
AT MOST REASONABLE RATES
ow up the Show with a Sandwich or Light Meal

IN THE TAFT TAPROOM
NCH and HIS COLLEGE ALL-STARS
Saturday 9:00 P. M. to 1:00 A. M.
NO COVER   NO MINIMUM
T OVER - - YOU'LL BE WELCOME
J. O. VOIT, Manager.

PROGRAM—(Continued)

TIME:
t After the Turn of the Century.

PLACE:
Indian Territory, Oklahoma.

ACT I.
Scene I. Laurey's Farm House
Scene II. The Smoke House
Scene III. A Grove on Laurey's Farm
ACT II.
Scene I. The Skidmore Ranch
Scene II. Stable Shed
Scene III. A Meadow
Scene IV. Laurey's Farm

11

PROGRAM—(Continued)

MUSICAL NUMBERS

Scene I: Oh, What A Beautiful Mornin' .... Curly
The Surrey With Fringe On Top .... Curly, Laurey, Aunt Eller
Kansas City .... Will
I Cain't Say No .... Ado Annie
Reprise of I Cain't Say No .... Ado Annie and Will
Many A New Day .... Laur...
It's a Scandall It's a Outrage! .... Ali Hal...
People Will Say ....

Scene II: Pore Jud Is Daid ....

Scene III: Out of My Dreams .... La...
Laurey Makes Up Her Mind ....
Danced by: Katharine Sergava as Laurey, Marc Platt as ...
George Church as Jud, Bambi Linn as the Child.

Laurey's Friends: Rhoda Hoffman, Rosemary Schaeffer, Nona Feid, M...
Adams, Billie Zay. Cowboys: Gary Fleming, Eric Kristen, Jac...
rison, Kenneth LeRoy, Eddie Howland, Kenneth Buffet. Jud...
McCracken, Kate Friedlich, Margit DeKova, Bobby Barrentine...

15

PROGRAM—(Continued)

ACT II.

Scene I. The Farmer and the Cowman .... Sung By Fred, Aunt Eller, Will, Curly.
Danced by Marc Platt and Eric Victor .... Ado Annie, Carnes and Ensemble
Scene II. Boys and Girls Like You and Me
All 'er Nothin' .... Ado Annie and Will
Scene III. Oklahoma .... Curly and Laurey
Danced by George Church .... Curly, Aunt Eller, Ike, Fred, Laurey and Ensemble
Finale—Oh, What A Beautiful Morning .... Curly, Laurey and the Entire Company

SINGERS: John Baum, Edwin Clay, Hayes Gordon, George Irving, Carl Nelson, Herbert
Rissman, Paul Schierz, Robert Penn, Elsie Arnold, Harvey Brown, Suzanne Lloyd,
Ellen Love, Dorothea MacFarland, Virginia Oswald, Faye Smith, Vivienne Simon.
DANCERS: Kenneth Buffet, Jack Dunphy, Gary Fleming, Eddie Howland, Ray Harrison,
Eric Kristen, Kenneth LeRoy, Diana Adams, Margit DeKova, Bobby Barrentine,
Nona Feid, Rhoda Hoffman, Maria Harriton, Kate Friedlich, Bambi Linn, Joan
McCracken, Katharine Sergava, Vivian Smith, Billie Zay, Rosemary Schaeffer.

PLEASE NOTE!!

SMOKING IS PROHIBITED IN ALL PARTS OF THIS BUILDING.
MAY WE ASK YOUR CO-OPERATION? THANK YOU!

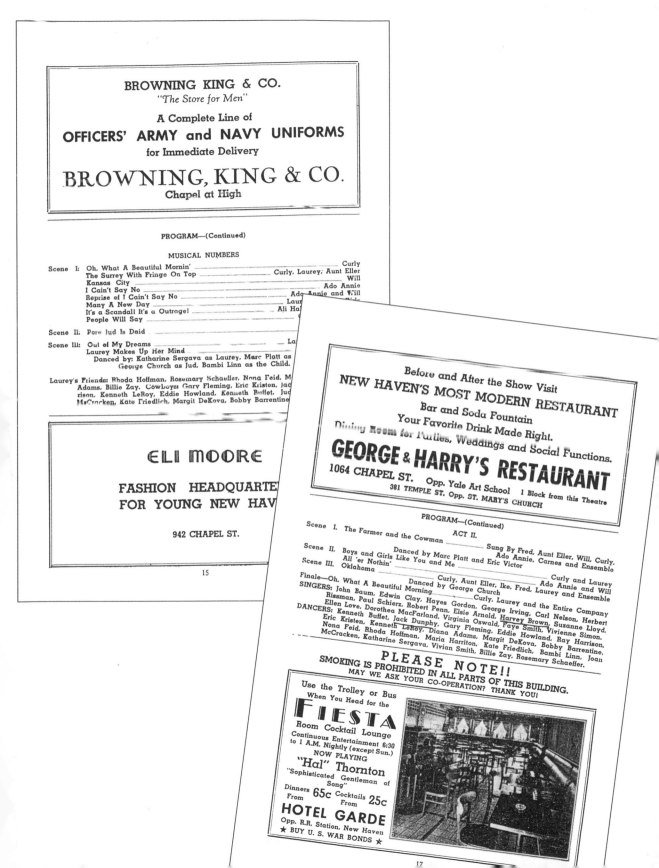

17

Then, silence. The curtain rose.

"Alfred Drake's lovely, familiar sound filled the theatre," Celeste Holm recalled, "now abetted by a marvelous orchestration, and as I waited, listening, I thought to myself, 'Well, now it's up to God and the audience and me to work it out together.'"

When Ado Annie's cue came, Celeste opened her parasol and ran onstage. "I'd never been in a musical before, so I didn't know what to do when the audience didn't stop applauding after I had finished 'I Cain't Say No.' I kept trying to continue with the dialogue, but they wouldn't let me. It was embarrassing, but it was glorious!"

De Mille stood at the rear of the theatre, in the narrow carpeted space traditionally reserved for anxious production people who needed room to pace up and down, fight back nausea, or dash out through the lobby doors into deserted areas where they could weep and groan and argue without disturbing the paying customers inside. When her dancers finished their first number, "Many a New Day," their performance again stopped the show cold. "Dick Rogers, standing beside me, threw his arms around me and hugged and hugged," she remembered.

On went the first act. On this March night an event of major importance to the American musical show was taking place; the audience was being treated to history. A new form was being born, one in which the integration of plot, music, lyrics, and ballet with character would triumphantly affect the creators of musical theatre for years to come.

But tonight the event was as yet unrecognized.

In fact, from the Shubert stage, behind the footlights, the cast could see an audience that was often far from overwhelmed. "I'd worked for Mike Todd in *Star and Garter*," says Kate Friedlich. "So I knew his looks without seeing every feature, and I can distinctly remember seeing him walking out *during* the show."

"Oh, they were all there," says de Mille. "The 'wrecking crew' from New York, that's the name Ruth Gordon gave them, up to New Haven to see this show. It certainly wasn't the show you see today, but all the good songs were there. So a lot of them left early, and most of their reactions were, 'Well, too bad. This means the end of the Theatre Guild. . . . This is their last flop.'"

After intermission, most of the others returned for the second act. They applauded the rousing "The Farmer and the Cowman," to which Marc Platt and Eric Victor performed their ebullient solo dances. They beamed fondly at the young lovers, parading back and forth to a lovely ballad, "Boys and Girls Like You and Me," then chuckled to the lyrics of "All Er Nothin'" performed by Celeste Holm and her intended, played by Lee Dixon.

Then in the third scene there came a song called "Oklahoma," a paean to a "brand new state." Tonight it featured George Church, and in front of the ensemble he performed his tap solo. "I did a pirouette," he recalls, "an inside pirouette, in which you turn right, with your left leg dragging, and as it drags, you do a tap with it. A real flash solo, turning and turning . . . and it got a big hand." Successful or not, that solo number would be performed only a few times more.

Meanwhile the Hammerstein libretto came to its climactic scene. Curly and Jud had their fight. Jud was inadvertently stabbed. Curly was eventually released from custody and reunited with his new bride, Laurey. All ended happily, to a reprise of "People Will Say We're in Love," and the curtain fell.

Applause.

The audience filed out into the night.

Was this going to be a hit?

Who knew? Maybe. Maybe not.

Not much sense saying "It needs work." Every show that opened at the Shubert in New Haven did. A very wise showman once remarked, "Anybody with enough dough can call himself a producer and bring a show up to open at the Shubert. But my definition of 'producer' is the guy who can take a half-baked show *out* of the Shubert, and bring it into New York a *hit!*"

It now remained to be seen whether the Guild, and Rodgers and Hammerstein, and Mamoulian and de Mille would fit his definition.

Yes, certainly there was work to be done, but not tonight. Tomorrow, after they'd had some sleep. Then the work would begin.

Without one member of the crew. "I left right after the opening," says Miles White. "Went back to New York on the late train! Can you imagine—I didn't realize I was supposed to stick around for the next couple of days of meetings? I was perfectly satisfied that all had gone well with my costumes and Lem's decor, so home I went!"

"My wife and I just found ourselves a place where we could have a snack and go to bed," remembered Blackton. "We didn't congregate with any of the cast. I was beat . . . and remember, I was doing this show with one foot still in the St. Louis Municipal Opera! *I* still wasn't sure it would last."

Right after the show the producers filed into Celeste Holm's dressing room.

"Lawrence said, 'That's just what I meant!'

"Armina said, 'I'm so glad I was wrong.'

"And Terry said, 'Will you sign a run-of-the-play contract at the same salary?'

"And I said, 'No.'

"Most of the 'experts' who'd come up from New York thought the show charming and ineffectual," said Blackton. "But the audience had loved it. . . . Later I signed my run-of-the-play contract, which actually meant a year from June 1st, and asked, and got, $100 more, or $350 a week, which seemed at the time an enormous sum."

According to Helburn, the Theatre Guild's own backers were still uncertain. "You cannot have a murder in a musical show," they said, referring to the stabbing of Jud. "The love story's weak," pointed out someone else. Said another, "Build up your jokes, give the comedian more to do. . . ."

But there were others who sensed something marvelous was in process up there on the stage that night. "A young man in the audience turned to me impulsively," Helburn recalled, years later. "'This show is just great!' he said. "Can I put all the money I have into it?'"

"He had just one hundred dollars.

"At that stage," she said, "even we didn't know what we had. But we did know that the New Haven audience had liked the show . . . for whatever that was worth."

Which at this moment wasn't enough. Far from it, in fact.

Max Gordon was not the only one dubious about the show's future. (He would send a note to Hammerstein later which said, "Did I tell you that I thought you ought to try to bring the girls in sooner in Act I?") But when Walter Winchell's legendary Rose, the dreaded seeress, had filed the wire from New Haven to her boss that read NO LEGS NO JOKES NO CHANCE, Winchell, always a point man for disaster, would show that wire to a Theatre Guild backer, an investor who had previously agreed to make a substantial check out to Helburn et al. But as a result of Rose's dire wire, the backer was about to renege on his promise.

Small wonder that the ensuing days would be filled with a certain amount of panic.

"I was an undergraduate at Yale in 1943," recalls Philip Barry, Jr. "Just before *Away We Go!* opened at the Shubert, I had a long-distance call from my father, who was down in his winter home at Hobe Sound, Florida. It seems that Terry had called Dad—remember, he'd had a long association with the Guild, and his plays had often made big money for them, especially *The Philadelphia Story*.

"Terry reminded Dad that there was a royalty account in a New York bank where the Guild had been channeling a considerable amount—his money from Guild productions. Just sitting there, earning interest. 'She's offered me twelve and a half percent of this new musical—it's budgeted at around eighty thousand—if I'll let her have ten thousand from the royalty account,' said Dad. 'Why don't you go have a look at the show, and let me know your opinion of it.'"

Barry Jr. promptly made his way to the Shubert box office and managed to grab a seat in the fourth row balcony for the Thursday night opening.

"So I was there," he says today. "I can remember it all so well—it was

long; there were things that needed pruning, sure, but I was absolutely en-
tranced by it! I loved the score—the dancing, the singing—I couldn't wait
to call him the next day. 'Go ahead!' I said. *'Give them the money!'*

"Well, alas, my father disagreed with my enthusiasm."

Why not invest? "It took me a while to find out. Seemed he felt that
Green Grow the Lilacs was one of the dullest plays ever written, and impossible to turn into a success. More importantly, he had very little faith that
the Guild could ever produce a successful musical. And so, . . ." he sighs,
"*you* figure out how much we'd have earned from his ten thousand, if he'd
given it to Terry. We've long since stopped—it's too painful."

"Of course," Barry Jr. adds, "it was consistent of him. Dad also turned
down Howard Lindsay and Russel Crouse when they asked him to invest
in *Life with Father*."

Friday and Saturday in New Haven were filled with rumor and contra-
diction. "We heard a lot of stories," said Alfred Drake. "One of them was
that the Guild was insecure about the director, and they were going to
replace Mamoulian. I didn't believe that was possible until Saturday. You
see, I had a habit of going down to the stage before a performance. . . . If
you ask me why I did that, I cannot tell you. Just a habit I've had, all my
life. I'd go down on the stage and walk around the set; it's not as though
I'm looking at it for the first time, but it's a way of getting myself into the
character, I guess.

"And that day, in New Haven, I came down on the set, and there was
George Abbott, sitting on one of the benches! I knew Mr. Abbott, I'd
worked for him, so I walked over to ask him what he was doing there. He
said, 'Well, they're asking me to direct this.'

"I said, 'Oh, are you going to?'

"He said, 'I don't think so. Why should anybody offer *me* a show like
this?'

"I was surprised at that. 'You think it's all right the way it is?'

"He said, '*Sure,* it's all right!'

"A pretty smart man, Mr. Abbott. Certainly made me feel a lot more secure. The Guild had somebody else up to see the show, I don't remember who. . . . But eventually they must have responded to Mr. Abbott's reaction. They stayed with Rouben; they were feeling less insecure. Which turned out to be very wise."

Mamoulian may not have been in complete control during earlier rehearsals, but after the New Haven opening he took a firm hold of the situation. "The morning after the opening he called us all together on the stage," says George Church. 'Ladies and gentlemen,' he said, 'I have to cut an hour and a half out of this show and this means that some of you are going to be unhappy.' Well, I for one was unhappy because my second-act solo tap dance to 'Oklahoma' was axed. Moo-Moo said it was too much like 'The Farmer and the Cowman,' which opened the second act. 'Anticlimactic' was how he put it."

The second casualty was the delightful solo dance that Eric Victor had done with Bambi Linn as part of "The Farmer and the Cowman." "It was a charming piece which Agnes had created," said Vivian Smith. "Bambi following Eric around, loving everything he did in the solo, and it ended up with a special finish, with Eric going up into a tree right there on stage!" On opening night Victor's solo had gotten a big hand. By the weekend the general analysis was that it interfered with the flow of the book.

Both featured dancers had lost their solos. By the time the company entrained for Boston, Victor had given his notice. "He settled for a small sum," says Church. "He had a run-of-the-play contract, but he knew this flop show wouldn't run and figured that he'd get more money by being paid off now. . . . A colossal mistake, as it turned out. I gave my two weeks' notice because I didn't see any future for myself, no solo, nothing that would give me any involvement when we got to New York. But Dick Rodgers got after me again and pleaded with me not to leave. 'Just give us the opening night in New York,' he said, 'which,' he added, 'may also be our closing night.' Some indication of how we were all feeling at the time.

"Well, I couldn't walk out; after all, I was still in the first-act closing ballet, in which I danced Jud and Marc Platt danced Curley. That ballet was very important; I didn't feel I could let Dick down. So I stayed, with the proviso that he'd take my name out of the billing; that meant nobody would know I wasn't a featured soloist any more."

"At the New Haven opening," said Alfred Drake, "for some reason or other the producers had decided to cut Jud Fry's second-act solo, 'Lonely Room.' Perhaps it was because Howard Da Silva wasn't singing it too well; after all, he was an actor first, not a singer. But they felt it didn't work.

"Next day I went to Dick Rodgers and I said, 'This is all wrong, that song is very important; it illuminates Jud's whole character. If you'd let me work with Howard on it I think I may be able to help him.'

"So he agreed, and Howard and I went off by ourselves into one of those little public meeting rooms off the lobby of the Taft Hotel and we worked together on that song. . . . I did my best to coach him so that it would be a dramatic solo. That he could do. When they heard him do it again, they decided to put it back into the show. And in Boston it worked!"

"Boys and Girls Like You and Me," that lovely ballad, was marked for the blue pencil. "The most Agnes had been able to do with it was to have the boys arm in arm with the girls, strolling up and down as they sang Hammerstein's lyrics," says Drake. "It was a sixteen-bar chorus, and within that length it was difficult to give the staging a great deal of variety."

According to singer Hayes Gordon, Mamoulian was far more assertive on the subject of that song. "After one run of it," he recalls, "Mamoulian came onstage and said in his heavy Armenian accent, 'Years from now, when I am sitting in my padded cell, someone will come in and ask, "You are Rouben Mamoulian?" and I will answer, "Yess," and they will say, "You directed *Away We Go!*?" And I will say, "Yess." Then they will say, "And you staged the number 'Boys and Girls'?" And I will scream, "*Yaaaaaahhhhh!*"' And with that, the number was out. He insisted it didn't advance the show; he was right."

A valuable lesson was being learned here in this split-week as the troupe prepared to leave New Haven to go to Boston. Nothing in *Away We Go!*—song, ballet, or solo—would be retained in the final version unless it was

Curly (Alfred Drake, right) contends that Jud (Howard Da Silva) will be missed as they lament "Pore Jud Is Daid." Jud's collection of cigarette-card girls decorates the walls of his shack. (Lynn Farnol Group, Inc./Courtesy of The Rodgers & Hammerstein Organization)

totally and deeply integrated with the text of the libretto, and most important, unless it contributed something valid to the characters Hammerstein and Rodgers had extrapolated from *Green Grow the Lilacs*.

Once that lesson had been applied (and it would include changing the show's title, as well), the show would begin to find its legs.

If some of the Theatre Guild's potential backers had lost faith in New Haven, Boston audiences would restore it.

What about the cast?

"All I can tell you," said Drake, "is that if anybody in that cast had had a penny they would have invested it in the show. They *believed* in it."

Last Night's Play

By F. R. J.

"Away We Go" Has Good Premiere

A lusty, swashbuckling musical play, "Away We Go!" had its premiere at the Shubert last evening under the auspices of The Theatre Guild, which means The- and Lawrence Lang- nd in it. Based on en Grow the Li- Riggs, the piece boisterous life of ndian Territory at e century.

gers has written music which is at l and yet contains strain in ballad ch will go well ooms. It's some- ny rate, adapted very old.

stein 2d, has and written le show and as directed features c s unusual am arrang le all the of the v West princi 'Miss dance ie n

Many of the players are well known and there are many who are not well known now but who will be soon if the work they did last night is kept up to any degree. Joan Roberts as Laurey and Alfred Drake as Curly, form the main romantic team, followed by Celeste Holm as Ado Annie and Lee Dixon as Will Parker. All of these young people sing well and dance well, with Miss Holm proving herself a charming commedienne and Miss Roberts, a fine singer with good stage sense. Joseph Buloff as the sly little peddler, Ali Hakim, provides many of the laughs in this hearty piece about love and life in the early West. Betty Garde as Aunt Eller, eeps order now and then, Silva as Jud, the with

---

THEATER

MUSICAL COMEDY AT THE SHUBERT IS REAL SPRING TONIC

A rollicking musical comedy, "Away We Go!", all about the territory of Oklahoma and its people, just after the turn of the century, had its world premiere last night at Shubert's and caught the fancy and praise of a large and enthusiastic audience. Many months have passed since a musical show has graced the Shubert stage, and last night's offering, jammed to the hilt with tuneful melodies, pleasant voices, unique dancing and a merry cast, proved the ideal escapist entertainment long anticipated.

The Theater Guild offered the musical version of its former hit, "Green Grow the Lilacs," by Lynn Riggs; Richard Rodgers composed t e music; Oscar Hammerstein, 2nd, is responsible for the book and lyrics; and Rouben Mamoulian served as director. Those two veterans of the Guild, Theresa Helburn and Lawrence Langer supervised the entire production.

"Away We go!" has no spectacular name in its cast, but instead it is composed of a bevy of talented young men and women. An engaging plot involves the courtship of Curly, played by Alfred Drake, and the winsome and attractive Laurey, in the person of Joan Roberts. That the course of true love never progresses at a smooth pace is proven before the final curtain. Howard deSilva is the villain.

For the comedy elements, there is Celeste Holm as Ado Annie, a gal, who by her own admission "Cain't Nay" Her suitors are Lee Dixon,

---

VARIETY
Wednesday, March 17, 1943

Play Out of Town

AWAY WE GO!

New Haven, March 11.

Theatre Guild production of two-act (seven scenes) musical comedy based on a play by Lynn Riggs. Book and lyrics, Oscar Hammerstein 2d; music. Richard Rodgers; staged by Rouben Mamoulian; dances, Agnes de Mille; settings, Lemuel Ayers; costumes, Miles White; orchestrations, Russell Bennett; music conductor, Jacob Schwartzdorf; production supervised by Theresa Helburn and Lawrence Langner. $3.30 top; opened at Shubert, New Haven, March 11, 1943.

Aunt Eller	Betty Garde
Curly	Alfred Drake
Laurey	Joan Roberts
Ike Skidmore	
Fred	
Slim	Edwin Clay
Will Parker	Barry Kelley
Jud Fry	Lee Dixon
Ado Annie Carnes	Howard da Silva
Ali Hakim	Celeste Holm
Gertie Cummings	Joseph Buloff
Ellen	Jane Lawrence
Andrew Carnes	Ellen Love
Cord Elam	Ralph Riggs
Mike	Owen Martin
Joe	Paul Schierz
Cowboy	George Irving
	Jack Harwood

Having tried practically everything else this season, from fantasy ('Mr. Sycamore') to stark realism ('Russian People'), the Theatre Guild is now offering a package of nostalgia neatly wrapped in a talented cast and tied up with a blue-ribbon score. They've jigsawed Lynn Riggs' 'Green Grow the Li sembled

number of lusty laughs. Miss Holm is a surprise click as a singing comedienne, registering in a solo, 'I Cain't Say No,' and teaming with Dixon on 'All or Nothin',' whose straight stuff scores, too. Jane Lawrence handles a bit easily.

Guild has dug into the sock to put this one on. Although not so sumptuous as the golden era extravaganza musicals, there's quality in the trappings for 'Away.' On costumes, Miles White has succeeded in making his feminine contingent attractive even though swathed in early century dress—no small trick in these days when female allure depends more or less on a certain amount of exposure. Sets by Lemuel Ayers feature a water-color effect with a simplicity that makes them distinctive. Backdrop perspectives are cleverly done. Staging by Reuben Mamoulian is expert and largely responsible for smoothness of performance.

Film possibilites are bright.

e will have Bone. night and there are two ormances tomorrow.

BOSTON

heatrical legend has usually had it that *Away We Go!* not only suffered indignities in New Haven from opening-nighters but was also mauled by the local critics.

Far from true.

In fact, the local boys smelled a hit long before the Bostonians and the New York big-leaguers.

The perspicacious *New Haven Register* critic (he remains, alas, anonymous to this day) who'd attended Thursday night's opening characterized the show as "a rollicking musical . . . jammed to the hilt with tuneful melodies . . . ideal escapist entertainment, long anticipated." He loved the de Mille dances, had high praise for the new Rodgers and Hammerstein

COLONIAL THEATRE
BOSTON
Direction Boylston Theatre Co.

now, as

THE THEATER
By ELINOR HUGHES

COLONIAL
"Away We Go!"

A musical play in two acts with score by Richard Rodgers, book and lyrics by Oscar Hammerstein, 2d, based on the folk drama, "Green Grow the Lilacs," by Lynn Riggs; directed by Rouben Mamoulian, with dances by Agnes de Mille, settings by Lemuel Ayars and costumes by Miles White; presented last night by the Theater Guild at the Colonial Theater as the fourth in a series of six subscription attractions, with the following cast:

Aunt Eller..................Betty Garde
Curly.......................Alfred Drake
Laurey......................Joan Roberts
Ike Skidmore................Barry Kelley
Fred........................Edwin Clay
Slim........................Herbert Rissman
Will Parker.................Lee Dixon
Jud Fry.....................Howard de Silva
Ado Annie Carnes............Celeste Holm
Ali Hakim...................Joseph Buloff
Gertie Cummings.............Jane Lawrence
Ellen.......................Ellen Love
Andrew Carnes...............Ralph Riggs
Cord Elam...................Owen Smith
Mike........................Paul Schierz
Joe.........................George Irving
Cowboy......................Jack Harwood
Sam.........................Hayes Gordon

The Theater Guild has gone into the musical comedy business with "Away We Go!" the Richard Rodgers-Oscar Hammerstein, 2d, show which opened last night at the Colonial Theater before a packed and enthusiastic house, and though there may be a few lifted eyebrows—the Guild promoting song and dance antics (tsk, tsk!) — the results were so satisfactory that I can't think of any reason why they shouldn't keep right at it. Big, handsome, picturesque and generally entertaining, the production isn't quite ready yet for Broadway, being as yet on the lengthy side and having some first act doldrums, but the virtues are numerous and the failings can be remedied. Meanwhile, Boston has a fine new musical to take to its heart —and you know Boston.

"Away We Go!" (the title could be improved on) has its foundation in Lynn Riggs's "Green Grow the Lilacs," a folk play set in the Oklahoma Territory about 1900 which the Guild did here 13 years ago; pleasing many and shocking a few. No one's going to be shocked by it now, how-

by Rodgers without Hart, but in Oscar Hammerstein, 2nd, Mr. Rodgers has found an admirable lyric and libretto writer, and the partnership promises extremely well. The songs that went over best last night were Curly's solo "Oh, What a Beautiful Morn[...] ple Will Say," "Many a New [...] "Out of My D[...] comic duet for [...] Jud Is Dead," [...] Nothin'," and [...] "Oklahoma."

The company [...] ing than on [...] Drake has a po[...] tone which he [...] Jean Roberts [...] soprano, and [...] an exceptionally [...] heroine, easy [...] Though Cele[...] wasn't trained [...] how to put a s[...] lent comic ef[...] when she sugg[...] Greenwood, a[...] either—Lee Di[...] the best of th[...] drawling cowh[...] lusty and a[...] Joseph Buloff [...] funny despite [...] frankest over[...] da Silva is a co[...] Jud.

A special pa[...] Agnes de Mille [...] an outstanding [...] and at one poi[...] ing "Away W[...] drama rather [...] As she proved [...] this year, Miss[...] ture the flavor[...] freedom and fi[...] patterns, and [...] the good work [...] her dancers, [...] and it is goo[...] an artist, as [...] chance to disp[...] Joseph Buloff [...]

'Away We Go' Is Adapted From Play by Lynn Riggs
By L. A. Sloper

For the second time in its history, the Theater Guild has undertaken a musical show. The first one, called "Parade," leaning well toward the Left, was not too well received by the public. The second, called for no apparent reason "Away We Go," and dealing with the folkways of Oklahoma just after the turn of the century, obviously pleased its first-night audience Monday.

The subject, borrowed from Lynn Riggs' play, "Green Grow the Lilacs," is good material for musical comedy. Toned down from its original verism, the story supplies folksy romance with space for tunes in folk style from the fecund pen of Richard Rodgers.

At present, the piece is too long for its matter, and contains too much rural humor and homely sentiment. Mr. Rodgers has been careful to make his songs simple, in keeping with the time and place, but unfortunately their simplicity, in common or in waltz time, becomes tiresome as the first scene drags on.

Later he injects changes of tempo and rhythmic variety to liven things up, and his dance music is excellent. The best song in the show is a satiric duet called "Pore Jud is Daid." There is vitality too in "I Cain't Say No," and in the chorus "Oklahoma."

But it is fortunate that the Guild has enlisted the help of Agnes de Mille to design the dances, and of Joseph Buloff to play the pedler.

Buloff were not the whole show. Alfred Drake and Joan Roberts did some good singing and some pleasant romantic acting as Curly and Laurey; and when their scenes have been cut a little they will seem even better.

Lee Dixon was an agreeably gauche cowboy with a talent for tapping, Celeste Holm an amusing comédienne and Howard da Silva a suitably sinister Jud Fry, capable, too, of a good comic touch in the duet with Mr. Drake lamenting his own demise.

The character of Jud poses a difficult problem for the makers of a musical comedy. To end a musical show with a fatal fight is a little unusual, is it not? It is true that a tragic note was struck in "Yeomen of the Guard," but "Yeomen of the Guard" is not musical comedy and Mr. Rodgers is not Sir Arthur Sullivan.

The Guild has followed the original play pretty closely, but a less faithful treatment of the disposition of Jud would make a better prelude to the departure of the bridal couple.

The settings are appropriately regional and the costumes attractive. The stage direction was efficient; there was some lagging which doubtless will be corrected as the whole show is cut and tightened.

It is reported that when the production arrives in New York, will be called "Oklahoma." That will help, too.

partnership, and heralded their work as "an excellent theatrical tonic to greet the approach of spring!"

Variety's resident New Haven critic, Harold M. Bone, did not file his review until after the show departed for Boston. Bone (as he signed himself) was a jovial New Havenite; a fixture at the Shubert for many seasons, he had been in an aisle seat for the birth of literally dozens of shows in the Elm City. Bone was a fair-minded critic and a theatre enthusiast. He bent over backward to be fair to the various talents who'd arrive in town for the ritual split-week bloodbath. Rather than rely on his reactions to what happened on those hectic opening Thursdays, Bone always made it a point to return on Friday, and on Saturday as well. Thus he could not only gauge the show in its current state, but he could also talk to the creative hands to get some sense of how they planned to repair, revise, or make changes. Bone was well aware of the blood, sweat, and anguish which went into each new arrival. Since he truly loved the theatre, his contribution to the cause was his understanding. A caring review in *Variety* from Bone would be a big help to an out-of-town show, especially one such as *Away We Go!*, which was already being bad-mouthed in Manhattan.

On Wednesday, March 17th, St. Patrick's Day, Bone's review appeared in *Variety*. His assessment of the show's possibilities was remarkably optimistic. "Paced on a par with the fine music," he wrote, "are the superb dance creations of Agnes de Mille. Though dance angle absorbs a bit too much running time, it's all sterling stuff. . . . Guild has dug into the sock to put this one on. Although not so sumptuous as the golden-era extravaganza musicals, there's quality in the trappings for *Away*. Songs are appropriately sentimental, peppy, and comic, as situations require, and the score as a whole comprises a succession of melodious moments. Overall high calibre of score augurs well for future possibilities of the new tunesmith duo. It got off to a good start here, and should stretch into a sizable stay on Broadway," predicted Bone.

And he added, "Film possibilities are bright."

*　　*　　*

By the time Bone's review appeared, spreading his optimistic bulletin through the world of New York show business, *Away We Go!* had opened in Boston, at the Colonial Theatre. And a good deal of important work on the show had already begun. If anyone in the cast or crew had hoped for a breathing space between Saturday night's closing at the Shubert and the arrival in Boston, he or she had not counted on Helburn and Langner's desperate determination to make the show into a success.

"I'd hoped to spend the trip to Boston reading a detective story," remembered de Mille, "but I'd reckoned without the Guild. They hired a dressing room on the train. We all crowded into it and in three and a half hours rewrote the play, chiefly the second act. I was ordered to produce a small three-minute dance in twenty-four hours. I did. But the skin came off the dancing girls' ribs from continuous lifting, and I couldn't seem to stop throwing up."

"Cuts and changes were made, and we worked constantly," says Celeste Holm. "Oscar gave me an encore, which was the funniest chorus of all to 'I Cain't Say No.' . . . But what I was so impressed with, working with Oscar and Dick, was to see the skill with which they knew what to put in and what to take out. That's when most people doing a new show get into trouble. The show's opened and now they're not sure what should be changed. But Dick and Oscar *did*.

". . . I could see Oscar standing in the back of the theatre with his back to the stage," she says. "He'd stand there during the performance and *listen*. . . . Why? The minute anybody in the audience at the Colonial coughed, Oscar would check the spot in his script which came thirty seconds *before* that spot. That's how he finally came to see that there was an emotional sag near the end of the second act . . . right after the murder.

"Oh yes, the murder," she smiles. "People do forget there's a murder in *Oklahoma!* All they usually talk about is that sunny sweetness and light coming off the stage . . . and I tell them, 'Yeah? Look again.'"

By the time the Boston reviews hit the streets, Hammerstein and Rodgers were already aware of the trouble spots in the second act. The Boston reviews were helpful.

Elinor Hughes of the *Herald*, the city's most important critic, was very optimistic:

> The Theatre Guild has gone into the musical comedy business with *Away We Go!*, which opened last night at the Colonial before a packed and enthusiastic house . . . and the results were so satisfactory that I can't think of any reason why they shouldn't keep right at it. Big, handsome, picturesque and generally entertaining, the production isn't quite ready for Broadway, being as yet on the lengthy side and having some first-act doldrums but the virtues are numerous and the failings can be remedied. Meanwhile, Boston has a fine new musical to take to its heart—and you know Boston.
>
> . . . A special paragraph must go to Agnes de Mille's dances, which are an outstanding feature of the show and at one point come close to turning *Away We Go!* into dance drama rather than musical comedy. . . . In Oscar Hammerstein, Mr. Rodgers has found an admirable lyric and libretto writer, and the partnership promises extremely well [sic]. The Theatre Guild has made no mistake with the production, and Broadway has a very agreeable experience in store for it. Right now, we can enjoy it.

But in the *Christian Science Monitor*, L. A. Stoper was far more critical. He suggested that "At present, the piece is too long for its matter, and contains too much rural humor and homely sentiment. Mr. Rodgers has been careful to make his songs simple, in keeping with the time and place, but unfortunately their simplicity, in common or in waltz time, becomes tiresome as the first scene drags on. . . . The character of Jud poses a difficult problem for the makers of a musical comedy. To end a musical show with a fatal fight is a little unusual, is it not? It is true that a tragic note was struck in *Yeomen of the Guard*, but *Yeomen of the Guard* is not musical comedy, and Mr. Rodgers is not Sir Arthur Sullivan. The Guild has followed the original play pretty closely, but a less faithful treatment of the disposition of Jud would make a better prelude to the departure of the bridal couple."

One final note in Stoper's review: "It is reported that when the production arrives in New York, it will be called *Oklahoma*. That will help, too."

There exists a certain amount of understandable confusion as to which of crew at the Colonial actually came up with the idea of retitling the show. Helburn remembered that Hammerstein had originally titled his libretto *Oklahoma*, but the title had been turned down, "as people might confuse it with Oakies. Armina, who was born on the Cherokee Strip, suggested the name *Cherokee Strip*, but there were objections to this, too. People might think of 'strip tease.' "

Agnes de Mille is equally uncertain. "*Oklahoma* was suggested," she says, "but it didn't seem like a very good title. Lawrence declared himself satisfied if an exclamation point was added. Would people go to see something with a plain geographical title? we asked. Armina had been born out there, and she thought, with great fervor, they would."

However, Hammerstein's biographer, Hugh Fordin, has it that the new title had been agreed upon by all when Hammerstein said "Why don't we add an exclamation point to *Oklahoma* and be done with it?"

It's certainly possible that the origin of the title may lie in the emphasis that would soon be placed on that song . . . or it may have been the reverse: that the revised title impelled the emphasis on the song—and caused it to be expanded into the blockbuster chorale version that would eventually emerge in the second act.

We can only conjecture. This was, remember, the first week in Boston. Hammerstein and Rodgers were doggedly wrestling with their problems. "Boys and Girls Like You and Me" was out; "Lonely Room" was back in. So, if Mr. Stoper of the *Monitor* had done anything in his review, he had fortified Hammerstein's understanding that the last half hour of the show wanted something . . . something musically solid, and exciting, some sort of a blockbuster.

Blockbusters are not easily come by. Yet as any seasoned veteran of musicals will testify, some of the most exciting changes in a show out of town take place under the gun.

Under which it now most certainly was.

"Lawrence made a list of everything to be done on a yellow pad, with a program," remembered de Mille. "The various departments were allotted time on stage, exactly like astronomers scheduled for the hundred-inch telescope. Lawrence policed the theatre with a large watch in his hand and there was no reprieve possible from his 'I'm very sorry, my dear.' Every night after the show, sharp councils were held. I have never seen a group of people work harder and faster, except perhaps the same group during my *Carousel* tryout. The entire play was reorganized in two weeks."

A phenomenal course of obstacles had to be overcome. For instance, the measles.

"That's where they really broke out," says Bambi Linn. "I don't know about other cities, but up in Boston, evidently, if you had more than a certain number of people having measles they'd shut down the show and you'd be quarantined. Naturally, the management was petrified! I think five people already had the measles, and we knew that if five people had it, it would go right through the cast. . . ."

"Diana Adams and I were staying at a girls' club—the Charlotte Cushman Club. I ran home and I said, 'I've had the measles, so I probably won't get it.' But Diana hadn't had them, so we put her in a hot tub and we watched the measles come out! And then Maria Harriton got them. She was the girl in 'Many a New Day' who ran across the stage, wearing red petticoats."

"In pure exhaustion," says De Mille, "I decided one night to forego dinner and have a nap instead. I was barely bedded when the phone rang. Maria had broken out in spots and no understudy was ready. An hour later I was onstage in Maria's dress and bonnet."

"Next, one of the girls in the dance hall scene got the measles," says

Finding a new title is never easy. Unearthing one for Lynn Riggs's Green Grow the Lilacs involved the usual complicated process, a community venture in which everyone in the Guild management participated.

Herewith, an interesting series of memos containing suggestions, from Helburn to Langner to Riggs and back, which finally concluded with the temporary Away We Go!

Memorandum from
THERESA HELBURN

SWING YOUR HONEY

OKLAHOMA HONEY

PARTY TONIGHT

SINGIN' PRETTY

GOIN' TO THE PARTY

PLAY PARTY TONIGHT

Memorandum from
LAWRENCE LANGNER

LAUREY AND ME

[handwritten notes]

LAWRENCE LANGNER

HOTEL DORSET
30 WEST 54TH ST.
NEW YORK
CI 7-7300

[handwritten notes]

One Two Three

Away we Go

Let Her Go, Laurey

Now altogether

Party on the Prairie

Prairie Song

[handwritten line] away we go.

Prairie Party

[handwritten notes at right]

Swing Your Honey

Oklahoma Honey

Party Tonight

Singin' Pretty ?

Goin' to be Party

Play Party Tonight

February 13, 1943.

Dear Lynn,

We went into rehearsal Monday and life has been
chaotic since then, but the play looks good. Dick has done
some lovely music and I think Oscar's book has shaped up
extremely well. We've tried to keep as much as possible of
the original spirit, but of course a musical entails an
enormous amount of change. Unfortunately, we can't keep the
title, because of the picture situation, and after much travail
and agony we finally got everyone to agree on

                    "AWAY WE GO!"

which I'm sure you won't like at all since GREEN GROW is in
your blood, but it has action and gaiety and it is the only one
that has so far gotten a majority vote from the six or seven
judges involved.

        Alfred Drake, who plays Curley, is going to be
excellent and has a lovely voice. The girl, Joan Roberts,
has a fine voice though she is not as good an actress as we
would like. Betty Garde is a tower of strength as Aunt Ella.
Howard deSilva is going to be fine as Jud (your Jeeter). Buloff
will, I think, be excellent as the peddler and Celeste Holm is
enchanting as Ado Annie. There's a new comed[...]
introduced into the book - he is in love with [...]
is being played by Lee Dixon.

        Agnes deMille is working on the da[...]
will produce results that have both humor and [...]
got a new number for the last act called Okla[...]
would delight you.   I'll ask Joe Heidt to s[...]
from time to time.   More Anon.

        I hope you'll be able to get a fur[...]
show.

        Cordial greetings.

March 2, 1943.

Dear Lynn,

        Have you any ideas for titles
that would have more quality than AWAY WE GO!
and yet a gaiety and a lightness that would
suit a musical version?   We can't use
GREEN GROW THE LILACS because of the picture
situation as you know and also we don't use
the Green Grow song in the musical.   We've
thought of a great many, including "Oklahoma"
and "Sing Oklahoma", etc. but people feel that
"Oklahoma" is too heavy.   We would like
something that would have the quality of the
earth or the sun and at the same time something
happy.   It seems to me you were very good at
titles, and maybe you'll have some brilliant
idea.

                    All best to you.

                              Sincerely,

Corporal Lynn Riggs,
Company "C",
846th Photo Bn.,
Wright Field,
Ohio.

P.S. We can change the title for New York though
the paper is out for New Haven where we open on
the 11th and Boston where we open March 15th.
The show gets better every day.   More anon.

Prior to the show's arrival at the Colonial Theatre in Boston, where the original title would be jettisoned, these flyers (now truly collector's items) were slipped into Colonial programs.

THE THEATRE GUILD

PRESENTS

A NEW MUSICAL COMEDY

AWAY WE GO!

(Based on the play "GREEN GROW THE LILACS" by Lynn Riggs)

MUSIC BY
RICHARD RODGERS
BOOK AND LYRICS BY
OSCAR HAMMERSTEIN 2d
DIRECTED BY
ROUBEN MAMOULIAN
Dances by AGNES deMILLE

with

BETTY GARDE • ALFRED DRAKE • JOSEPH BULOFF • JOAN ROBERTS
LEE DIXON • HOWARD DaSILVA • CELESTE HOLM

AND A CAST OF SIXTY

Settings designed by
LEMUEL AYERS

Costumes designed by
MILES WHITE

Production under the supervision of
LAWRENCE LANGNER & THERESA HELBURN

•

COLONIAL THEATRE
Beginning Monday, March 15th
MATINEES THURSDAY AND SATURDAY

Prices: Evenings $3.30 to $1.10; Matinees $2.75 to $1.10

Bambi, "and Agnes went on for *her*! For a time up there in Boston she became our 'swing girl,' filling in for anybody who was out sick. . . . She replaced all the measles cases! She was wonderful, of course. She had her own special way, she was the choreographer, she knew exactly what she wanted to do onstage, and as one of the dance hall girls she was marvelous. Exhausted at the end of the week, of course."

"Even though we got better reviews in Boston, I gave my two weeks' notice," says George Church.

> I knew my solo was being cut and that I was left with only my part in the ballet. Again, Dick Rodgers and I had a talk. "Where the hell are we going to find another six-foot, two-hundred pound ballet dancer?" he asked.*
>
> "I don't know," I told him, "but I can't afford to appear in such a small part on Broadway, Dick. It would be a backward step." "I appreciate that," said Dick, "but please just give us the opening night in New York!"
>
> I knew very well that the first-act ballet, in which I danced the role of Jud and Marc Platt danced Curley and in which I ended up choking him, was very important to the show; it motivated the entire second act. Dick promised he'd make it up to me later, so we came to a compromise. I'd do "Laurey Makes Up Her Mind" for the first week in New York without any billing either in the program or outside the theatre, and that way nobody would know it was me and it couldn't hurt my future.
>
> That settled, we proceeded to play Boston, and by the second week "Oklahoma" was totally transformed, without my solo.

* "May I tell you about George in that ballet?" said Marc Platt. "At the end of the ballet, I'm choked, I'm dead. I die. George turns to Katya Sergava, she's Laurey, and she's slight, about one hundred fifteen pounds, but George picks her up, not in an accustomed ballet lift, but he picks her up by the waist, his arms are almost straight, and she's dead weight, and he walks very slowly off the stage. That is almost impossible . . . it takes a lot of strength. No wonder they didn't want to lose him."

"Up in Boston the audiences were enjoying the show," says Jay Blackton. "But I still hadn't settled my situation with the St. Louis Municipal season. Dick Berger, my boss out there, had promised me he'd wait to see what happened to us in New Haven. Well, after that opening he went back to New York and he called. 'I don't know, Jay,' he said. 'It's not a bad show, but I still have my doubts. Let me wait on things until you open in Boston; after that, we'll know whether we have to replace you out in St Louis.'

"Then we opened in Boston. Dick came up to see it, and we went out to have lunch in Faneuil Hall Market. 'Well, Jay,' he said, 'I'll give it six months. Which means I'm going to lose you—because you'll open March 31st . . . April, May June—I've got to get somebody to replace you, so would you please suggest somebody?' And I went back to the hotel, and I said to my wife, 'Well, we can eat for the next six months!' "

And how and when did "Oklahoma" metamorphose from a pleasant second-act dance number (too similar to "The Farmer and the Cowman" was Mamoulian's correct appraisal) in which George Church did his virtuoso tap routine solo into the eventual smashing chorale showstopper?

It started with an inspired guess by one of the show's singers, Faye Elizabeth Smith. "She had the loveliest voice in the show, incredible voice," says Celeste Holm. "All I do is just think of her, even today, and it makes me sing better.

"It was *her* suggestion. She went up to Rodgers—and she said, 'Richard' —we all called him Richard; it was before he became a living legend, he was simply a darling guy who wrote wonderful music—and she said, 'You know, with the voices you have in this show, why are you having us do this song in unison? If we did "Oklahoma" in *harmony* we could take the roof off every theatre in this country!'

"And Dick said, 'You're right!' "

Arranger Robert Russell Bennett had returned to his New York home. The majority of his work was completed, but he was on standby.

"If we needed him to do anything he could hop the train to Boston and come right up," says Jay Blackton. "He'd fix things for Rodgers, and then go home. So we phoned him and told him the problem. 'Robert, we need a full chorale arrangement for the song "Oklahoma." Everyone on stage, singing. Can you get it up here as soon as possible?'

"Now this is a *major* piece of work," says Blackton. "Because from one master copy of such an arrangement we would need all sorts of copies, for each member of the orchestra. But Bennett was a helluva guy, and a hard worker. He started in immediately down in New York, got on the train, and I believe he finished some of it as the train was pulling into Boston!"

Precious copy in hand, Bennett grabbed a cab and hurried to the Colonial Theatre.

"All he had was that one copy of the vocal arrangement," says Blackton. "This was Sunday, our day off—there weren't any copyists available to go to work on it. But it had been decided we had to put this new number into the show as soon as possible."

What ensued was a screenwriter's dream, a climactic moment that would have thrilled any audience. In came the cast, eager and willing to learn the new arrangement; and from improvisation there would emerge pure theatrical gold.

"Margot Hopkins, who usually worked with Dick, couldn't read Bennett's arrangment, so I had to sit at the piano," says Blackton. "They hauled one into the lobby of the Colonial, which was closed. Everybody—all the dancers and singers—piled around me in this very small space, and there was I, at the piano, with Russell's new arrangement on my music stand, plunking out the parts!"

Giving up their one day off, the ensemble enthusiastically piled in. "I was the conductor, so I had to assign the parts to the various singing groups arbitrarily. I'd say, '*You* sing tenor; *You* sing bass here,' just by rote. I was banging out the melodies and the harmonies. . . . The people were learning it on their feet, or on their haunches, or wherever they were perched on stools, whatever—everybody! Alfred Drake stood by, he had the first chorus, and of course Betty Garde was in it—that was the first part, which was easy. But the second part, that fancy part with all those countermelodies and so on—I had to teach it all!" He sighs today at the recollection. "But fortunately, in my experience I'd worked with choruses at Juilliard and out in St. Louis, so I knew how to do that. . . . Just plunking tediously away, teaching them all their notes."

Little by little the Bennett arrangement came to life, growing in strength bit by bit, all of the harmonies coming together. A showstopper was being born.

"Now, while I'm rehearsing all this," continues Blackton, "waiting behind us there were Mamoulian, and Agnes, Rodgers and Hammerstein, and the producers, impatient to have me prepare the cast well enough so it could be staged. The kids were marvelous—they were eager to learn it quickly, so they were a great help. Some of them were such good sight readers that they'd peek over my shoulder, get the notes, and then pass it around!

"So finally I thought it was well enough prepared to have a go at the number up on the Colonial stage. We all went upstairs, and we sang it, with me leading, and it sounded marvelous. But it had to be *staged*. Mamoulian was our director, so it was up to him to do it—but evidently he couldn't handle chorale numbers, they just weren't his thing."

"I remember exactly what happened after that," says Vivian Smith. "Agnes said, 'Wait a minute, I know how to do this,' and she got us all positioned, assigning us places in a sort of a wedge-shaped formation, in rows —she had us starting upstage, and then we moved down, in that **V**-shaped formation—we called it 'the flying wedge' because it came straight at the audience. You knew when you moved because it was your group which moved. We started in the rear, and came closer, and closer, and then we came together, at the footlights. A marvelous effect!"

"And remember, it was all done to the music," says Blackton. "There I was, on the stage, holding on to that one copy of the score as de Mille worked with the people, making sure the right singer was in the right place melodically—guarding Russell's arrangement. There was Alfred, standing in the middle at the apex of the **V**, and the kids all singing this complicated thing, half doing the melody, the other half doing countermelody. . . . Oh, it was wild, we were all working from scratch, staging that number right on the spot, without an orchestra—and me, holding that orchestration in my hand."

Out of such a convulsive Sunday creative explosion would come true theatrical excitement. Anyone who's ever seen a cast perform that great number, assembled in one afternoon at the Colonial, will testify to that.

The revised "Oklahoma" went into the show in the second week in Boston, and the effect was immediate.

"The first night we did it I was conducting, and so I couldn't see the audience behind me," says Blackton. "But I certainly could *hear* them. They went wild! The number stopped the show, dead. The applause was so great that first time we did it that right after the performance Dick came to me and we decided to establish an encore chorus of the song; that meant going back and repeating the ensemble part—the one I'd taught them all."

"I had only one problem with it," said Alfred Drake. "When Dick asked me to do the encore solo, I asked him, 'Richard, may I take it down a half a tone? I think it will sound better.' He agreed, Jay and I made the adjustment, and from then on that's how we did it. We did the number, down came Agnes's flying wedge, and we did the finish with the cowboy yell— '*Yee-ow!*' and then came the applause. And *then* the encore—and we had our showstopper!"

This eleven o'clock showstopper would invariably bring down the house; it also propelled *Oklahoma!* into a smash hit and performed a critical service: it wafted the second act past the sagging spot after Jud Fry's killing and carried the audience happily into the finale, the reprise of "People Will Say We're in Love." "It gave the show a *punctuation*," says Blackton today. "A real exclamation point. In fact, I'm certain that's where the exclamation point in the title came from—that same excitement we'd generated."

"Funny thing," de Mille reported in her diary. "People went home, down the sidewalks singing, and they wanted to come back. No one seemed very excited, but suddenly we were sold out."

The audiences were humming happily on their way out of the Colonial, but behind the scenes there were serious problems. Now de Mille fell victim to the measles. Helburn went to bed with icebags on her head to quell a fever but left her hotel room to attend rehearsals with a trained nurse. Mrs. Hammerstein was taken to Peter Bent Brigham Hospital with a raging fever, and her husband commuted back and forth from her hospital room. Marc Platt accidentally hurt his foot and was ordered not to dance for a week; he ignored the doctor's warning and continued to perform. "Margit DeKova fainted every time she jumped," recorded de Mille. "Two of the leads and one of the best girls out of every number. The matinee [March 27th] went on in good order. This," she proudly concluded, "is a remarkable troupe. The actors are dumbfounded. They've never seen such stamina before; they've never worked with real dancers."

"I think we did as good a job on *Oklahoma!* as I've ever done on a show," mused Elaine Steinbeck, looking back. "Constructive, good work. Everybody pulled together. They took out a number, and they added a number, but most of all they added *authority* to the show. They tightened it. They gave it a viewpoint. I think Mamoulian was superb in Boston. He saw what he had in New Haven, and then he went to work and put it into operation at the Colonial.

"And as for Oscar," she adds, "well, he was brilliant. I certainly think you have to give Dick Rodgers enormous credit for having chosen exactly the right man to be his collaborator."

Down in the Manhattan offices of the Guild, Helene Hanff toiled away at her press department chores:

Joe Heidt phoned from Boston with instructions about the opening-night press release, to be sent to the ten thousand Guild subscribers. He said that the whole second act had been thrown out and that the company was working around the clock on a new second act. With a new second act, Joe felt, it would really be a great show.

. . . For the next few days we were busy addressing envelopes and grinding out ten thousand copies of the press release on the mimeograph machine, to tell the world about the new American folk opera *Away We Go!* We had about eight thousand mimeographed when Joe came back from Boston and broke the news to us that we'd have to throw them all away and start over. There had been a title change.

It sounds fine to you; you're used to it. But do me a favor and imagine you're working in a theatre and somebody tells you your new musical is going to be called *New Jersey*, or *Maine*. To us, *Oklahoma* remained the name of a state, even after we'd mimeographed ten thousand *new* releases and despite the fact that *Oklahoma* appeared three times on each one.

We had folded several hundred of them when the call came from Boston. Joe picked up the phone and we heard him say "Yes, Terry" and "All right, dear." And then he hung up and he looked at us, in the dazed way people who worked at the Guild frequently looked at each other.

"They want," he said in a faraway voice, "an exclamation point *after* Oklahoma."

Which is how it happened that, far, far into the night, Lois and I, bundled in our winter coats, sat in the outer office putting thirty thousand exclamation points on ten thousand press releases while Joe, in the inner office bundled in his overcoat, phoned all over town hunting down and waking up various printing firms and sign painters. We were bundled in our coats because the heat had been turned off by an economy-minded management, now happily engaged in spending several thousand dollars to alter houseboards, playbills, ads, three-sheet posters, and souvenir booklets, to put an exclamation point after *Oklahoma*.

"Boys and Girls Like You and Me" was gone. "The advance sales for the

You are looking at five very rare items.

As the Away We Go! company headed for New Haven, a music publisher was already printing the Rodgers and Hammerstein score so that it would be available for sale in theatre lobbies and music stores while the show tried out.

But in Boston, after the title of the show had been changed, overnight all of this sheet music was rendered obsolete. And doubly so was "Boys and Girls Like You and Me," which was cut from the show.

Some collectors did buy these music sheets, however, before they were withdrawn. Today each title is worth at least $350. And if you're lucky enough to unearth the lovely ballad "Boys and Girls Like You and Me" somewhere, in an attic or at a flea market—bingo! Name your own price.

sheet music of that lovely tune presaged a hit," Helburn commented later. "But we had to sacrifice it and go to the reprise of 'People Will Say We're in Love.' But that revision of 'Oklahoma,' sung in a rousing chorale, struck audiences with the power of a thunderclap, and the sheet music began to sell in the theatre lobby like wildfire."

By the end of the second week in Boston, *Oklahoma!* was, in theatrical argot, "frozen." What the Boston audiences saw and cheered on that final Saturday night was what the much tougher New Yorkers would see on the coming Wednesday night, March 31st, at the St. James. The work had been done; this show that had amused and pleased the New Havenites but struck out with the blasé Broadway "wrecking crew" was now energized to the point where Bostonians were calling for encores. But Boston had traditionally been a town that loved musicals. Certainly something remarkable had happened since the show had left New Haven. The question remained: Was that something sufficient to contradict the professional New York carpers and turn an almost-hit into an honest-to-God smash?

Nobody dared to answer.

Oscar Hammerstein wrote to his son Bill, now serving in the navy, and said, "I think we have something this time." Hammerstein was shrewd enough to see that in all these past frenetic Boston days the cast had lost the pace of the show while all the changes had been in rehearsal. But, he added, "We gave them a good drilling, and the result was so successful that one night we suddenly took on the aura of a hit. . . . All this is said in the hope that a handful of beer-stupefied critics may not decide that we have tried to write a musical comedy and failed. If they see that this is different, and higher in its intent, they should rave. I *know* this is a good show. I cannot believe it will not find a substantial public. There! My neck is out."

Jay Blackton was optimistic, but guardedly so. "I wasn't sure we'd be a hit, enough of a hit so that I'd lose my job in St. Louis. So I kept on worrying . . . 'Is this show going to make it?' "

He was far from alone. A good many futures, perhaps even more than in most Broadway ventures, hung in midair. There was enough money in the

Theatre Guild bank account to keep the show running in New York for a week or so. At the St. James box office there were hardly any advance sales. The work was done. A couple of dress rehearsals away loomed Wednesday night's opening.

Then it would be up to the New York critics.

In his biography of Oscar Hammerstein, Hugh Fordin recounts how Oscar and his wife, Dorothy, went for a walk in Doylestown, near their Pennsylvania home, on the day of the show's opening. It had certainly been a long pull for Hammerstein. An optimist by nature (he would give the audience his credo when he wrote 'A Cock-Eyed Optimist' for Mary Martin), he was also a seasoned pragmatist who'd spent the past decade or so swimming upstream against an increasingly hostile tide. Certainly the past year with *Oklahoma!* had been an uphill struggle. That day Hammerstein told his wife, "I don't know what to do if they don't like this. I don't know what to do because this is the only kind of show I can write."

One member of the company was, however, already convinced of the show's success. "We were rehearsing in the foyer, one day after the matinee," recalls Kate Friedlich. "Agnes, Joan and I, I think it was 'All Er Nothin'.' When we came upstairs, everyone had gone to dinner except Lawrence Langner. Under the arc light, on stage, he was bowing right and left and acknowledging the cheers from the balcony, and we could hear him saying 'This has never happened to me before.' Obviously he was rehearsing for the New York opening night when the audience would shout 'Producer, producer!' Happily, he didn't see us."

OH, WHAT A BEAUTIFUL EVENING

he scenery, lighting, and costumes left Sunday on a train from Boston and by Monday, the 29th of March, were being unloaded into the St. James Theatre on West Forty-fourth.

"I got back to New York, picked up my mail, and found the well-known summons from my Uncle Sam ('Congratulations: you have been accepted into the United States Army!')," says George Church. "I went over to the St. James, where we were due to open in two days. There, out front on the houseboards, was my name, in large print, and in the program also, big as life!

"I ran into Dick Rodgers inside. 'Hey, Dick,' I asked, 'what happened to our deal?'

"'Looks like somebody goofed, George,' he said, and he apologized;

THE PLAYBILL

FOR THE ST. JAMES THEATRE

June 13 - '43

he hoped it wouldn't make me a problem. It was too late now to make a fuss. What was my problem? The word seemed to have gotten around town that this show was very shaky. Nobody really figured it was going to make it, so I could play out a few days and then I'd go off to take care of Mr. Hitler, right?"

"I wrote to my family and I told them I'd gotten them opening-night tickets," says Bambi Linn. "I said, 'You have to come opening night, because we may not be running much longer than that.' Big Broadway dancer that I now was, I was talking as if I really knew what I was talking about!

"So we came down to New York, and I walked over to the St. James, and I saw my *picture* up in front of the theatre! And then there was an article about me in the *Brooklyn Daily Eagle*, because I was a local girl making her debut—and I thought to myself, 'How can this be? I'm the lowest of the low in this production, and here they have me out in front of the theatre?' . . . Oh, for me, it really didn't matter if the show was a hit—it was just so wonderful to be there!"

Inside the theatre, as the production was being set up on stage, Jay Blackton assembled his New York pit orchestra and ran a musical rehearsal while Jerry Whyte and his cadre of stage managers checked out every under-the-gun last-minute detail backstage.

"During the last dress rehearsal in New York, some musician struck a wrong note," recalled de Mille. "And Diana Adams's face contorted with pain. It was not annoyance, or amusement, it was agonized concern. Richard Rodgers saw the expression and marveled. That look had never crossed a chorus girl's face; he was aware (as were not all of us?) that responsible artists had entered the ranks. Diana's expression marked the beginning of a new era."

There was precious—and rationed—heat on in the St. James, there were lights on inside the lobby box office, but outside that ticket window there was no line of eager buyers, and in the cash drawers there wasn't much of a "wrap," theatre talk for the day's take. The prospective audience for *Oklahoma!* was nowhere to be seen.

HIRSCHFELD

ma!' New Musical,
p Homespun U. S. A.

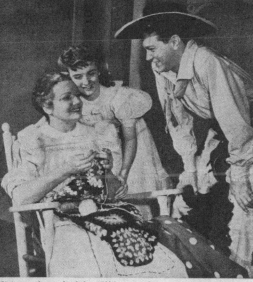

Something a little different in the way of musical comedy is due here tonight with the opening at the St. James Theater of *Oklahoma!* the Theatre Guild's musical version of the Lynn Riggs play, *Green Grow the Lilacs*. For though the results were aimed straight for Broadway and most of the people connected with the enterprise are old hands at show business, the production has such unusual features as a 28-piece orchestra (very large for a musical comedy), a generous sprinkling of graduates of the Juilliard School of Music and various ballet schools, and such people as the ballet's Agnes de Mille plotting the choreography and the movies' Rouben Mamoulian, directing.

What Richard Rodgers, who wrote the music, Oscar Hammerstein II, who wrote the book and lyrics, and Mamoulian are trying to do is to concoct something approaching a folk operetta. The book has a hero-heroine-villian, "curse you, Jack Dalton," kind of plot that leaves plenty of room for wild West square dances, gittar playing, and fights to the death. It also allows for colorful, Grant Woodsy sets by Lemuel Ayers and costumes by Miles White that play up petticoats and ten gallon hats.

Oklahoma opened out-of-town on March 11 and comes to New York after a "tryout" of only 20 days—something of a record for a big musical show. And that, as the wise birds on Shubert Alley will tell you, is a good sign.

Most of the comedy in *Oklahoma!* is supplied by these two screwball characters — Ado Annie (Celeste Holm) and Ali Hakim (Joseph Buloff)

Sitting on the porch of their Oklahoma ranch house are the show's three principals (l. to r.): Aunt Eller (Betty Garde), her niece, Laurey (Joan Roberts) and Laurey's boy friend Curly (Alfred Drake). The cast has plenty of talent, but no big-name stars.

A fair sample of Agnes de Mille's dances is this dream sequence, in which the heroine has a nightmare about her forthcoming wedding. Katharine Sergava, at left in the bridal gown, dances the dream version of Laurey. The three dancers at right represent Laurey's friends "marching" down the aisle of the church with hands folded in caricatured solemnity.

Photos by Graphic House

This "fancy lady" of the early 1900s is one of five such gals who also appear in Laurey's dream. Kate Friedlich dances the role.

Obviously the word from Boston, the news of the second ˅
and their impact on the audience, hadn't reached New Y˅
hadn't caused any ground swell. But considering th˅
this enterprise had been, ever since that summe˅
Green Grow the Lilacs had been revived in Wesֈ
After dozens of auditions, and actual performances,
shunned the show. And if the word around town was thֈ
not, could not possibly make it, can anyone blame ticket buֈ
ning the St. James window?

The Guild's subscription list had dwindled seriously in the pֈ
seasons, eroded by a parade of sixteen flops. Then came the final obstֈ
On the morning of March 31st, it began to snow.

Is it any wonder then that on that opening night the St. James was not
sold out?

It continued to snow.

"I remember going up to the Ballet Arts School the day of the opening
and finding Diana Adams and Bambi Linn sweating through two classes,"
said de Mille. "I ordered them to rest, but I had to enlist the help of the
teacher to make them leave the floor!

"I had ten front-row balcony seats, and I didn't know whom to give
them to," said de Mille. "I think a couple remained empty."

"We hear they went out and started bringing people in," says Linn.
"They found as many servicemen as they could; they literally went out and
dragged them in; whenever they'd see servicemen walking down Forty-
fourth or Forty-fifth, and there were lots of them on the streets headed for
the Stage Door Canteen or movies or trying to get into a show, they'd say,
'Come see a new show, come on in.' They had to do it. You know how big
the St. James is, and if those last few rows were empty downstairs, they
couldn't let it look like that. Not to have a full house on *opening night*?

"So they papered the house, and in fact I remember somebody said to
us, 'Is there anybody you could invite?' I mean, to the *cast*! Of course, I'd

opֈ
Arts aֈ
section.) ֈ
years have pֈ
and Oklahomaֈ
carries on; so,
gratefully, does
Mr. Hirschfeld. A
low bow, then, to
both of these great
American institu-
tions! (Courtesy of
Al Hirschfeld)

already paid for my family's tickets, and when I heard that I said, 'Gee whiz, I could have got them in for free!'"

Helene Hanff was still laboring up in the Theatre Guild press department.

At six, that evening, the snow had turned to sleet, and the cold I'd developed now included a cough. As I left the office to go home and climb into a drafty evening dress, Joe Heidt took pity on me. "I don't need you there, dear," he said. "Don't come unless you feel like it."

I felt guilty about not going as I ate a quick dinner at a cafeteria. But by the time I'd fought my way home through the sleet, guilt had given way to self-preservation. I undressed and crawled thankfully into bed. In bed, I reached for the wet newspaper I'd brought home and opened it to the theatre page. Our big opening night legend leaped out at me: OKLAHOMA! •

Slowly, surely, with that foggy bewilderment you were bound to feel sooner or later if you worked at the Theatre Guild long enough, I saw that Terry and Lawrence were right. About the exclamation point.

I did not allow myself to speculate on the insane possibility that they might also be right about such brainwaves as a clean, corn-fed musical with no legs and no jokes and with a score by Richard Rodgers and Oscar Hammerstein II, who'd never collaborated before, a full-blown ballet by an unknown young choreographer named Agnes de Mille, and a cast of unknowns, including Celeste Holm, the ingenue from *Papa Is All.*

I switched off the lamp, thinking how typical it was of both this epic and the Guild that the notices would appear on the morning of April Fool's Day. . . . I coughed, pulled up the blankets as I drifted off to sleep, said a silent "Good luck" to Alfred Drake, the juvenile from *Yesterday's Magic* who was at that moment about to stroll onto the stage of the St. James Theatre to sing "Oh, What a Beautiful Mornin'."

Marc Platt's foot, which he'd injured in Boston, was still troubling him. But the young ballet dancer, who'd lately been in three successive flop musicals, *The Lady Comes Across*, *My Dear Public*, and *Beat the Band*, told his doctor he'd be damned if he'd miss being in what he hoped would be his first hit. So the doctor taped Marc up as best he could to protect him from further injury, and in order to make certain the dancer could go on agreed to be around on opening night at the theatre. And Marc sat backstage, preparing to go on.

"That took a lot of guts on Marc's part," says George Church. "He and I worked up a very strenuous routine in the first-act dream ballet. We used to kill each other every day out of town. We had a lot of fun, but we ended up black-and-blue."

"We used to bring gasps from the audience at some of the stuff we did; very acrobatic stunts," said Platt. "George used to throw me ten, twelve feet in the air, and then when I landed I'd slide another six. Very flashy acrobatic stuff."

"Of course," adds Platt sadly, "none of that was ever seen after opening night. By that time I was out, and George had left to go into the army."

By nightfall the weather hadn't improved.

Bundled in winter coats, the opening-night audience sloshed up Forty-fourth Street to the darkened marquee of the St. James and filed inside.

The audience dispensed the customary waves and greetings (New York openings were clubby affairs, a form of movable theatrical feast), the house lights went down, and the conductor, Jay Blackton, took his place in the pit, in front of his orchestra. He raised his hands to give a downbeat (he did not yet use a baton, but would later—a collision with a music stand would give Blackton a permanently gnarled left pinky).

The music began.

When the overture ended, there was silence.

Outside the St. James, in a darkened, browned-out city, there were shortages and rationing, uncertainty. There were few families who were not bereft of sons and husbands. But here, inside the theatre, a thousand-odd people sat and watched the lights come up, bright and strong, bathing Lem Ayers's vista of Oklahoma prairie in a warm, golden aura.

There sat a placid lady in simple clothing, beside her a butter churn, and as she did her chores there was a sense of peace and quiet and complete security.

"Was there ever a more magical moment in the theatre than that one of small, early sounds that preceded Alfred Drake's song of rejoicing in the morning?" wrote Celeste Holm years afterward.

And then, from offstage, came the voice of Curly, singing.

When he finished there was a wave of applause.

"Then they fell in love with 'The Surrey with the Fringe on Top,'" said Celeste. "Alfred had never been more wonderful. They adored Lee Dixon doing 'Everything's Up to Date in Kansas City.' And then it was my turn. I tried to remember everything that those two-and-a-half weeks of acting and reacting to audiences had confirmed. . . . My opening night nerves really attacked; a tight band of hope around my head, and a tighter one of fear around my chest. . . ." Then she made her entrance, and soon she was enchanting the audience with "I Cain't Say No."

The laughs were delighted, and the applause was hearty. If they wanted an encore Hammerstein's second chorus was all a comedienne could ever dream about.

"With each song," said Celeste, "the show rose higher and higher!"

On rolled the first act. After this night, with this one performance of *Oklahoma!*, the American musical theatre would never be the same. Farewell to those years of European-based operettas, to the Ziegfeld extravaganzas, to claptrap books designed for star performers, and to rowdy semiburlesque shows. By 11:20 P.M. on this night they were all history. This simple and winning story of America's growing up on the frontier, set to a wonderful score, with its honest characters and brilliant choreography all melded into a theatre piece, was something new. A successful vision, a prototype from which everything would now flow.

But how could the St. James audience know that its opening night tick-

*It would appear
that the entire
state agrees, "The
farmer and the
cowman should be
friends." (Courtesy
of The Rodgers &
Hammerstein
Organization)*

Laurey has hopes to marry Curly, in a scene from the "Out of My Dreams" ballet. (Courtesy of Photofest)

As the "dancing Jud," George Church turned Laurey's "dream" into a nightmare. (*Courtesy of Dorene Church*)

Oklahoma! hits the road. Members of the touring company find Ado Annie's problems persist. (*Vandamm Photography/ Courtesy of Photofest*)

ets had purchased it a place in history? At that moment, those thousand-odd people were too busy enjoying.

At the end of the first act, when the curtain fell on the de Mille ballet, "the boys started hitting each other backstage with their big hats," Celeste remembered. " 'It's a *hit,* it's a *hit!*' "

Outside, the lobby was buzzing with excited responses.

Upstairs in the backstage dressing rooms there was also excitement, but of a different nature.

"At intermission," said Agnes de Mille, "I bucked the tide of spectators and fought my way to the stage door. Marc's leg was in a terrible state. Upstairs, Kate Friedlich was crying; she'd torn two ligaments from her heel."

"It was in the ballet at the end of the first act," says Friedlich. "I was dancing with a young man whose first show this was. I'm sure I was keyed up and nervous; he was probably even more so. . . . But he took me up in a lift, way up, he was a six-footer, and he lifted me eight feet up there, off the stage. And in his nervousness he forgot to bring me down properly, and he just dropped me—and I smashed down to the stage! And I badly sprained my ankle.

"Since Marc Platt's doctor was backstage, it was decided they would shoot me full of something called ethyl chloride, which froze your foot up like a block of ice . . . so then I could go on spraining my ankle four or five more ways, without feeling it, not knowing what the hell I felt!" says Friedlich. "Later a sports doctor told me that was a very dangerous treatment; they use it on athletes sometimes to kill the pain, but *never* allow them to go back in action afterwards. But that night, at the St. James, I didn't feel I had much choice not to go back and do the second act—I was duty bound. We didn't have any understudies.

"Agnes claims she fed me and Marc both some brandy. I don't remember much about that. But by the time the second act began we were both ready, and off we went."

"I stood at the back," said de Mille, "beside Rodgers and the staff. Oscar, who was calm, sat down front with his wife. The barn dance for 'The Farmer and the Cowman' opened the second act. Marc, in an ecstasy of excitement, rode the pain to triumph! Virile, young, red-headed, and able, he looked like Apollo and moved like a stallion!

"'Oh, Agnes,' said Rodgers, 'I'm so proud of you. I hope this opens doors.'

"'Dick, Dick,' I said, melting into his arms. 'I love you! Thank you!' Then Morgan Lewis, our rehearsal accompanist, started beating us on the back and shrieking, 'Will you two stop courting and look what's happened to the theatre?'

"They were roaring. They were howling. People hadn't seen boys and girls dance like this in so long. Of course, they had been dancing like this, but just not where this audience could see them!"

"When the show was over," says Friedlich, "I had myself six or seven sprains. I was out of the show for eight weeks; Marc was out for a long, long time. But we'd danced that opening night!"*

On rolled that second act, gathering momentum as it went, resonating to an enraptured audience that laughed and sighed in all the right places to the Rodgers and Hammerstein score and followed the fortunes of Curly and Laurey, the complex love affair of Will Parker and Ado Annie and Ali Hakim. The box social. The auction, at which Curly sacrifices all his possessions to wrest Laurey away from Jud Fry's dark attentions. The wedding, and then, to celebrate it, that exultant eleven o'clock chorale version of "Oklahoma" with the cast down front belting out to the New Yorkers a hymn to a brand new state: "Oklahoma, O . . . K!"

*"The way it worked out, with Marc Platt and Katie injuring themselves," comments Vivian Shiers, "we only had the original cast of the show on that *one* opening night. After the opening, they started drafting the guys, not only George Church but George Irving, too."

"Knocked everybody for a loop," says Blackton. "I couldn't see the reaction of the audience behind me, but I could certainly hear it! Amazing."

The encore, second chorus, was as powerful and exciting as all that had gone before. Or more so.

Hammerstein's brilliant stagecraft wound it all up. The shivaree on the wedding night. The struggle with Jud Fry, Curly's intervention, Jud's inadvertent death at the hands of Curly by Jud's own knife, that symbolic weapon we'd known about since the first act . . . The accusation of Curly, then the reprieve. "We ain't gonna let you send the boy to jail on his wedding night!" cries one of the Oklahomans; justice triumphs—it was self-defense! And away go the happy bride and groom in their surrey with the fringe on top, headed for a truly happy ending . . .

Finale. Applause, and more applause, roars of it . . .

And bows from the happy cast, beaming at an equally happy audience.

Which eventually gathered up its coats and hats and reluctantly began to leave the St. James. A majority of them were floating, wafted out of that theatre on a cloud of delight that carried them into the darkness of the cold, wartime city. Away from the golden glow of that Oklahoma prairie and its staunch pioneer people.

But they were newly equipped with memories for a lifetime, set to music, which they could not wait to rave about to anyone who hadn't been at the St. James. Half a century later Mrs. Ethel Heyn, who was then married to comedian Charlie Butterworth, remembers that opening night somewhat ruefully. "I was having dinner at '21,' and my escort was our good friend Nunnally Johnson, who was in from Hollywood and doing the town. Anyway, as we finished our dinner he pulled out a pair of tickets and showed them to me. 'These are for the opening night of some new show,' he said. 'Do you have any possible interest in seeing something they're calling 'Oklahoma'? Well, we could see outside how it was snowing, and it was so pleasant inside '21,' and so we both finally agreed, not a chance, we'd stay at our table and pass up the show. We were there much later, right up until the time people came back from the opening for a drink, and we knew some of them who'd seen the show, they came by our table and said, 'My God, *what you missed!* ' "

Agnes de Mille took her mother to Sardi's for a sandwich. A thin, bespectacled gentleman crossed over to her table, shook her hand, and congratulated her. He was Wolcott Gibbs, the drama critic of the *New Yorker*, well known for his waspish reviews and acerbic tongue. But not on this night. "I want to congratulate you," he said. "This was most distinguished."

"I chewed on, in a sort of stupor," she relates.

In Sardi's, as was the custom, applause greeted each member of the *Oklahoma!* crew as he or she entered that traditional theatrical watering hole. Everyone knew how important the newspaper reviews would be; especially the one being written a block away, on West Forty-third, at the *New York Times* office, not by the dean of New York critics, Brooks Atkinson, who'd gone off to war, but by his replacement, Lewis Nichols.

Meanwhile there were congratulations all around. Dick Rodgers was suddenly accosted by a small man grinning from ear to ear who threw his arms around him. It was Larry Hart, who'd seen the show from a Row B seat and roared with laughter and applauded all the way through. "*Dick!*" he cried, "I've never had a better evening in my life! This show will be around twenty years from now!"

An error on Hart's part, this time one of underestimation.

Later the *Times* review would arrive, but before it did Helburn had gone home and turned on a radio. At midnight she heard the first commentator. "The show," he said, "won't last a week."

One is forced to speculate which theatre he'd attended that night.

Probably the happiest member of that opening night audience—certainly the most possessive—was playwright Lynn Riggs, in New York on an army pass from his post. His escort to the show was Miranda Masocco Levy, an old friend from Santa Fe who had taken a job in Bergdorf-Goodman. "Lynn absolutely loved the show from beginning to end," Levy

remembers. "He laughed, he applauded, he was delighted with what they'd all done with his play. When it was over we went backstage so he could congratulate everyone; what a thrill for me, a small-town girl, meeting all those performers!"

Next day, euphorically, Riggs would hurry up to Bergdorf's, where he bought presents for the cast. "By that time he'd read the reviews and knew what a hit they all had," she says. "He was so happy—he spent so much money on gifts that Andrew Goodman gave me the rest of the day off!"

Jules Glaenzer, the head of Cartier's and a veteran Broadway habitué, threw a large celebratory cast party after the Sardi's gathering. When he offered Rodgers a drink, the composer refused, saying, "No, thanks, I don't want to touch a drop. I want to remember every second of this night!"

The revised sheet-music cover for the Oklahoma! score. The lower left-hand corner note (which urges us to buy U.S. War Savings Bonds and Stamps) provides evidence that this is an original printing, circa 1943–45. Should you unearth such a copy today, cherish it.

THE SURREY WITH THE FRINGE ON TOP

THE THEATRE GUILD *presents*

Oklahoma!

A MUSICAL PLAY

(Based on the play "GREEN GROW THE LILACS" by Lynn Riggs)

Music by
RICHARD RODGERS

Book and Lyrics by
OSCAR HAMMERSTEIN 2ᴰ

Directed by
ROUBEN MAMOULIAN

Dances by
AGNES DE MILLE

Production under the supervision of
LAWRENCE LANGNER and
THERESA HELBURN

BUY UNITED STATES
WAR SAVINGS
BONDS AND STAMPS

WILLIAMSON MUSIC, INC.
Sole Selling Agent
CRAWFORD MUSIC CORPORATION
RKO BLDG. · RADIO CITY · NEW YORK

OKLAHOMA
MANY A NEW DAY
THE SURREY WITH THE FRINGE ON TOP
OH, WHAT A BEAUTIFUL MORNIN'
PEOPLE WILL SAY WE'RE IN LOVE
OUT OF MY DREAMS
I CAIN'T SAY NO

Years later, in his memoirs, Rodgers summed up the experience. "I was forty at the time, with a number of hit shows behind me, but nothing had ever remotely compared to this. It was a rebirth, both in my associations and in my career."

The *Times* review was good. "For years they have been saying the Theatre Guild is dead," wrote Nichols, "words that obviously will have to be eaten with breakfast this morning. . . . A truly delightful musical play. . . . Wonderful is the nearest adjective, for this excursion of the Guild combines a fresh and infectious gaiety, a charm of manner, beautiful acting, singing and dancing, and a score by Richard Rodgers that doesn't do any harm, either, since it is one of his best."

Howard Barnes of the *Tribune* called it "Jubilant and enchanting . . . a superb musical." Walter Winchell, who hadn't made it up to New Haven, was less excited. "When the ladies of the ballet are on view," he remarked, "*Oklahoma!* is at its very best. . . . The audience last night had a happy time." Burns Mantle gave it three stars and a plus in the *Daily News*.

The rave reviews would be joined by those in the afternoon papers, and they would mount in crescendo in the following Sunday assessments.

Jay Blackton, his evening chores done, left the St. James Theatre and took his wife, Louise, and his assistant to a nearby Italian restaurant. After a plate of spaghetti he went uptown with his wife and they retired. "We figured what must be must be," he remembers. "We could read the papers tomorrow morning. Now we needed sleep.

"In the morning, we're still in bed. Very early. The phone rings. It's Dick Berger, my patient boss from the St. Louis Municipal Opera, who's been waiting for *weeks* now to see how things would be with this show and if I'd be able to do his summer season or not.

"He said, 'Jay, did you read?'

"I said, 'Read *what*?'

'Oklahoma!' a Musical Hailed as Delightful, Based on 'Green Grow the Lilacs,' Opens Here at the St. James Theatre

OKLAHOMA! a musical play in two acts and five scenes, derived from "Green Grow the Lilacs," by Lynn Riggs. Music by Richard Rodgers; book and lyrics by Oscar Hammerstein 2d. Staged by Rouben Mamoulian; choreography by Agnes de Mille; settings by Lemuel Ayers; costumes designed by Miles White; produced by the Theatre Guild. At the St. James Theatre.

Aunt Eller	Betty Garde
Curly	Alfred Drake
Laurey	Joan Roberts
Ike Skidmore	Barry Kelley
Fred	Edwin Clay
Slim	Herbert Rissman
Will Parker	Lee Dixon
Jud Fry	Howard da Silva
Ado Annie Carnes	Celeste Holm
Ali Hakim	Joseph Buloff
Gertie Cummings	Jane Lawrence
Ellen	Katharine Sergava
Kate	Ellen Love
Sylvie	Joan McCracken
Armina	Kate Friedlich
Aggie	Bambi Linn
Andrew Carnes	Ralph Riggs
Cord Elam	Owen Martin
Jess	George Church
Chalmers	Marc Platt
Mike	Paul Schierz
Joe	George Irving
Sam	Hayes Gordon

By LEWIS NICHOLS

For years they have been saying the Theatre Guild is dead, words that obviously will have to be eaten with breakfast this morning. Forsaking the sometimes somber tenor of her ways, the little lady of Fifty-second Street last evening danced off into new paths and brought to the St. James a truly delightful musical play called "Oklahoma!" Wonderful is the nearest adjective, for this excursion of the Guild combines a fresh and infectious gayety, a charm of manner, beautiful acting, singing and dancing, and a score by Richard Rodgers which doesn't do any harm either, since it is one of his best.

* * *

"Oklahoma!" is based on Lynn Riggs's saga of the Indian Territory at the turn of the century, "Green Grow the Lilacs," and, like its predecessor, it is simple and warm. It relies not for a moment on Broadway gags to stimulate an appearance of comedy, but goes winningly on its way with Rouben Mamoulian's best direction to point up its sly humor, and with some of Agnes de Mille's most inspired dances to do so further. There is more comedy in one of Miss de Mille's gay little passages than in many of the other Broadway tom-tom beats together. The Guild has known what it is about

'Oklahoma With

"Oklahoma," musical play ba Lilacs;" music by Richard Rodge stein, 2d. Produced by the The New York, March 31, 1943.

★

Aunt Eller	Betty Garde
Curly	Alfred Drake
Laurey	Joan Roberts
Ike Skidmore	Barry Kelley
Fred	Edwin Clay
Slim	Herbert Rissman
Will Parker	Lee Dixon
Jud Fry	Howard da Silva
Andrew Carnes	

By BURN

"Oklahoma," which the St. James Theatre last night, "Green Grows the Lilacs" ar let, if you can picture the co joining of the arts of drama

With the songs that Richar Rodgers has fitted to a collectio of unusually atmospheric and in telligible lyrics by Oscar Hammer stein 2d, "Oklahoma" seems to m to be the most thoroughly and at tractively American musical com edy since Edna Ferber's "Show Boat" was done by this same Ham merstein and Jerome Kern.

It has color, and rhythm an harmony plus. It is held to th native idiom and kept sufficientl clean to give it standing in th Western country from which i springs. And it has been modestl but handsomely staged by th Guild.

Ballet and Drama.

There may be some little objec tion advanced by subscribers wh have little liking for the moder ballet. They may insist that th dance numbers dominate both th drama and the songs.

"OKLAHOMA," a musical play based on the play "Green Grow the Lilacs," by Lynn Riggs, music by Richard Rodgers, book and lyrics by Oscar Hammerstein 2d, production directed by Rouben Mamoulian, settings by Lemuel Ayers, costumes by Miles White, dances by Agnes de Mille, presented by The Theater Guild at the St. James Theater with the following cast:

Aunt Eller	Betty Garde
Curly	Alfred Drake
Laurey	Joan Roberts
Ike Skidmore	Barry Kelley
Fred	Edwin Clay
Slim	Herbert Rissman
Will Parker	Lee Dixon
Jud Fry	Howard da Silva
Ado Annie Carnes	Celeste Holm
Ali Hakim	Joseph Buloff
Gertie Cummings	Jane Lawrence
Ellen	Katherine Sergava
Kate	Ellen Love
Sylvie	Joan McCracken
Armina	Kate Friedlich
Aggie	Bambi Linn
Andrew Carnes	Ralph Riggs
Cord Elam	Owen Martin
Jess	George Church
Chalmers	Marc Platt
Mike	Paul Shiers
Joe	George Irving
Sam	Hayes Gordon

SYNOPSIS—Time: Just after the turn of the century. Place: Indian Territory (now Oklahoma) Act I—Scene 1: The front of Laurey's farmhouse. Scene 2: The smokehouse. Scene 3: A grove on Laurey's farm. Act II—Scene 1: The Skidmore ranch. Scene 2: Skidmore's kitchen porch. Scene 3: The back of Laurey's farmhouse.

Lilacs to "Oklahoma"

SONGS, dances and a story have been triumphantly blended at the St. James. "Oklahoma!" is a jubilant and enchanting musical. The Richard Rodgers score is one of his best, which is saying plenty. Oscar Hammerstein 2d has written a dramatically imaginative libretto and a string of catchy lyrics; Agnes de Mille has worked small miracles in devising original dances to fit the story and the tunes, while Rouben Mamoulian has directed an excellent company with great taste and craftsmanship. Is it any wonder, then, that this Theater Guild production is one of the most captivating shows of the season?

* * *

Plots are generally a nuisance in musical comedies, but the narrative line in "Oklahoma!" is arresting and even dramatic. It is based on the Lynn Riggs play of a dozen years ago, "Green Grow the Lilacs." That work, as I remember it, was lean on substantial subject matter for a straight play, but it has been transmuted into a brilliant frame for songs and dances. The melodrama which Riggs invented for the Indian Territory at the turn of the century has been given exciting elaboration at the St. James, with the vocalists and the dancers picking

What a ple Will Dreams" a lot, bu tunes, suc 'er Nothin at the St freshing.

So ma after "O rather sh cult to them for The ball act, whe a fight b and the has wha designs a superb raphy, and the house is matic sc for the homa" a knock is somet

There known, but that show wh cal exci first rat Howard

'Oklahoma' At St. Jam[es]

Theatre Guild Gives Lynn Riggs' 'Gree[n]

By JOHN ANDERSON

When the Theatre Guild goes gay anything can happen—sometimes the best and sometimes the worst, but from the uproar of welcome at the St. James last night there was no mistaking the fact that in "Oklahoma" the Guild has a beautiful and delightful show, fresh and imaginative, as enchanting to the eye as Richard Rodgers' music is to the ear. It has, at a rough estimate, practically everything. Even Guild First Nighters, suspected for years of not having hands, applauded.

Though the horse has recently returned to fame, both on the streets and on the menu, no one could have guessed (as did the astute Guild) that the horse's late companion, the cowboy, would achieve a similar urban popularity. "Oklahoma" is about cowboys and their girls, so the home-state of Will Rogers herewith makes its second gift to Broadway. Actually the show is based on Lynn Riggs' "Green Grow the Lilacs," a folk play of the Indian territory days of 1901, which never had the success it deserved when the Guild did it without music and dances these years ago.

Delightful Score

Now the second Oscar Hammerstein has turned Mr. Riggs' play into a light and colorful libretto, and written the lyrics for Mr. Rodgers' music. Lemuel Ayres has tossed out a stage-ful of handsome scenery, suggesting the wide, windswept, rich rolling land of Grant Wood paintings and Agnes deMille has inserted some superb dances into the proceedings with the fine energy of splashing movement, and the boldness of fresh design, all helped by Miles White's brilliant costumes.

THEATER
By Burton Rascoe

The Guild's Oklahoma Opens at the St. James

The Theater Guild, once so austerely intellectual and aristocratic, has joined the march of democracy, let down the bars to a musical show—and has a hit on its hands. With its Oklahoma, which opened at the St. James last night, the Guild has combined some of the best features of the ballet at the Met with some of the best features of the great tradition of Broadway's own indigenous contribution to the theater—a girl show with lovely tunes, a couple of comics, a heavy, pretty costuming and an infectious spirit of gayety and good humor.

Oklahoma is fresh, li[vely] Richard Rodgers has writte[n] scores any musical play eve[r] it with a touch of genius, [and] over the musicians who pl[ay] proud symphony orchestra[s].

Next to Mr. Rodgers, [is] de Mille, whose choreogra[phy] ballet is actually the bigg[est] already won fame with her of Les Six of Paris in the teurish and mechanical; b[ut] danced to the music of th[e] Nothin'—which are such st[uff] anything the Met can prod[uce] out of this world.

Why No Encore.

(I have a quarrel wit[h] these numbers. In spite applause at the end of Ou[t] and, moreover, allowed onl[y] Marc Platt, of the ballet nu[mber] of course, but there was [no] program to be either Rho[da] was the outstanding hit of was the girl who danced th[e] such sprite-like and unutt[erable]

Among the principals, Holm simply tucked the under her arm and just [let] others touch it. This is [as] tounding young woman, Holm. It seems that only weeks ago she was do[ing] straight part exceedingly [well] The Damask Cheek, as a fully meretricious lady o[f] theater whose morals were of the alley fence; and he shows up as an excellent and still an eyeful, with a[n] caressing voice. When y[ou] and hear her sing the naughty song, I Can't Say N[o] are in for a tickling thrill. you just wait for her next

The Guild is probably too [late]

It's Right Nice In Oklahoma

PM Reviews

OKLAHOMA! a new musical comedy by Richard Rodgers and Oscar Hammerstein 2d, based on Lynn Riggs' *Green Grow the Lilacs*, presented by the Theatre Guild at the St. James; with Betty Garde, Alfred Drake, Joseph Buloff, Joan Roberts, Lee Dixon, Howard da Silva, Celeste Holm, Ralph Riggs, Marc Platt, Katharine Sergava, Kate Friedlich, Joan McCracken and George Church; directed by Rouben Mamoulian; dances by Agnes de Mille; settings by Lemuel Ayers; costumes by Miles White.

By Louis Kronenberger

Oklahoma! is a little more than a musical comedy without being pretentiously so. Based on Lynn Riggs' *Green Grow the Lilacs,* it is a folk musical laid at the turn of the century, for which Richard Rodgers has written one of his most charming scores, and into which Agnes de Mille has introduced some picturesque and lively dancing, and a very good first-act-finale ballet. The whole show has just enough of an old-fashioned period quality to be pleasantly refreshing.

The book, to be sure, is just one of those things, if that, and the comedy is neither subtle nor extensive. But they play so minor a part in the evening's business that they can play an equally minor one in this review. *Oklahoma!*—for the record—tells of the trouble a couple of nice guys in cowboy boots have in winning a couple of pretty farm girls. A comic peddler and a villainous

"He said, 'You haven't read the papers? The *Times*—the Trib?" He was so excited.

"I said, 'No, we just got up—'

"He said, 'My God—you have got to read them!' And then he added, 'Jay—*good-bye!*' "

Ever-hopeful ticket buyers were confronted with this sad news in the St. James lobby.

We have no tickets for OKLAHOMA!

YEE-OW!

By noontime of the next day Agnes De Mille was back at the St. James rehearsing Marc Platt's understudy for the Thursday night performance.

The afternoon papers were out. John Anderson, in the *Journal-American*, called *Oklahoma!* "A beautiful and delightful show, fresh and imaginative, as enchanting to the eye as Richard Rodgers's music is to the ear. It has, at a rough estimate, practically everything."

Ward Morehouse, in the *Sun*, was less effusive and pointed to slowness and monotony, "But by the time they're singing the lusty title song near the finish," he said, "you're under the spell of it." Burton Rascoe, in the *World-Telegram* (should we not relish this long-gone era in which fortunate readers had a choice of so many drama critics?), enjoyed himself. "The Theatre Guild, once so austerely intellectual and aristocratic, has joined the march of democracy, let down the bars to a musical show—and has a hit on its hands." He was particularly effusive about de Mille's ballets. "She has two numbers, danced to the music of 'Out of My Dreams' and 'All Er Nothin',' which are such supreme aesthetic delights as to challenge anything the Met can produce this season. They are spinetingling and out of this world."

That Thursday morning Rodgers and Hammerstein, recovered from the previous night's festivities, decided to have lunch.

"Should we sneak off to some quiet place where we can talk, or shall we go to Sardi's and show off?" asked Rodgers.

"Hell, let's go to Sardi's and show off!" replied Oscar.

They came down Forty-fourth Street and passed the St. James Theatre. It was after 10, the box office was open, and there was bedlam. Ticket buyers were pushing and shoving to get to the window and buy seats to this new sleeper hit. A New York policeman had been sent over from the precinct to try and keep order.

Inside Sardi's there was another triumphant lunchtime scene as congratulatory friends and pseudofriends surrounded the pair, offering handshakes and hugs and of course requesting house seats for the first available date. "All the while assuring us that they'd known right from the start that the show would be a hit," commented Rodgers sardonically.

The strongest form of advertising in show business is word of mouth. A scant twelve hours after the curtain had fallen the night before, the word was spreading all over New York, and by telephone out to California.

By the end of the week everyone was writing about this newly arrived smash hit. *PM*, Ralph Ingersoll's innovative tabloid, summed up the various physical problems which had beset the cast out of town, i.e., measles, illness, and injuries. "The casualties were not suffered in vain," the paper reported. *Oklahoma!* seems to be well established in the hit category, and ticket brokers are reporting a tremendous demand for seats. The Theatre Guild, which seems a bit bewildered at having such a bonanza on its hands, reports in awed tones that the first five shows in New York netted

$18,000 and 151 standees—capacity—and that advance sales are something like $25,000.* That news makes up for a lot of sprained ankles and German measles."

"There were a few vacant seats at the first Thursday matinee," Helburn recorded. "That night, the house sold out for the next four years."

"The real raves came in the Sunday papers," said Alfred Drake, "after they'd had time to think about what they'd seen. Florence Reed, who was playing in Thornton Wilder's *The Skin of Our Teeth*, loved the show so much that she bought tickets for the next thirty-odd Thursday matinees! Hers were on Wednesday, so she had Thursdays free, and she'd sit out there in the mezzanine every week; every time she was there, I'd know. I'd finish singing 'Surrey,' and this deep bass voice, unmistakeable, would boom out from the mezzanine . . . '*Bravo!*'"

Shortly afterward, the Guild exercised its option on the screen rights to *Green Grow the Lilacs* from Metro-Goldwyn-Mayer. The film version of the show would not be produced for many years, prosperous years in which the Broadway company ran at capacity, the national company and other touring companies would crisscross the United States. In London when it opened at the Drury Lane it would be a tonic for the war-weary British audiences and would have the longest run of any show that had ever opened at that venerable theatre. A USO touring company went off to play *Oklahoma!* for the troops in the Pacific, and after the war there would be productions in Europe.

The bonanza that Helburn's Folly had induced brought this amused comment from H. I. Phillips, the resident humorist of the *New York Sun*, in his column "The Sun Dial."

---

* Bear in mind we are discussing 1943 dollars. Half a century later, the rate of inflation has been so rapid that it's safe to estimate that $25,000 as being worth ten times more today. Certainly not as impressive as the $32,000,000 advance sales figure quoted for *Miss Saigon*, but based on the original production cost of the Guild's 1943 production and the pay-back to its investors over the years (Miss Helburn estimated it at a staggering 2,500 percent), who, one may ask, came out ahead?

The Guild and The Gold

Eugene O'Neill was no playwrighting heel;
For the Theatre Guild oft he made money.
And that fellow G. Shaw made its life less than raw,
With a play that was often a honey:
But the records all fell to a sweet fare-thee-well,
And prosperity followed (and how!) boys,
When the Guild so sedate pulled a big thirty-eight
And went in for the musical cowboys!

With the big problem plays it had plentiful days
The "significant" stuff was its baby;
Any genius who had little notes on a pad
Got production at once, and not maybe.
But the bankroll grew fat when the Guild went to bat—
(And the fates did it one of their best turns)—
With those cowboys galore and a musical score,
As the dignified group fell for "westerns."

But Pygmalion's through, for she won't spit or chew
And Electra cannot get a hearing.
For the Guild's gone all out with a rodeo shout
As the cow ponies tear through the clearing.
Broadway's all in a daze over what type show pays
As the Guild goes to town with its furs on;
It once razzed the old girl and her old-fashioned curl,
BUT SHE AIN'T THE SAME GAL WITH THOSE SPURS ON!

There were only a thousand-odd seats in the St. James, and the show played eight performances a week. (A ninth was played, but the seats were reserved during the war for servicemen only.) It doesn't take a mathematician to figure out the odds involved in the availabilities of those St. James seats: tiny supply, untold-of demand. Getting a pair for *Oklahoma!* would be the equivalent of winning the lottery. The Theatre Guild files, which are stored away for posterity at the Beinecke Library at Yale, contain cartons of correspondence from the *Oklahoma!* years. Dozens of them deal with the problems involved in the show's preparation and production. But there are two bulging file cartons that deal with one particular subject; namely, requests for precious "house" seats to the show!

Day after day, from 1943 on, Langner and Helburn (as well as Rodgers, Hammerstein, Mamoulian, and de Mille, certainly) would be the recipients of a steady stream of begging letters from friends, relatives, friends of friends, friends of relatives, in-laws of same, business acquaintances, anyone with whom they might have had, somewhere in the past half century, a brief chat, a cup of coffee, or shared a train seat—the entire world seemed to want only one boon from Helburn or Langner—a precious pair of on-the-aisle tickets!

An entire body of legends grew up on the subject.

Oscar Hammerstein's tenant farmer in Doylestown asked his landlord for a pair for his son and his future bride, to enable them to see the show after their wedding reception. Oscar promised to arrange it and asked, "When's the wedding?"

"The day you can get us the tickets," promised the farmer.

Lines at the St. James box office never varied. They were long and determined. The box-office people reported threats, cajolery, and out-and-out bribery offers. One of the treasurers reported turning down steaks, nylon stockings, and similar wartime rarities for valuable two-on-the-aisles. Al Hildreth, the head treasurer at the theatre, finally had enough of the daily stress involved in dealing with the crowds, and in September 1944 he turned in his resignation!

A cartoon of the day depicted two affluent businessmen chatting at their club.

Says the first, "I hear you sold your seat on the Exchange."

"Yeah," says the second, "I got a seat at *Oklahoma!*"

Another story, possibly apocryphal, dealt with an undertaker gleefully

During the run of Oklahoma! *at the St. James Theatre, full-size photographs of the principals in the cast were mounted under the Forty-fourth Street marquee. Miraculously, this one of young Bambi Linn has survived for almost half a century, and is reproduced here as a greatly diminished but charming tribute to the dancer. (Courtesy of Bambi Linn)*

arriving at the theatre and announcing he was the bearer of two tickets. When asked where he'd managed to snag them he said, "A body was
brought in, and they were in the coat pocket."

One day there came to the box office a letter mailed from a German
prison camp. It read, "Please reserve tickets for *Oklahoma!* for the following prisoners of war," and it then listed the thirteen names of the senders,
with their ranks.

On a matinee a lady showed up at the theatre bearing a matinee ticket.
It had come in her mail, even though she hadn't ordered it and certainly
hadn't paid for it. The box-office man checked it and reported that the
pasteboard was absolutely valid. Didn't she want to see this show today?
The dubious lady finally agreed to do so. . . . When she returned home,
she discovered that her apartment had been thoroughly burgled.

"The smart set," reported one columnist, "isn't showing off diamonds
at the supper clubs around town. The real flash item is a pair of Saturday
night ducats to *Oklahoma!*"

On another evening, two British officers just arrived in New York turned
up at the St. James to ask for tickets. They were in remarkable luck; the
treasurer was able to produce a precious pair for that very night that had
just been turned in! The two Britishers hesitated and then turned down
the tickets. "Can't be much of a show if you can get tickets *that* easily,"
sniffed one, and they strolled away.

"The New York Fire Department allowed us to bring in a couple of servicemen each night, and we'd have them stand in the wings, backstage,
so they could watch the show," says Elaine Steinbeck. "Of course, they'd
never allow that today, but remember, this was wartime, and everybody
was patriotic about it."

But it was the impact on those fortunate audiences who did manage to get
scarce tickets to the show, who nightly came into the St. James, who sat
back and basked in the glow of the music and its lyrics, the love story,

the ballets, who savored that ultimate, triumphant ending that is the truly remarkable phenomenon that was *Oklahoma!*

Half a century later the show still exercises the same effect on an audience. "If you say to anyone today, 'Yes, we were in *Oklahoma!*'" comments Vivian Smith, "immediately they can remember. Their faces light up, and they can tell you exactly what they were doing and what was happening in their lives when they first saw the show."

"It's as important an evening in their lives as, say, where they were when Pearl Harbor was bombed, or the Kennedy assassination," says Paul Shiers.

Dick Rodgers himself attempted an appraisal of that incredible magnetism the show exercised when he wrote his memoirs. "People would come to see *Oklahoma!* and derive not only pleasure but a measure of optimism. It dealt with pioneers in the Southwest; it showed their spirit and the kinds of problems they had to overcome in carving out a new state; and it gave citizens an appreciation of the hardy stock from which they'd sprung. People said to themselves, in effect, 'If this is what our country looked and sounded like at the turn of the century, perhaps once this war is over we can again return to this kind of buoyant, optimistic life.'"

"Every one of us who was involved in the show suddenly became a star, in a way," remembered Jay Blackton. Suddenly, outside the theatre, every one of us was recognized! People would stop me on the street to tell me how much they enjoyed watching me! Some newspaperman wrote a whole column about me—how I conducted, and when things were going right how I would suddenly burst into a big smile. There I was, leading the orchestra, working and enjoying myself at the same time!"

"Oh, the days after the opening were just magic," says Elaine Steinbeck. "It was *such* a hit! It absolutely blew everyone's mind! The thing I've always regretted was that I didn't stay longer with it. But my first husband, Zack Scott, got himself a Hollywood contract, and I followed him out there, so I had to leave."

The impact was different for Bambi Linn, a hit in her first show. "For me, it was a *school*," she observes today. "I learned how to perform. I learned how to keep a performance up. And Agnes would come in as much as she could, but when she was out front, you knew, of course, and then we really worked like dogs for her. I was grateful that I had two years of *Oklahoma!* It was the very best schooling in the world." When the young ballerina left the show it would be to move on to a leading role as an actress in another Rodgers-Hammerstein-de Mille-Guild success, *Carousel.*

"To have been in the show was a real feather in your cap," says Kate Friedlich. "We all went on to bigger and better things, Agnes took Diana Adams out of the show and put her in as the dance lead in *One Touch of Venus*, and Joanie McCracken went into *Bloomer Girl.* I stayed fifteen months, until my husband came home from the war."

What also took off like a prairie wildfire was the Rodgers and Hammerstein score. Two mornings after the show opened Rodgers was spending the night in a New York hotel off Park Avenue while his family stayed in their Connecticut home. He was awakened in the morning by the sun pouring into his hotel room window and the sound of childish voices below singing something familiar. He looked down below to find a group of children singing, "Oh, What a Beautiful Mornin'." "The show had just opened and they knew the song already!" he said. "What a lovely feeling it was to realize that I was reaching not only the theatregoing adults but their children as well." Nothing Rodgers had written with Larry Hart had ever enjoyed such instant popularity. "People Will Say We're in Love" was the top radio tune of 1943 and sold nine thousand copies a day; "Oh, What a Beautiful Mornin'," four thousand. Less than a year after the opening of the show the millionth copy of the *Oklahoma!* sheet music was presented by the authors to Mayor Fiorello LaGuardia at City Hall.

One of the side effects of this incredible success was the birth of a new kind of recording, the original-cast album. For years the Broadway theatre, which had offered such bounties of music and lyrics during the twenties and the thirties to its audiences, had been ignored on records. Major recording companies would deign to issue singles by star singers and comedy performers, or song hits played by popular orchestras of the day, but

The one millionth copy of the song "Oklahoma" had been printed by December 1943. To commemorate this event, Mayor Fiorello La Guardia came backstage at the St. James and accepted the millionth copy of the sheet music for permanent inclusion in the archives of the City of New York. Left to right are Lawrence Langner, Governor Ernest Gruening of Alaska (obviously happy to have been presented with a pair of choice seats), Mayor La Guardia, Richard Rodgers, Theresa Helburn, and Oscar Hammerstein II. Joining them in the background are Betty Garde, Joan Roberts, Celeste Holm, and Alfred Drake. (Courtesy of Beinecke Library)

rarely, if ever, were record buyers offered the performances of complete Broadway shows by the original cast.

Right after the opening in 1943, Jack Kapp, the visionary, aggressive head of Decca Records, came up with a terrific idea. He approached Rodgers and Hammerstein with a bold concept; he would use the original cast of *Oklahoma!* plus the pit orchestra, conducted by Jay Blackton, playing Robert Russell Bennett's arrangements, and produce an album of recordings which would provide customers with an entire Broadway show. If they couldn't get precious tickets to the show, at least they could take it home in an album and enjoy it there, indefinitely!

If *Oklahoma!* would prove to be a bold watershed event in American musical theatre, Kapp's plan was equal to the event. A deal was quickly struck, and the album went into production. "We brought the whole gang into Decca's studio on West Fifty-seventh Street," says Blackton. "Jack Kapp supervised the recording, with the help of his brother Dave. You have to remember they were making this album on seventy-eight rpm, on twelve-inch records, where the length would be about five minutes. Sometimes a song we'd be recording would time out too long for the record side and Jack would come out of the control booth and say, 'How about it, a little faster, maybe?' So I'd speed up the tempo a bit to fit the record. Take 'Surrey with the Fringe on Top.' I had to cut a whole chorus out of it so it would fit on one side of a twelve-incher."

The album went into the stores and sold steadily thereafter. By the time *Oklahoma!* closed on Broadway, Decca had sold an astonishing eight hundred thousand copies. And from then on, Broadway shows have been preserved for the future with their original casts.

That original-cast album recording from 1943, transferred to an LP, then to a tape cassette, and now to a compact disc, remains on the shelves of your local music store, under BROADWAY. The clerk will attest to its popularity.

And the financial rewards?

Those staunch souls the backers, who'd stood up to be counted, who'd written out the precious checks that enabled the Guild to take *Away We Go!* to New Haven and bring it back to New York as *Oklahoma!* would participate in a long-term bonanza comparable only to winning the lottery.

Contemplate these figures.

In 1943, for the week ending December 25th (traditionally a very poor week in the theatre financially, since ticket buyers are out shopping), the Guild books reveal the following:

On the week's gross (capacity, of course) of $30,814.50, the producers paid their landlords, the Shuberts, a rental for the St. James Theatre of $8,704.00; that left the Guild with $22,110.50. After deducting all the running expenses, i.e., salaries, royalties, expenses, publicity and advertising, taxes, crew expense, office expense, and a special item marked "Christmas Gifts," the operating profit for the week, including "Souvenir Books Income,"* came to a lusty $7,796.56.

* Refers to the souvenir book that was sold in the lobby by the same Al Greenstone who'd purchased a share of the show in the New Haven Shubert.

The week before Christmas is historically considered to be the poorest one for theatre grosses; ticket buyers are out shopping and are too busy to go to shows. Not so for Oklahoma! By December 1943 it was obviously the one show everyone had to see. Selling out each performance, the New York company and the newly launched Chicago company were grossing a remarkable $60,846.50 each week! As you can see from the Guild's own figures, the net weekly profit was an amazing $14,852.01— with much more to come, for many years.

Note, if you will, the income from Mr. Al Greenstone's souvenir book sales in the lobby of the St. James Theatre. Lucky Mr. Greenstone, the satisfied backer who'd bought a "piece" of Oklahoma! in the lobby of the New Haven Shubert. How could he have imagined, in his fondest dreams, that he'd acquired a "piece" of a bonanza?

		No. 1 New York	No. 2 Chicago
Oklahoma			
Week Ended December 25, 1943			
Box Office Receipts.		$30,814.50	$30,032.00
Company Share.		22,110.50	22,524.00
EXPENSES:			
Salaries:			
Company.		6,123.06	5,770.09
Crew		855.00	670.00
Wardrobe		321.00	388.50
Musicians.		250.00	765.02
Press Agent.		165.00	200.00
Company Manager.		125.00	165.00
Pianist.		45.00	
Extra Musicians.		1,355.70	831.60
Extra Stage Hands.		126.68	378.00
Authors Royalty.		2,465.17	2,382.56
Directors Percentage		505.15	375.32
Dance Director		50.00	75.00
Department Expenses:			
Carpenter.			150.77
Property		19.59	68.78
Electric		25.73	339.60
Wardrobe		53.91	52.35
Publicity:			
Newspaper.		711.79	544.18
Printing			345.00
Billposting.		186.92	
Photos		170.67	
Frames		16.34	
Mailing.			43.30
Press Agent Expenses		52.28	18.62
Other.		12.50	12.50
Railroad			40.63
Rehearsal Expense.		50.00	
Insurance.		44.94	46.13
League Dues.		10.00	10.00
Company Manager Expenses		9.26	51.28
Social Security Taxes.		110.93	296.09
City Excise Taxes.		11.06	
Audit.		25.00	25.00
Crew Expense		189.00	
Christmas Gifts.		1,190.20	259.08
Office Expense		250.00	250.00
TOTAL EXPENSES		15,317.19	14,465.50
OPERATING PROFIT		6,793.31	8,058.70
Add: Souvenir Books Income		1,005.25	
TOTAL PROFIT		$ 7,798.56	$ 8,058.70

$100.00 REWARD

HAVE YOU BEEN VICTIMIZED ON YOUR TICKETS FOR "OKLAHOMA!"?

If you have been victimized by speculators in your purchase of seats for "Oklahoma!", you can help us put a stop to this by furnishing us with information as to where and when you and your friends were forced to pay excessive prices.

You will be rendering both us and the theatregoing public a service by furnishing us with this information, and we will gladly pay the above reward for your assistance in disciplining speculators. Please write us enclosing your ticket stubs and a letter stating all the facts, addressed to the personal attention of Miss Theresa Helburn or Mr. Lawrence Langner, Theatre Guild, Inc., 245 West 52nd Street, New York City 19.

The theatre tickets for "Oklahoma!" are sold: (a) at the Box Office. (b) by mail orders addressed to the Box Office. (c) through ticket brokers under the Theatre Ticket Code established by The League of New York Theatres and the Actors Equity Association and licensed by the Commissioner of Licenses. Under the New York State Law, Licensed ticket brokers are not permitted to charge more than 83c on orchestra seats and 55c on 1st balcony seats over and above the price printed on the ticket. If you have paid more, you have been victimized, and we will be glad to pay the above reward for information resulting in the disciplining of such law breakers.

Ticket buyers who had been forced to pay "speculators" as much as $50 a pair for precious Oklahoma! seats—not outrageous at all by today's prices, but in 1943 a staggering sum—were cautioned by the Guild to help stamp out this practice.

Since by that month the national company was already thriving in Chicago and showing a weekly net profit of $8,058.70, the total profit for that one week would be a heartwarming $15,855.26. Multiply that sum by fifty-two weeks and we come to a total of $824,473.52 in profits, to be divided between the Guild and the investors.

According to the Guild's own recap, when *Oklahoma!* closed on Broadway on May 29, 1948, after playing 2,212 performances, it would have been seen by over 4,500,000 paying customers and amassed a total gross of over $7 million for the fortunate few who'd invested. Their eventual payoff from all sources would be over 2,500 percent on their original investment.

Translation into dollars? One thousand dollars would return a staggering $2,500,000.*

A staggering return, indeed. Small wonder that for months after the opening Helburn and Langner would meet with Rodgers and Hammerstein for weekly luncheons to discuss strategy and future plans. They called such get-togethers meetings of "The Three Hour Gloat Club." But, as Cap'n Andy said in *Show Boat*, "only the beginning, folks, only the beginning!"

By 1944, when *Oklahoma!* was awarded a special Pulitzer Prize, it had already become something of a phenomenon. No Broadway musical had ever had such an impact on audiences. A national company had been quickly assembled and was touring, so successfully that the Guild promptly launched a second road company. In Chicago, the show settled down for a sold-out run of fourteen months.

The army and navy asked for a production to tour the Pacific, and eventually the "War Company" played its first one-night stand, on a far-off (and unnamed) tropical island. "By floodlight," Helburn later reported. "In the

---

*"I remember Phyllis Langner, Lawrence's daughter from his first marriage, had a birthday during the winter of 1943," says Elaine Steinbeck. "And Lawrence gave her a piece of the show as a gift. Phyllis mentioned it to me and she said, 'Isn't that the lousiest, crummiest birthday present you ever heard of?'"

steaming hot darkness. The cyclorama was a tangle of twisted banyans and cabbage palms. The curtain was a sheet of silver rain. . . . Thousands of wounded boys, stretcher cases, lay there watching at the jungle's edge. They lifted their bandaged hands in applause. The boys whistled in the dark 'Oh, What a Beautiful Mornin'.' Our youngsters played to the most distinguished first night they were ever to face. They sang with tears in their throats. . . ." Before its travels ended, that USO touring company had played to an estimated million and a half homesick troops, who'd gratefully absorbed its message from home of joy and strength.

An English company, produced by the Guild, opened at the venerable Drury Lane Theatre in London on May 1, 1947. Some thirty-six hours before the curtain rose, lines of ticket buyers formed at the box office and continued to pack that huge theatre for the next three and a half years. The gross "takings" would reach an astonishing 1,324,500 pounds, paid in by nearly three million war-weary British, grateful for the opportunity to bask in the glow of the sunlit sagebrush and prairie, exported to them from the colonies.

"Agnes de Mille took the musical out into the Middle West and invented for it a jollier, more masculine style of dancing that the English never attempted," wrote Quentin Crisp, forty-odd years later. "In Britain, when I was young, a musical had a love-misunderstanding-reunion storyline enacted by a pretty boy and girl while behind them a line of chorus boys and girls did nothing more than link arms and kick their height. When *Oklahoma!* arrived, the theatre—nay, the entire city—shook."

Figuring in the revenues from all these sources, plus what would eventually be derived from the film rights, stock rights, and amateur royalties et al., it's a safe assumption that in the past half century no single Broadway show has ever returned as much for its dauntless investors as has Helburn's Folly.

And lest anyone suspect that those same backers were unmindful of their great good fortune, consider the following letter from Mr. Al Greenstone, that gentleman who'd invested during the intermission in the

AL GREENSTONE

145 WEST 45th STREET :·: NEW YORK

Telephone: BRyant 9-3591

June 21, 1943

Mr. Lawrence Langner
Theatre Guild
245 West 52nd Street
New York, N.Y.

Dear Mr. Langner:

This letter and enclosure will surprise you, as I do not think you know who I am.

I am the man who has been making the
souvenir programs for the Theatre Guild for nearly
twenty years. I recently invested a little money in
"OKLAHOMA", and I feel that I must show my appreciation,
not only for making these books for the Theatre Guild
for all these years, but also for the fact that I was
allowed to buy a small share in this wonderful show.
My investment was not strictly business. I never do
this, but I thought possibly I could be lucky to the
Theatre Guild. My good intentions turned out very lucky
for me, and I feel I want to share my good luck with
the people who have been responsible for the great
success of "OKLAHOMA", and also for the fact that I have
been with your organization for so many years. I have
also sent one of these checks to Miss Helburn.

Hoping for more "OKLAHOMAS", and that
I will be able to say hello to you in the near future,
I remain,

Gratefully,

AL GREENSTONE

OKLAHOMA!

Cast in order of appearance :

Aunt Eller ... ... , ...	MARY MARLO
Curly	HAROLD KEEL
Laurey	BETTY JANE WATSON
Ike Skidmore	THOMAS SPENCER
Fred	ELLIOT MARTIN
Slim	Wm. SUTHERLAND
Will Parker	WALTER DONAHUE
Jud Fry	HENRY CLARKE
Ado Annie Carnes...	DOROTHEA MACFARLAND
Ali Hakim	MAREK WINDHEIM
Gertie Cummings ... ...' ...	JACQUELINE DANIELS
Ellen	SUZANNE LLOYD
Kate	MARJORIE AUSTIN
Sylvie	BEATRICE LYNN
Armina	ISABEL BIGLEY
Aggie " Pigtails."	MARGARET AULD NELSON
Andrew Carnes	WM. J. McCARTHY
Cord Elam	LEONARD MENCE
Jess	REMINGTON OLMSTEAD, Jr.
Chalmers	ERIK KRISTEN
Joe	WALTER PETERSON
Sam	ROBERT PATTERSON

TIME
Just after the turn of the century

PLACE STATE OF
Indian Territory (Now Oklahoma)-U S A.

ACT I
Scene 1. The Front of Laurey's Farm House
Scene 2. The Smoke House
Scene 3. A Grove on Laurey's Farm

ACT II
Scene 1. The Skidmore Ranch
Scene 2. Skidmore's Kitchen Porch
Scene 3. The Back of Laurey's Farm House

(handwritten notes in margin: "DENIZE DE LANOE", "X?")

When the American troupe arrived in 1947 to open the show at the Drury Lane, London was a tired city, one whose population had endured years of wartime blitzes, shortages, and devastation. Despite the fact the war was over, it appeared to the troupe that Londoners had had little opportunity to express their collective joy. When the curtain fell on that first Oklahoma! finale, the English audience stood and cheered. They refused to leave the theatre without hearing some of the songs again. As one witness remarked, "That night was such magic. The show touched a responsive nerve in all of us. We never wanted to go home."

Take a moment to examine these two programs closely and you will become aware of one of the major issues in the theatre, i.e., billing.

In June 1943 the program for the new hit carries the demure line, "Production under the supervision of Theresa Helburn and Lawrence Langner." Now turn to the following year. For July 1944 the billing has been reversed (as per prior agreement between Helburn and Langner). But even more revealing is the positioning of said billing. Since the show had become such a major, roaring success, is it not only right that the producers ordained that their names be moved up, to a position above the cast? And be set in bold type?

Week beginning Sunday, June 13, 1943 • Matinees Thursday and Saturday

THE THEATRE GUILD

presents

OKLAHOMA!

A Musical Play
Based on the play "Green Grow the Lilacs" by Lynn Riggs

Music by RICHARD RODGERS
Book and Lyrics by OSCAR HAMMERSTEIN 2d
Production directed by ROUBEN MAMOULIAN
Dances by AGNES de MILLE

Settings by   Costumes by
LEMUEL AYERS   MILES WHITE

With

BETTY GARDE   ALFRED DRAKE   JOSEPH BULOFF   JOAN ROBERTS
LEE DIXON   HOWARD da SILVA   CELESTE HOLM   RALPH RIGGS
                 MARC PLATT   KATHARINE SERGAVA

Orchestra directed by Jacob Schwartzdorf
Orchestrations by Russell Bennett
Production under the supervision of
Theresa Helburn and Lawrence Langner

Week beginning Sunday, July 2, 1944 • Matinees Thursday and Saturday

THE THEATRE GUILD

presents

OKLAHOMA!

A Musical Play
Based on the play "Green Grow the Lilacs" by Lynn Riggs

Music by RICHARD RODGERS
Book and Lyrics by OSCAR HAMMERSTEIN 2nd
Production directed by ROUBEN MAMOULIAN
Dances by AGNES de MILLE

Settings by   Costumes by
LEMUEL AYERS   MILES WHITE

Production supervised by
LAWRENCE LANGNER and THERESA HELBURN

With

BETTY GARDE   HARRY STOCKWELL   JOSEPH BULOFF   EVELYN WYCKOFF
LEE DIXON   MURVYN VYE   EDNA SKINNER   RALPH RIGGS
DAVID TIHMAR   KATHARINE SERGAVA VLADIMIR KOSTENKO

Orchestra directed by Arthur Norris

Orchestrations by Russell Bennett

Shubert lobby in New Haven on opening night by taking on some of Max Gordon's "piece"—and who enjoyed his subsequent profits with such gratitude that he decided to respond in kind.

As for Hammerstein, when he journeyed back to Doylestown to begin work on his adaptation of Bizet's *Carmen*, he couldn't possibly know that he had turned a major corner in his career.

On January 4, 1944, when *Variety*, the bible of show business, published its yearly holiday issue in which show business figures traditionally take full-page advertisements to let the world know of their latest achievements, Hammerstein took an ad of his own. In the past year, he had produced the libretto and lyrics for *Oklahoma!* and had done the same for *Carmen Jones*. Both shows were smash Broadway hits. To paraphrase one of his own lyrics, success was busting out all over for Oscar. Hammerstein's ad, which has since become a show business legend, read:

Holiday Greetings
from
Oscar Hammerstein, II
author of
Sunny River (6 weeks at The St. James)
Very Warm For May (7 weeks at The Alvin)
Three Sisters (7 weeks at The Drury Lane)
Ball At The Savoy (5 weeks at The Drury Lane)
Free For All (3 weeks at The Manhattan)

"I've Done It Before And I Can Do It Again!"

Such modesty is rarely, if ever, memorialized in print. But then, as he demonstrated so often in his lyrics, Hammerstein had a gift for honesty, one he was never afraid to express in public.

Browse through a Playbill from 1943, the year that Oklahoma! arrived, and it would seem there was a dazzling array of entertainments available to wartime theatregoers.

But now examine the following season. By 1944, consider all the various attractions from the previous year that have closed and been trundled off to Cain's Warehouse, to be replaced by new and hopeful offerings. Of the sixteen shows that were running the previous year, only Oklahoma!, Angel Street, and Ziegfeld Follies remain. Truly, there is no business like show business, is there?

If *Oklahoma!*'s amazing success was beneficial for its management and creators, it was equally helpful to the careers of actors and actresses in the cast. Alfred Drake would sign a contract with Columbia, the fiefdom of

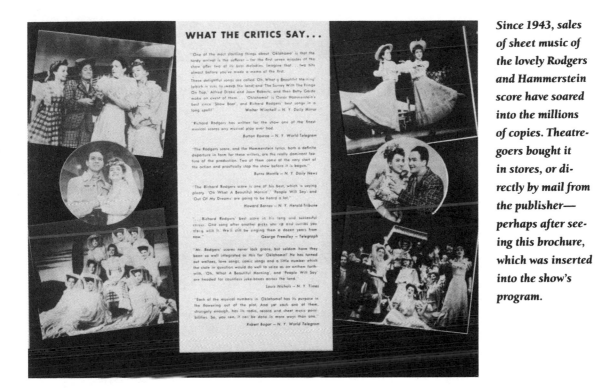

WHAT THE CRITICS SAY...

Since 1943, sales
of sheet music of
the lovely Rodgers
and Hammerstein
score have soared
into the millions
of copies. Theatre-
goers bought it
in stores, or di-
rectly by mail from
the publisher—
perhaps after see-
ing this brochure,
which was inserted
into the show's
program.

Harry Cohn, who'd stepped in where other angels feared to tread. Cohn also signed up Marc Platt, who went to the Coast and proceeded to appear in a series of Columbia musicals. Drake did only one, *Tars and Spars*, and then returned to New York. "The theatre was always my turf," he said. "Films weren't for me." In the years following he would star in *Kiss Me Kate*, *Kismet*, *Kean*, and a string of other shows.

Howard Da Silva, whose career following his role as Jud Fry would go into eclipse due to political blacklist, survived to reemerge on Broadway, starring as Benjamin Franklin in *1776*. George Irving, who left *Oklahoma!* to join the army, returned after the war and has been ever since a very busy musical comedy star.

Since she first explained to us that she couldn't say no, Celeste Holm continues with affirmatives, without pause. Long before anyone defined the term "bicoastal", the lady went to Hollywood to win an Academy Award for her performance in *All About Eve* then returned to New York. Onstage she starred in *Bloomer Girl* and a string of other successes; to this day she plays leads in films, television, and the theatre.

Before her untimely passing, Joan McCracken played leads in *Bloomer Girl*, *Billion Dollar Baby*, and Rodgers and Hammerstein's *Me and Juliet*.

For another member of the cast there was a sad finale. Lee Dixon, that agile and charming hoofer who stopped the show with *Kansas City*, was an alcoholic. "We adored him, and the audiences loved him—Oscar said he'd written the part of Will Parker for Lee, but it was difficult having him," says Elaine Steinbeck. "We would always keep his understudy, Paul Shiers, ready to go on for Dixie, every day that first year, because he just sometimes wouldn't show up. He always delivered when he went on, and the audiences adored him, he was a wonderful performer, but it was a losing battle."

"He was a trouper, even when he was drunk," comments Paul Shiers, remembering back to those early days. "It began when he was in the touring company at the St. Louis Municipal Opera. They'd tell him his first line and push him out on the stage, and once he was out there off he'd go, and he could do it—by reflex! But you could never be sure, so Jerry Whyte, the stage manager, would have me standing by, to sing either the first, or the second act—who knew if Lee could finish it?"

"When I got out to California I met Lee—after he'd left the show," says Celeste Holm. "Oh, it was so sad. He wasn't well at all, had some awful things wrong, and he said to me, 'Oh, God, Celeste, I wish I were back in *Oklahoma!* again.'"

And what of Larry Hart?

Riggs's play *wasn't* his kind of show. It was a joyful, high-spirited affair, about honest-to-God rough-hewn frontier types, with ballet dancing and two young lovers and a brooding menace overhanging their simple story.

It was nothing at all like the flip, glib, highly sophisticated Rodgers and Hart musicals that he and his partner had turned out with such success. Larry could write wonderful love songs, certainly, but his true metier with its sardonic overtones was as far removed from Oklahoma at the turn of the century as Oscar Hammerstein was from Pal Joey's saga amid John O'Hara's nightclubs.

Alan Jay Lerner, who would become a very successful librettist and lyricist in his own right, came down from Harvard and was living in Manhattan. A dedicated Larry Hart fan, he became a close friend of the man in 1943, and when he wrote his own autobiography, years later, he remembered Hart well. "Larry's pain must have been unbearable. One of the saddest moments I can remember happened a few months after the musical opened. We were in Fritz Loewe's living room. There was a blackout, and the room was pitch dark. The only light was from Larry's cigar. Fritz turned on the radio and an orchestra was playing something from *Oklahoma!* The end of the cigar flashed brighter and brighter with accelerated puffs. Fritz immediately switched to another station. Again, someone was playing a song from *Oklahoma!* And Larry's cigar grew brighter and the puffs became faster. It happened three times and then Fritz turned off the radio. The glow from the cigar subsided and the breathing became so slow Larry's cigar almost went out. The whole incident probably took less than two minutes and during it not a word was said, but I wept for him in the dark. The moment the lights came on, Larry continued the conversation that had been interrupted by the blackout without a trace of what had happened in his voice or on his face."

In the style of an operatic libretto, the unhappy coda to Hart's life ground on to an inevitable closing.

Rodgers, empathetic to the pain which Hart must be suffering, did not turn away. Eventually, he and their old mutual friend and fellow worker Herbert Fields came up with a solution. They proposed a revival of their twenties success, *A Connecticut Yankee*.

Rodgers approached Warner Brothers, a film company that had a record of investing successfully in Broadway shows, one dating back to 1929, when it had bankrolled Cole Porter's *Fifty Million Frenchmen*. He offered the project to Jake Wilk, my father, who was the executive story editor and who also had complete charge of the company's theatrical activities. The prospect of such a revival was a tempting one, especially since Rodgers was now certainly the hottest composer in the business. Quickly and enthusiastically, Warner Brothers bankrolled Rodgers.

In the early fall of 1943 the revival of *Connecticut Yankee* began rehearsals, destined to open at the Martin Beck Theatre. According to Rodgers, Hart went to work on a regular schedule; he collaborated on the new songs that were needed, and he abstained from liquor. The results were remarkable. Hart's work was consistently completed on time, and he applied himself, usually up at Rodgers's Connecticut home, all through the writing and then during the New York rehearsals. He supplied Rodgers with his customary brilliant lyrics; the wit of "To Keep My Love Alive," with its three choruses of incredibly clever jokes in which Morgan Le Fay, played by Hart's old friend Vivienne Segal, describes how she disposed of her many husbands, has long been treasured by Hart's fans.

But once the show went out of town, to Philadelphia, Hart fell off the wagon; he went back to the bottle with a vengeance. Obviously the stress of the enforced abstinence was too much. By the time *Connecticut Yankee* began previewing in New York, Hart was totally out of control. On opening night Rodgers was so worried about Larry's condition that he instructed two men from the company to stand by Hart as he weaved back and forth in the rear of the theatre. Rodgers's concern was correct; in the midst of the first act Hart began babbling incoherently to the actors onstage. The two men picked him up and took him home.

"I believe Fritz [Loewe] was the last one to see him alive," wrote Lerner. "Larry had a cousin who was a close friend of Fritz, and late one night he called Fritz, worried because he could not find Larry. It was about three in the morning and raining heavily. Fritz went out looking for him. He found him sitting in the gutter outside a bar on Eighth Avenue, drunk and drenched to the skin. He put him in a cab and took him to Delmonico's, where Larry was staying at the time. He made Larry promise he would go upstairs and go to bed, and he stayed in the cab until he saw him enter the hotel. Then he went home. Larry, true to his promise, went up to his room and got into bed. When he fell asleep he never awakened. He had contracted pneumonia. . . . Life had ended for him much earlier, and death was but a formality."

He died in Doctors Hospital, on the night of November 22, 1943. Rodgers and his wife were keeping vigil downstairs; suddenly there was an air-raid alert in Manhattan and the lights went out. When the doctor emerged from the hospital room to tell Rodgers that Hart had died, suddenly the lights went on again. "To those of us in the hospital that night," wrote Rodgers, "the lights going on again at that moment was some sort of cosmic assurance that the darkness which had always surrounded Larry had suddenly disappeared—that in death he could at last enjoy the warmth and brightness that had eluded him all his life."

Hart wrote his own epitaph and farewell to Rodgers.

It is the verse to a song in *Connecticut Yankee* and it goes:

> You can count your friends
> On the fingers of your hand,
> If you're lucky, you have two.
> I have just two friends,
> That is all I demand,
> Only two, just me and you.

The title of their last collaboration was "Can't You Do a Friend a Favor?"

To mark the first anniversary of Oklahoma! the Guild hosted a heck of a hoe-down in The Hay Loft at the Astor Hotel. Invitations 19½ inches long, printed on heavy parchment, promised the singing and dancing talents of Mister Ali Hakimstein (aka Oscar Hammerstein) and Mister Will Parker Rodgers (aka Richard Rodgers). Two-Gun Larry (Langner) and Oklahoma Terry (Helburn) were also expected to appear, "By Special Arrangement with The Theatre Guild."

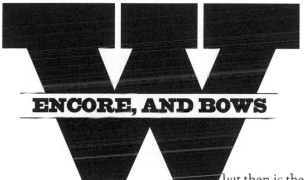

ENCORE, AND BOWS

hat then is the reason that this remarkable musical show goes on, season after season, for a half century now, pleasing ticket buyers everywhere, from Las Cruces, New Mexico, to Darien, Connecticut, and points south? Charming customers of every age group, from energetic high-schoolers to AARP members? *Oklahoma!* is by far the most popular work in the Rodgers and Hammerstein catalogue; it is performed in over six hundred different theatres each and every year.

New audiences keep discovering it; old audiences keep coming back to it. What accounts for this insistent popularity?

Interviewed some years back, Oscar Hammerstein remarked, "It has no particular message. It imparts a flavor which infects the people who see it.

It's gutsy. *Oklahoma!* is youthful, and irresponsible, and not very intellectual, but it has a heartiness of life."

Other musicals have emerged from Broadway in recent years that can certainly be said to spread heartiness, and they may or may not be revived this year in Las Cruces. Why then *Oklahoma!*?

Stephen Sondheim, our primary composer-lyricist for more than thirty years in the ever-narrowing Broadway musical arena, believes *Oklahoma!* has retained such a permanent presence on the American scene for very pragmatic reasons.

It has to do firstly with kids, even though the show is not about kids. Here's a show with seven or eight principal roles, a dancing chorus, and from a performance point of view that makes it very attractive. Easy to do on a number of levels.

Carousel is much more difficult to do. *South Pacific* is topical; and remember, there are lots of people who don't know about World War II. *The King and I* is tough to cast. *Sound of Music* is done a lot, but it's a much more complex show. *Oklahoma!*—well, it's a reliable. Wonderfully high-spirited, and it won't offend anybody. Take *Gypsy*. It can be a hit on Broadway, or on tour, but it *won't* be done in high schools or community theatres—it's vaguely raunchy, remember, it has some four letter words, and it's a vehicle for one strong leading lady and two strong supporting actors.

Or there's my own *A Funny Thing Happened on the Way to the Forum*, which the kids may also want to produce but which gets stopped in many local high schools simply because it has the word "virgin" in it! But *Oklahoma!*—well, there are those terrific songs, and most of all, it's a very *comfortable* show, both for the cast and the Middle American audience.

Is it the sheer efficiency, then, that keeps *Oklahoma!* so popular year after year? Well, it certainly helps.

But there are other shows equally as efficient for production that do not

WE HAVE
NO TICKETS
for "OKLAHOMA!"
AND CERTAINLY NONE
for "Carousel"
AND DON'T EVEN MENTION
"O MISTRESS MINE"

For years following its opening in 1943, tickets for Oklahoma! continued to be scarce. This sign appeared at the St. James (both Carousel and O Mistress Mine were Guild hits).

The original Curly and Laurey, Alfred Drake and Joan Roberts. Ten sell-out years later, the Guild had replaced them with Florence Henderson (later to be a star in her own right) and Ralph Lowe. (Courtesy of Beinecke Library)

The happy participants came together in October 1947 to celebrate the fourth anniversary of their wildly successful musical. On Broadway, on tour, and in London, Oklahoma! was well on its way to becoming an American classic. Who can blame all these creative people for smiling?

Left to right are Helburn, Hammerstein, de Mille, Marshall, Rodgers, and Langner. (Courtesy of Beinecke Library)

Agnes de Mille and ballerina Joan McCracken joyfully demonstrate a ballet movement in preparation for the gala fourth anniversary show celebrating the opening of Oklahoma!

Three of the dancers who were associated with Oklahoma! during its five-year run on Broadway join choreographer Agnes de Mille (second from right) in celebrating the fifth birthday of the show, on March 31, 1948. Left to right are Dania Krupska, a member of the cast for two years, and original members Joan McCracken and Bambi Linn. (Associated Press photograph/Courtesy of Mark Barrow)

A fifth-anniversary cake is the centerpiece of this celebration. Left to right are Langner, Rodgers, Helburn, Mamoulian, Ayers, Hammerstein, de Mille, and White. (Courtesy of Beinecke Library) faze the most nervous of groups. *Bye, Bye Birdie*, for one, and *The Fanta-sticks*, for another. Somehow they do not touch the same nerve in audiences as does *Oklahoma!*

Miles White offers another reason. He looks back on the show that he costumed and he murmurs fondly, "It has truth imbedded in it."

Just so.

Dick Rodgers, who for years afterward was fond of quoting his laundry list of reasons why *Oklahoma!* could not possibly have succeeded (Oscar Hammerstein hadn't had a hit in twelve years or so; the Theatre Guild on the verge of bankruptcy; a totally starless cast in a story that dealt with cowboys and farmers; a choreographer who'd never done anything on Broadway; no girls until forty-five minutes after the rise of the curtain and then none of them revealing a single shapely leg, and even less showing above; no rousing number to open the show; and on and on), later tried to articulate what positive force *was* the core of the show's powerful and lasting impact.

In his autobiography he said, "The chief influence of *Oklahoma!* was simply to serve notice that when writers come up with something different, and it had merit, there would be a large and receptive audience waiting for it. From *Oklahoma!* on, with only rare exceptions, the memorable productions have been those daring to break free from the conventional mode."

Certainly, during those World War II years, the magical glow that the St. James Theatre stage gave off each evening toured up and down the land and eventually went to war-weary Great Britain is easier to understand. Those of us who were lucky enough to have snagged precious tickets to the show when it was playing back then have no problem explaining our joyful if almost Pavlovian reaction to the story of Curly and Laurey. *Oklahoma!* gave us and our families a reason to get this war over. Happier times, it promised, lay ahead. We didn't need a Yellow Brick Road; that Oklahoma prairie would more than suffice. What Rodgers and Hammerstein et al. had presented us with was a lovely two-hour promissory note set to music that we could take back home. It sent us out of the theatre charged with hope (remember those servicemen always standing in the back, ready to leave for parts unknown), it did good work in the military hospitals (where its songs were sung), and it traveled out to the tropical atolls and to the army camp theatres where USO troupes could spread the reassurance in those two acts. It said to the servicemen, *Be of good cheer*—the time will soon come when you and your lady will climb into your own private surrey with the fringe on top, and you'll ride off to a happy ending.

But the war years are long over. Even though in the past fifty years we've traveled through two more ugly periods and weathered dreadful back-washes from them that tore us all apart, *Oklahoma!* audiences are no longer preoccupied with wartime tensions. New generations who aren't service-men separated from their families or parents waiting for them to come home have grown up with the show.

Perhaps audiences today are far more sophisticated than the crowd at the St. James that stood up and cheered on opening night. Perhaps that's why they respond to the simplicity of the show. It's the same reason that Hammerstein himself would brush away a tear when Curly and Laurey went riding in the surrey. Their innocence touched him.

As it will touch others, tonight, when Ado Annie explains her sexual appetites, or when Laurey and Curly embrace, or when the dancers begin to leap through de Mille's choreography.

Never forget the impact of her ballets, those marvelous creations that Agnes de Mille assembled in such a frenzy of creativity down in that drafty, dusty lobby of the Guild Theatre as she sipped from endless containers of lukewarm coffee and urged on her young dancers to leaps and bounds of near-perfection.

John Martin, then the dance critic of the *New York Times*, commented soon after the show opened, "She has a genius for capturing human people of whatever locale or social level in their simplest and most honest phrases, ridiculing them sometimes, fairly devastating them at others, and still making them seem like members of a mighty likeable race." Those ballets

had an enormous impact on audiences then, as now. In fact, from that 1943 opening night on, for years to come, it was the rare Broadway musical that would raise its opening curtain without some form of ballet derived (often forthrightly stolen) from the basic patterns provided by de Mille.

Alan Jay Lerner, himself a respected craftsman in the field, wryly assessed de Mille's enormous impact of what followed in his 1963 summing-up. "Year after year," he wrote, "up and down Broadway, everybody was 'integrating' all over the place, until sadly, but inevitably, the dream ballet became a veritable nightmare. Because *Oklahoma!* had mined its gold in American soil, and early American soil at that, from *Bloomer Girl* down to *The Music Man* and *The Unsinkable Molly Brown* hardly a season passed on Broadway without girls having fellers and everybody singin' and dancin'." (Ironically, Lerner chose to omit any mention of his own contribution to the genre; he and Loewe had succumbed to the call of the frontier and the mountains in 1951 with their own *Paint Your Wagon*.)

"But de Mille's special kind of lyricism required a special kind of lyricism in book and treatment," wrote Lerner, "and by the end of the forties, musical books started hardening up and heading down a more realistic road. In *South Pacific*, *The King and I*, *My Fair Lady*, and *Camelot*, choreography varied from nonexistent to the isolated ballet and local color. Only with Jerome Robbins did it retain its dramatic and theatrical lustre, as in *West Side Story* and *Fiddler on the Roof*."

Since then other choreographers have built entire shows on their individual styles: Gower Champion, Bob Fosse, Michael Kidd, Danny Daniels, Tommy Tune, and of course Michael Bennett. Bennett's *Chorus Line*, which is the ultimate dancers' show, outran *Oklahoma!* by a country mile. On Broadway. But will it remain as deeply imbedded in Middle America's affection? We shall need another half century before we can assess that.

Perhaps the magic response *Oklahoma!* induces comes from Lynn Riggs's play and that marvelous Hammerstein libretto. "Wholesome and sweet, in the unaffected way that a fairy tale is," said *Life* magazine's critic in 1943. Wholesome and sweet the show may be, but that critic's euphoria beclouded his memory of the threat of sexual violence that the character of Jud represents and of the second-act killing.

"A musical in the twenties and the thirties had no dramatic validity and the wit was the lyric writer's, never the characters'," Lerner commented in 1963. "Oscar Hammerstein, on the other hand, was very much a dramatic lyric writer, and with *Oklahoma!* he and Dick Rodgers radically changed the course of the musical theatre. The musical comedy became a play."

Certainly then we must look and listen to that great Rodgers and Hammerstein score, in which each and every song provides us with such insights into the character singing it and impels the show so beautifully toward the finale. Shall we assume that the music and lyrics are the major magic element of the show's lasting strength?

Perhaps, perhaps not. Has *Oklahoma!* a better score than, say, *Carousel*, with its lovely ballads, airy duets, and rollicking chorus numbers, even more melodious Rodgers waltzes, and for icing on the cake that marvelous party piece of every qualified baritone, the "Soliloquy"? Is it better than their score to *The King and I* or *The Sound of Music* or *South Pacific*, all of which are certain to be played and sung so long as there are the voices to perform them?

Such comparisons are foolish and make no point. Weighing *Oklahoma!* against the other R-and-H works, one merely ends up dealing with personal prejudices. It's as pointless an exercise as trying to compare Rodgers and Hart songs with those of Rodgers with Hammerstein. The argument reaches one conclusion. Wonderful either way, merely different.

Alan Lerner's final assessment of *Oklahoma!* was "not an operetta, nor a musical comedy, but a musical play, in which libretto, music and lyrics and dancing were all fused together into one living experience." Three decades later he seems to have found the precise word that explains the impact of the show. *Experience.*

Almost half a century since she made such a massive contribution to the show's success, Agnes de Mille agrees. "The show is good. I see it every so often and I say, 'My God, this is put together with real skill! The way the songs are introduced, and the way they are reintroduced—it's all done with such expertise!' " And what of the opinion, so long advocated by the critics and theatre historians, this author included, that *Oklahoma!* was *the* watershed show of the forties, the single production that would change, in that one night in March 1943, the entire direction of the American musical comedy? Miss de Mille sighs, and then she shakes her head. "Perhaps," she remarks, "but it has all come back to where it was, hasn't it?" she comments sadly. "Before *Oklahoma!*".

"Not so!" rebuts Hal Prince, our leading producer-director whose *Evita*, *Phantom of the Opera*, and a string of collaborations with Sondheim have provided milestones to what's left of our musical theatre. "*Oklahoma!* came at a time when there was an absolute surfeit of damned foolishness in the musical theatre," he remarks. "That show had the shivering, shattering effect of saying 'It *can* be different, totally different!'

"Remember, there had been other watershed shows before it arrived. *Show Boat*, which I'm preparing now for a new production—not a revival, but a restaged version, with new thinking. And another such a show was *Porgy and Bess*. Remember how it opened, with an empty stage and somebody off singing 'Summertime'? You had to know something was happening, something new. And not so far from 'Oh, What a Beautiful Mornin',' now, was it?

"I am one of Agnes's firmest admirers," says Prince. "She is a genius. She took the dancers in *Oklahoma!* and integrated them into Oscar's book—a massive step. Jerry Robbins came along, fourteen years later, took the dancers another step forward, in *West Side Story*, and made them all into leading characters. Major, massive steps forward.

"But I disagree with Agnes about Broadway being back to where it was before *Oklahoma!* People like to write that the Broadway musical is trapped where Steve and I put it, in *Company* and *A Little Night Music*. So be it. But the musical theatre has to move on to the *next* phase," he says firmly. "And right now, there's nobody around to nurture that next step. It won't be me—I won't work on Broadway. There's no *there* there. So when that next phase in the musical theatre comes, it'll probably have to be done somewhere else, not on 'Broadway,' which doesn't exist anymore!

"You know, I was just a kid when I first saw *Oklahoma!*" muses Prince. "And I also went to see the revival of Rodgers and Hart's *A Connecticut Yankee* that same week back in 1943. It was an amazing contrast. I remember saying, 'Look at that—there's a big change here!' In the one show, singers like Vivienne Segal doing chorus after chorus of brilliant Hart lyrics, such as 'To Keep My Love Alive,' and nobody could ever do that again, or even try it today—and in the other show, Oscar Hammerstein breaking *every* rule! Remarkable, the contrast.

"Oscar was totally revolutionary," says Prince from the perspective of almost five decades later, "and Dick was totally willing. But," he adds, "if Oscar were around today, he'd probably be asking questions about

An Oklahoma! revival at Connecticut's Broadway Theatre, 1991, in Darien, nine miles south of Westport, where it all began half a century ago. (Courtesy of Connecticut Broadway Theatre)

the libretto of *Oklahoma!* as it stands. And if somebody were interested in doing a first-class revival of it here on Broadway—or what passes for Broadway—Oscar would certainly be asking questions, say, about the chorus—'Do we really *need* the entire chorus here—could we maybe try to find some other way of doing this number without them?'

"So I repeat what I said," Prince concludes. "I think dear Agnes is wrong about today. It's not all back to where it *was* on Broadway, not at all. It's merely paused—waiting for the next phase." One hopes Hal Prince is correct.

Libretto? Truth? An experience, or a glorious example of creative rule-breaking that reaches out and touches its audience?

If we cannot agree on what specifically keeps *Oklahoma!* so alive all these seasons after it opened, one thing is certain. The more our world spins madly on, and Japanese cowboys now roam the Montana ranges, the more we need Curly and all his other Oklahoma pals. If factories are closing across the landscape, then Will Parker must still reassure us that things are up-to-date in Kansas City. And if heavy-metal rock and rapid-fire angry rap are reducing love to mere mechanically amplified sex, Laurey and Curly can reassure us there still remains another aspect to the male and female experience, something called romance. In a hard-edged world populated by Miss Saigon, de-clawed Cats, and French revolutionaries storming the barricades, *Oklahoma!* remains our precious promissory note on an America that was. Perhaps it is a fantasy. Is that so terrible when it's an America that most of us fervently hope will someday return even though we know it won't?

All we must do is dim the houselights, raise the curtain, and there it is, the prairie. The prairie that was, preserved for us, and, as Curly begins singing offstage, it comes floating out towards us.

For that permanent golden bounty should we not say a fervent "thank you" to Lynn Riggs, Dick Rodgers and Oscar Hammerstein, Agnes de Mille, Terry Helburn and Lawrence Langner, Armina Marshall, Rouben

Mamoulian, Lemuel Ayers and Miles White, Jay Blackton and Robert Russell Bennett, the stars, the character people, the singers and the dancers, the backstage crew and stage managers (and not forgetting the backers and loyal Mr. Al Greenstone), each one of whom took part in creating something unique in our lives?

The magic of *Oklahoma!* is reborn each night that the curtain rises on Aunt Eller, sitting there churning, as Curly strolls on, singing.

For that beautiful morning, then, folks—*take another bow!*

SOURCES

Dance to the Piper by Agnes de Mille, Da Capo, 1980.

Getting to Know Him by Hugh Fordin, Ungar, 1986.

Interview with Mrs. Dorothy Rodgers, *The New York Times*, April 22, 1990.

Lyrics by Oscar Hammerstein II, Hal Leonard, 1985.

Lyrics by Lorenz Hart, Knopf, 1986.

Mister Abbott by George Abbott, Random House, 1963.

Musical Stages by Richard Rodgers, Random House, 1949.

People Will Talk by John Kobal, Knopf, 1986.

The Street Where I Live by Alan Jay Lerner, W. W. Norton, 1978.

Take Them Up Tenderly by Margaret Case Harriman, Knopf, 1944.

Twenty Best American Plays, 1918–1958, edited by John Gassner, Crown, 1961.

Theatre in America by Mary Henderson, Harry Abrams, 1989.

They're Playing Our Song by Max Wilk, Moyer Bell, 1991.

Underfoot in Show Business by Helene Hanff, Moyer Bell, 1989.

A Wayward Quest by Theresa Helburn, Little Brown, 1960.

ORAL HISTORIES

Elaine Scott Steinbeck, New York

Mary Hunter Wolf, New Haven

George Church, Fort Myers, Florida

Hal Prince, New York

Edmund Hartmann, Santa Fe

Alfred Drake, New York

Miles White, New York

Jay Blackton, Los Angeles

Agnes de Mille, New York

Bambi Linn de Jesus, Massachusetts

George Irving, New York

Kate Friedlich Witkin, New York

Marc Platt, Florida

Celeste Holm, New York

Paul Shiers, New Jersey

Vivian Smith Shiers, New Jersey

Stephen Sondheim, New York

Miranda Levy, Santa Fe

Ethel Heyn, Westport, Connecticut

Hayes Gordon, Australia

Philip Barry, Jr., Waterford, Connecticut

PERMISSIONS

*Grateful acknowledgment is made to the following for permission to reprint
previously published material:*

INDEX

Page numbers in *italics* indicate illustrations.